FEMINISM AND
SOCIOLOGICAL
THEORY

KEY ISSUES IN SOCIOLOGICAL THEORY

Series Editors
JEFFREY C. ALEXANDER, *University of California, Los Angeles*
& JONATHAN H. TURNER, *University of California, Riverside*

This series of annual publications is designed to crystallize key issues in contemporary theoretical debate. Each year, the chair of the Theory Section of the American Sociological Association has the authority to organize a "conference within a conference" at the annual meeting. The intention is to provide a forum for intensive public discussion of an issue that has assumed overriding theoretical importance. After the miniconference, the chair assumes the role of volume editor and, subject to final approval by the series editors, prepares a volume based on the reworked conference papers.

We hope that this periodic focusing of theoretical energy will strengthen the "disciplinary matrix" upon which theoretical progress in every science depends. Theoretical consensus may be impossible, but disciplinary integration is not. Only if a solid infrastructure is provided can communication among different orientations be carried out in the kind of ongoing, continuous way that is so necessary for mutual understanding and scientifically constructive criticism.

Volumes in this series:

FEMINISM AND SOCIOLOGICAL THEORY

Edited by

RUTH A. WALLACE

4

KEY ISSUES IN
SOCIOLOGICAL THEORY

Series Editors: Jeffrey C. Alexander,
University of California, Los Angeles

Jonathan Turner,
University of California, Riverside

SAGE PUBLICATIONS
The International Professional Publishers
Newbury Park   London   New Delhi

For information address:

SAGE Publications, Inc.
2111 West Hillcrest Drive
Newbury Park, California 91320

SAGE Publications Ltd.
28 Banner Street
London EC1Y 8QE
England

SAGE Publications India Pvt. Ltd.
M-32 Market
Greater Kailash I
New Delhi 110 048 India

Printed in the United States of America

Library of Congress Cataloging-in-Publication Data

Main entry under title:

Feminism and sociological theory / edited by Ruth A. Wallace.
    p.   cm.—(Key issues in sociological theory : 4)
    Bibliography: p.
    ISBN 0-8039-3397-5.—ISBN 0-8039-3398-3 (pbk.)
    1. Sociology—Congresses.   2. Sociology—Philosophy—Congresses.
3. Feminism—Philosophy—Congresses.   4. Feminist criticism—
Congresses.   I. Wallace, Ruth A.   II. Series.
HM13.F46 1989
301'.01—dc20   89-10201
                                                    CIP

SECOND PRINTING 1990

CONTENTS

INTRODUCTION

RUTH A. WALLACE
George Washington University

MANY SOCIOLOGISTS WHO WERE in graduate school prior to the late 1960s probably did not make note of the fact that all of the theorists whose works were on their required reading lists for theory courses were men. Only a little more noticeable, because of daily encounters on campus, was the overwhelming preponderance of male professors and graduate students. Little wonder, then, that few graduate students ever pictured the "actor" mentioned by so many theorists as anything but a male. Indeed, George C. Homans's (1964) presidential address, "Bringing Men Back In," was, by its very title, an affirmation of the actor as male.

However, the rise of the contemporary women's movement in the late 1960s challenged such taken-for-granted assumptions. Questions like, "Why *shouldn't* there be more women faculty members, graduate students, researchers, and theorists?" were beginning to be asked. Throughout the 1970s and 1980s increasing numbers of women joined the ranks of sociology graduate students and faculty, making them a more visible minority.

What are some indicators that this influx of women has had an impact on theoretical sociology in the United States? In 1982, when the American Sociological Association listed members by areas of interest, 16% (201) of the 1,215 sociologists who listed theory as an area of interest were female. As of July 1988, the female percentage increased to 26% (552). Analysis of a recent (November 1988) membership list of the American Sociological Association's Section on Theoretical Sociology revealed that 113 of the 543 members, or 21%, were female. There is, then, indication of a growing interest in theory among women sociologists in the United States.

AUTHOR'S NOTE: I wish to thank Caroline Bugno, Section Coordinator at the American Sociological Association, for providing me with these data. In addition I want to thank Janet Chafetz for her helpful comments on an earlier draft of this chapter.

The impact is less strong with regard to leadership positions. Although the Theory Section was established in 1968, it was not until 1974 that the first woman was elected to its council. In the past 20 years only ten women have been elected to serve on the council, and only two women have been elected to chair the section. Given the minority position of women theorists, it is not surprising that feminist concerns have tended to suffer from a kind of benign neglect on the part of social theorists. This volume, and the conference upon which it is based, published under the auspices of the American Sociological Association Theory Section, is an attempt to reverse that trend by placing feminist concerns at the top of the theory agenda.

The threefold aim of this volume is to bring the theoretical efforts of feminist scholarship into the mainstream, to illuminate the directions of theoretical work already in progress, and to encourage more thinking and writing about the implications of feminism for sociological theory. The focus is on theoretical work that has been produced as a result of the contemporary women's movement. The basic question is this: What are the implications of contemporary feminism for sociological theory?

Most of the chapters in this volume were initially presented at the Conference on Feminism and Sociological Theory sponsored by the Theory Section of the American Sociological Association in Atlanta, Georgia, in August 1988. The chapters that follow, all of which appear here for the first time, exemplify the new directions in sociological theory emerging from the contemporary women's movement.

The contemporary feminist movement has produced a profusion of scholarly work in a variety of disciplines: history, literature, anthropology, psychology, and sociology, to name a few. While most of the sociological achievement has taken the form of empirical research into areas that had been virtually unresearched, contemporary feminism has inspired some important theoretical work as well. Much of that work, however, remains unnoticed and uncited by most sociologists. Stacey and Thorne (1985, p. 306) argue that the ghettoization of feminist insights was one of the major ways that feminist studies was contained in the discipline of sociology. A brief discussion of that containment is in order.

THE GHETTOIZATION OF FEMINIST SCHOLARSHIP

About 10 years ago, at a business meeting of the ASA Section on Sex and Gender, the issue of mainstreaming feminist issues throughout the various ASA sections was raised. It was noted that women's concerns and the insights of feminist scholars have often been directed to two areas of specialization in sociology: sociology of the family and sociology of sex and gender. Some of the leading voices at that meeting encouraged feminists to end this isolation and to become more involved in other sections.

In Chapter 1 of this volume, Jessie Bernard provides an overview of some of the journals launched by feminists in the late 1960s and early 1970s. Even today feminist sociological research tends not to be published in the mainline journals of the discipline but in such journals as *Signs, Sex Roles, Feminist Studies, Gender and Society,* and *Women's Studies International Forum.* It is true that some of the major journals, like *American Journal of Sociology, Social Problems,* and *Sociological Inquiry* have, from time to time, published an entire volume on gender issues or women's concerns, but this has been woefully inadequate to accommodate the outpouring of feminist scholarship in sociology. Because of the need for an outlet for publication of feminist sociology, a new journal, *Gender and Society,* the official publication of Sociologists for Women in Society, was created in 1987.

It is not surprising, then, that many sociologists are unaware of the theoretical contributions that feminists have made to the discipline. As the chairperson of the American Sociological Association's Section on Theoretical Sociology, I chose "Feminism and Sociological Theory" as the theme for the Theory Section's 1988 conference, with the goal of mainstreaming feminist theoretical scholarship. This book, a product of that conference, is sponsored by a section of the American Sociological Association that is quintessentially mainstream. Indeed, one could argue that only the section on methodology can rival the Theory Section for its central place in the discipline. This book, then, represents a movement away from the ghettoization of feminist scholarship in sociology.

I would hasten to add, however, that this is not the first effort toward the inclusion of feminist scholarship in the discipline. In 1976 the American Sociological Association approved a recommendation by the Committee on the Status of Women to create a new award named in honor of Jessie Bernard "in recognition of scholarly work that has enlarged the horizons of sociology to encompass fully the role of women in society."[1]

Another path-breaking effort was made by Alice Rossi in 1983 when, as President of the American Sociological Association, she chose as a theme for the annual meetings "Gender and the Life Course." The choice of this theme encouraged research on gender, and it resulted in a greatly increased proportion of women as presenters of research papers at that annual meeting.

Even theory textbooks are beginning to devote some space to a discussion of feminist theory. The second edition of George Ritzer's (1988) text includes a new chapter on contemporary feminist theory by Patricia Lengermann and Jill Brantley, and Janet Chafetz's (1988) new text is an overview of a variety of contemporary feminist theories in sociology. In addition, Norbert Wiley's (1987) introduction to the second volume of this series, *The Marx-Weber Debate*, includes a short section on feminist theory.

FEMINIST THEORY DEFINED

There are many sociologists who seriously question the labeling of a theory as feminist, and others who would vehemently deny even the possibility of the existence of feminist theory. Janet Chafetz, who admits that she was in the latter category when she first heard the term *feminist theory* in 1974, has recently presented one of the most articulate definitions of feminist theory. How does feminist theory differ from general theories of inequality? Chafetz argues that a theory is feminist if it can be used to challenge, counteract, or change a status quo that disadvantages or devalues women. The three elements of feminist theory, according to Chafetz (1988, p. 5), are as follows:

> First, *gender comprises a central focus or subject matter* of the theory. Feminist theory seeks ultimately to understand the gendered nature of virtually all social relations, institutions, and processes. Second, *gender relations are viewed as a problem*. By this I mean that feminist theory seeks to understand how gender is related to social inequities, strains, and contradictions. Finally, *gender relations are not viewed as either natural or immutable*. Rather, the gender-related status quo is viewed as the product of sociocultural and historical forces which have been created, and are constantly re-created by humans, and therefore can potentially be changed by human agency.

As we will see in Chapter 9 Rose Coser takes a nuanced position regarding feminist theory. Basically, she would rather label the enterprise as "theorizing by a feminist," rather than feminist theory. In her chapter titled "Reflections on Feminist Theory," Coser presents some examples of what she views as "fine feminist scholarship" and "fruitful social theory."

Some sociologists have pointed out that there is almost an overabundance of feminist-inspired empirical studies. Indeed, they have practically called for a moratorium on gender research, suggesting that it is time for some theoretical work to be done. Their underlying assumption is that research and theory are exclusive categories, or at least that they should be separated, a position with which I disagree. Rather than decry the over-emphasis on empirical work, I think we should rejoice that we have a gold mine of sociological data on gender inequality and other feminist issues, and begin to dig into it in order to extract some theoretical elements.

Recall that Robert K. Merton (1967), in a classic essay titled "The Bearing of Empirical Research on Sociological Theory" in his book *On Theoretical Sociology*, reminded us of the reciprocal relationship between theory and research. He questioned the ranking of theory over and above research, stating, "As a matter of plain fact the theorist is not inevitably the lamp lighting the way to new observations." Throughout this introductory essay, I will present illustrations of the bearing of feminist research on sociological theory.

FEMINIST CONTRIBUTIONS TO SOCIOLOGICAL THEORY

We now turn to a discussion of the types of contributions made by feminist theorists. At this point in time I can visualize four theoretical contributions of feminist sociologists: (1) the critique and reevaluation of existing theories, (2) the discovery of new topics and concepts, (3) interdisciplinary linkages, and (4) the creation of a new sociological paradigm. In the following sections I will briefly discuss each contribution, citing relevant feminist scholarship, including the work of the contributors to this volume.

Critique and Reevaluation of Existing Theories

The chief target of feminist criticism has been functionalist theory, and, in particular, Talcott Parsons's work on the family. Much of the critique has centered on his dualistic notion of expressive versus instrumental orientations in his pattern variable scheme. In his categorization of role expectations and the structure of relationships, Parsons tended to

view women's roles as predominantly expressive, and men's as instrumental. In general, feminists have criticized Parsons's theory of gender
socialization as oppressive for both genders, but particularly so for
women.

In my view (Wallace 1985, p. 28), the critique of Parsons should
begin with his earlier work, *Working Papers in the Theory of Action*
(Parsons et al. 1953), because a scrutiny of this work moves away from
a critique of the pattern variables and raises some questions about the
empirical basis of his AGIL model. Parsons's attempt to incorporate
propositions about the nature of goals into his theory of action evolved
from his collaboration with Robert F. Bales in experiments on leadership
in small groups. As these groups attempted to solve their task problems,
Bales observed changes in the quality of the activity among the group
members. The patterns emerging from these activities led him to develop categories that were later reconceptualized by Parsons to include
all systems of action, his AGIL model.

It is important to keep in mind that Bales's data base was the foundation on which Parsons built his four functional prerequisites. In my
rereading of *Working Papers,* I noticed for the first time that Bales's
small groups were made up entirely of Harvard undergraduates, all
males, whom Bales obtained through the Harvard employment service.
In the early 1950s those groups would have been made up almost
entirely of upper-middle- to upper-class, White Protestant males.

What theoretical issues might the group's homogeneity raise? Certainly it could call into question the number, type, and range of functional system problems. If the groups had included Blacks, women,
blue-collar workers, Catholics, and Jews, we might expect differences in
the quality and in the sequence of the activity of these groups. For
instance, we would expect that more tensions would arise in a less
homogeneous group; thus tension management and/or conflict resolution might emerge as a major category. Task orientation is seen and
accomplished differently by groups at the bottom of the social ladder,
for they have a different view of social control in general and of social
control agents in particular. Would the patterns emerging from more
heterogeneous groups have produced AGIL? Feminist psychologist
Carol Gilligan's (1982) work, for instance, would suggest that pattern
maintenance and tension management should be treated separately or
at least differently.

Another example of how a feminist rereading of sociological theory
can raise new questions comes from the work of Stacey and Thorne

(1985). There has been ongoing debate and discussion among feminists concerning the concept of role, centering on its functionalist underpinnings. Although many feminists use the terms *sex* and/or *gender roles* and emphasize the process of sex and/or gender role socialization, Stacey and Thorne (1985, p. 307) argue that

> the notion of role "focuses attention more on individuals than on social structure, and implies that "the female role" and "the male role" are complementary (i.e., separate or different but equal). The terms are depoliticizing: they strip experience from its historical and political context and neglect questions of power and conflict. It is significant that sociologists do not speak of "class roles" or "race roles." Functionalist assumptions linger more deeply in sociological conceptualizations of gender than of other forms of inequality. These functionalist assumptions have posed significant obstacles to feminist rethinking of basic orienting assumptions within sociology.

The analyses of some of the authors in this volume also exemplify a critique and/or reevaluation of existing theories. Miriam Johnson (Chapter 5) reevaluates Parsons's work on the family, and argues that he was aware of structured strains in both male and female socialization, as his early writings on the family illustrate. Johnson also applies Parsons's theory of social change to the contemporary women's movement. To my knowledge this is the first time a sociologist has used Parsons's evolutionary change theory to analyze the women's movement, and I predict that it will spark some discussion, particularly among neofunctionalists who are "pushing functionalism to the left" (Alexander 1985, p. 14).

Dorothy Smith, on the other hand, argues in Chapter 2 that Parsons's adaptation of psychoanalysis "as a theory of the internalization of practically everything" in effect treated individuals as expressions of a sociocultural system. Consequently, profound alteration of the family structure is problematic. She criticizes both Durkheim and Parsons for their view that the social is external to the particularities of people's lives, because the subject has no place or position in such disembodied theories. Joan Acker adds that functionalism, a dominant paradigm, participates in re-creating existing social structures.

Feminist critiques of sociological theorists have not, however, been fixated on Parsons. Recognizing the interconnections between race, class, and gender, feminist theorists have also turned their critical eye to Marxist class theory. In Chapter 3, Joan Acker criticizes Marx for defining the economy from the perspective of the male-dominated ruling system, and in Chapter 6, Thomas Meisenhelder points out the limitations involved in Habermas's male notion of human reason. In a similar vein, Smith argues that Weber's concept of class, based on economic interests in property, excludes aspects of economic and social organization in which women have traditionally been active. Likewise Edith Kurzweil, in Chapter 4, chronicles the work of women psychoanalysts who have had to modify Freud's theories in order to do away with the repression of women.

Discovery of New Topics and Concepts

When it turned the spotlight on gender and women's concerns, the contemporary women's movement produced a new kind of research approach, one less tangible than a computer or a new statistical formula. Through becoming "woman-centered," as Dorothy Smith (1979, 1987) urges, feminists have uncovered vast areas of research hitherto neglected, and these efforts have sparked a refocusing of theoretical interest.

Two feminists who have come to terms with emotionality, a topic rarely addressed by social theorists, are Nancy Chodorow and Arlie Russell Hochschild. In a path-breaking work titled *The Reproduction of Mothering*, Nancy Chodorow (1978) argues that male children see themselves as unlike the mothers with whom they have had their first emotional relationships, and they learn to repress and deny female qualities in order to accomplish their individuated male identities. Thus males grow up with an underdeveloped relational capacity, and they tend to see the feminine as inferior. Female children, on the other hand, strongly and continously identify with the mother, accept their emotions, and develop a high relational capacity.

Hochschild's work on emotional labor presses for what Merton (1967) would call the recasting of theory. In her book, *The Managed Heart*, Hochschild researched the emotion work required by two occupations: flight attendants (mostly women) and bill collectors (mostly men). She (Hochschild 1983, p. 137) found that the flight attendants were asked to "feel sympathy, trust, and good will," while the bill collectors were asked to "feel distrust and sometimes positive bad will."

Hochschild learned that the struggle to maintain a difference between feeling and feigning led to a strain for the people in occupations calling for emotional labor, a strain that she labeled "emotive dissonance." She

(1983, p. 90) states, "We try to reduce this strain by pulling the two closer together either by changing what we feel or by changing what we feign." The emotive dissonance involved in the management of feelings, which Hochschild discovered in her research, resulted in a recasting of the theory of cognitive dissonance, extending its margins to include emotive dissonance as well.

Another feminist discovery is exemplified in the recent resurgence of interest in research on friendship. As Bernard (1981, p. 293) argues, any discussion of the structure of the female world must pay attention to the phenomenon of friendships. She states: "There are many more female-female relationships in our society than there are female-male relationships. And the part they play not only in the lives of women but also in the structure of the female world is incalculable."

Wallace and Hartley (1988) point out that only a few social theorists have seriously analyzed the phenomenon of friendship; most theorists, in fact, have alluded to it only peripherally or implicitly in their writings. It is relatively unknown, for instance, that Durkheim's suicide research was begun very shortly after the suicide of his best friend, Victor Hommay. The depth of his friendship with Hommay was revealed in an as yet untranslated obituary Durkheim wrote for his closest friend (Wallace and Hartley 1988, p. 95). Other than this, Durkheim only mentions friendship in passing in *Division of Labor in Society* ([1893] 1964, pp. 54–56).

One could ask whether an obituary is one of the few acceptable avenues in Western society for males' admission of deep friendship bonds. Is this one of the prices of male "adulthood"? Gilligan (1982, p. 71) points to the dilemma between femininity, which involves responsibility to others, and adulthood (or masculinity), which involves autonomy. Chodorow's (1978) insights regarding male socialization also suggest why the majority of social theorists have tended to overlook friendship as an important topic for sociological analysis.

Rosabeth Moss Kanter's (1977) research led to the discovery of a new concept, tokenism. Her immersion in the daily encounters in a corporation enabled her to take a close look at the role of the "token" woman, and much of what she observed about women who were working in skewed groups (groups where women were numerically rare) was unanticipated. In Kanter's (1977, p. 212) words, "Visibility tends to create performance pressures on the token. Contrast leads to heightening of dominant culture boundaries, including isolation of the token. And assimilation results in the token's role encapsulation."

Although her insights regarding the plight of numerical minorities resulted from her focus on women in a corporation, Kanter urged researchers to examine other types of tokens, such as racial or ethnic minorities, younger workers, handicapped individuals, and males in predominantly female occupations. Because she was steeped in her data, as Merton (1967) predicted, Kanter hit upon a fruitful direction of inquiry that can extend sociological theory.

Janet Chafetz's work on role expansion in Chapter 7 of this volume provides us with another example of the discovery of new concepts. She argues that technological variation and changes in the demographic profile of a collectivity result in role expansion for women. Together with Gary Dworkin, Chafetz (1986) sets forth a number of hypotheses regarding the causes and results of women's role expansion.

Interdisciplinary Linkages

In Neil Smelser's (1988, p. 2) discussion of new integrative directions in sociological thinking, he points to an "increasing emphasis in the social sciences that is topical or problem-related in character, and reaches across disciplinary boundaries." Within the discipline of sociology, feminist theorists are among the most active in reaching across sociological boundaries.

Miriam Johnson, in Chapter 5, makes the point that feminism has been an interdisciplinary movement. In addition, Lengermann and Brantley (1988, p. 282) state that feminist theory actually emerged as an interdisciplinary effort, including scholars from such fields as philosophy, history, economics, anthropology, political science, psychology, literature, and religion, as well as sociology.

Edith Kurzweil argues, in Chapter 4, that American feminist theorists were slow in exploring psychoanalytic theory for their own ends because earlier applications had been connected to conservative sociology, in particular, to the work of Talcott Parsons. Kurzweil examines the debates between Freud and feminist psychoanalysts about the origins of femininity, which were renewed in France and Germany in the 1960s, and she demonstrates how psychoanalytic feminism, sparked by international contacts within the contemporary women's movement, brought psychoanalytic thinking more fully into sociology. In Chapter 8, Rae Lesser Blumberg's feminist theory of development is informed by the work of Esther Boserup, a Danish economist. In addition, Jessie Bernard's chapter on the dissemination of feminist thought utilizes statements from a number of feminist journals that are interdisciplinary in nature.

The Creation of a New Sociological Paradigm

What are the signs that feminist theorists are moving toward a new sociological paradigm? In Chapter 3, Joan Acker illustrates the strains and tensions involved in such a transformation. I agree with her assessment: The creation of a new sociological paradigm has not yet occurred. We do, however, have the beginnings of a movement toward a new paradigm. Acker suggests three emerging alternatives: a woman-centered standpoint, the gendered character of social relations and social processes, and the development of the concept of reproduction.

What will the new sociological paradigm look like? I predict that the new sociological paradigm created by feminists will be characterized by theoretical synthesis. In accord with my prediction, Charles Lemert (1988, p. 1), citing feminist theory as one of the powerful new theoretical traditions in sociology, stated recently: "It is especially impressive that those working in these areas share and cooperate across perspectival boundaries."

Some of the work by the contributors to this volume illustrates attempts on the part of feminist theorists to synthesize sociological perspectives. Smith combines the dialectical materialism of Marx and Engels with elements of Garfinkel's ethnomethodology. Blumberg attempts to bridge the macro-micro gap in development theory. Chafetz's eclectic approach includes elements from Marx, exchange theory, reference group theory, and cognitive dissonance.

CONCLUSION

The chapters presented here do not, of course, exhaust the theoretical work of feminist sociologists. Many of those scholars not included, however, have been cited by the authors in this volume. If space and time had allowed me to draw up a comprehensive list, I would have included the work of many more theorists.

As mentioned earlier, the threefold goal of this volume is to illuminate the directions of feminist theoretical work already in progress, to bring the theoretical efforts of feminist scholarship into the mainstream, and to encourage more thinking and writing about the implications of feminism for sociological theory. In the pursuit of that goal, the experience of editing this volume has been a gratifying one, from the inception of this project to its culmination. This has been entirely due to the cooperation and dedicated commitment on the part of the contributors, whose works draw on a variety of macro and micro sociological perspectives. I close this introduction with a word of gratitude to the authors who made this volume possible, and with a challenge to other sociologists to write and/or edit more books similar to this one. It is my conviction that this volume is only the tip of the iceberg.

NOTE

1. Part I of this volume is titled "Enlarging the Horizons of Sociological Theory" to honor Jessie's pioneering efforts. I am deeply grateful that she agreed to be a contributor to this volume.

REFERENCES

Alexander, Jeffrey C., ed. 1985. *Neofunctionalism*. Beverly Hills, CA: Sage.

Bernard, Jessie 1981. *The Female World*. New York: Free Press.

Chafetz, Janet S. 1988. *Feminist Sociology: An Overview of Contemporary Theories*. Itasca, IL: F. E. Peacock.

Chafetz, Janet S. and A. Gary Dworkin. 1986. *Female Revolt*. Totowa, NJ: Rowman and Allanheld.

Chodorow, Nancy. 1987. *The Reproduction of Mothering*. Berkeley: University of California Press.

Durkheim, Émile. [1893] 1964. *Division of Labor in Society*. New York: Free Press.

Gilligan, Carol. 1982. *In a Different Voice*. Cambridge, MA: Harvard University Press.

Hochschild, Arlie R. 1983. *The Managed Heart*. Berkeley: University of California Press.

Homans, George C. 1964. "Bringing Men Back In." *American Sociological Review* 29(December):809–18.

Kanter, Rosabeth Moss. 1977. *Men and Women of the Corporation*. New York: Basic Books.

Lemert, Charles. 1988. "Social Theory Beyond the Academy: Intellectuals and Politics." *Perspectives* 2(October):1–2.

Lengermann, Patricia M. and Jill N. Brantley. 1988. "Contemporary Feminist Theory." Pp. 282–325 in *Contemporary Sociological Theory*, edited by G. Ritzer. New York: Knopf.

Merton, Robert K. 1967. *On Theoretical Sociology.* New York: Free Press.

Parsons, Talcott and Robert F. Bales. 1955. *Family, Socialization and Interaction Process.* Glencoe, IL: Free Press

Parsons, T., R. F. Bales, and E. A. Shils. 1953. *Working Papers in the Theory of Action.* Glencoe, IL: Free Press.

Ritzer, George, ed. 1988. *Contemporary Sociological Theory.* New York: Knopf.

Smelser, N. J. 1988. "Sociological Theory: Looking Forward." *Perspectives* 11(June):1–3.

Smith, Dorothy. 1979. "A Sociology for Women." Pp.135–87 in *The Prism of Sex: Essays in the Sociology of Knowledge,* edited by J. A. Sherman and E. T. Beck. Madison: University of Wisconsin.

———. 1987. *The Everyday World as Problematic: A Feminist Sociology.* Boston: Northeastern University Press.

Stacey, Judith and Barrie Thorne. 1985. "The Missing Feminist Revolution in Sociology." *Social Problems* 32(April):301–16.

Wallace, Ruth A. 1985. "Religion, Privatization, and Maladaption: A Comment on Niklas Luhmann." *Sociological Analysis* 46(Spring):27–31.

Wallace, Ruth A. and S. F. Hartley. 1988. "Religious Elements in Friendship: Durkheimian Theory in an Empirical Context." Pp. 93–106 in *Durkheimian Sociology: Cultural Studies,* edited by J. C. Alexander. New York: Cambridge University Press.

Wiley, Norbert. 1987. *The Marx-Weber Debate.* Beverly Hills, CA: Sage.

PART I

Enlarging the Horizons of Sociological
Theory

Chapter 1

THE DISSEMINATION OF FEMINIST THOUGHT
1960 to 1988

JESSIE BERNARD
Pennsylvania State University

Sociological theory is entering a new and important phase. In the (*first*) postwar period, European theory was diminished and Parsons's structural-functional approach held the day. In the 1960s, there developed the challenges to Parsons's hegemony that became the major traditions in the *second*, post-Parsonian period: constructivist and logico-deductive trends; new waves of micro-theorizing; and the reemergence of macro-structuralist approaches. The polarization that defined these first two periods has come to an end. We are in the beginning of a *third* phase that (as yet) has a much less clearly defined character . . . . What will emerge from this (*third*) period of theoretical ferment remains to be seen. (Alexander and Turner 1985, p.2; emphases and parentheses added)

This book marks the coming of age of that third postwar period of ferment in sociological theory, referred to by Alexander and Turner above. Its character—not yet clearly defined when they first called our attention to it—has now become unmistakable. We can see clearly now how it differs from its predecessors: that, in brief, it is a *feminist* contribution to our discipline, long in gestation but not until recently achieving an autonomous identity freeing it from dependence on the male perspective, which has characterized our discipline until now. Watching the turns and squirms of our professional meetings year after year, under good leadership and bad, has convinced me—again—of the validity of "Deor's La-

---

AUTHOR'S NOTE: The sociological recognition of feminism in this book represents a critical step forward in the story of feminism as well as of sociological theory in this country. The members of the ASA Theory Section, which recognized its significance, deserve a salute, especially Ruth Wallace, not only for her early recognition of the importance of the subject but also for the energy she has invested in its implementation.

ment": "that was 'o'erpassed,' this will pass also." Past ignore-ance of the sociology of the female world may now be declared "o'erpassed." Or nearly so. For, in the efflorescence of thinking on the subject of feminism, our knowledge and data have been enormously enriched and the repercussions are rewarding for both feminism and sociological theory, as the authors of this book so convincingly demonstrate.

There is a fairly long and checkered history behind the achievement of recognition of the scientific legitimacy of the sociology of feminism. It was already adding whole areas to the boundaries of sociology a decade ago. In 1975, for example, Arlene Daniels was proud of what feminists had already achieved by then, not only in the area of the sociology of sex and gender—an area already granted or conceded to feminists—but elsewhere also, indeed, everywhere. Daniels (1975, p. 349) stated:

> The development of a feminist perspective in sociology offers an important contribution to the sociology of knowledge. And through this contribution, we are forced to re-think the structure and organization of sociological theory in all the traditional fields of theory and empirical research.

The harvest even then was already rich. Feminists could be proud of the "important, even cutting edge contributions" such work had already made to our understanding of society and increasingly, to our discipline. Much more was to come, although not without difficulties. Even this important book does not adequately convey the sociological significance of feminism in our hitherto predominantly male-oriented discipline.

THE 1960s: HIS

The decades of the 1960s and 1970s marked a series of eye-opening experiences for a generation of extraordinary young women activists trained in the civil rights and antiwar movements, who, despite their contributions, were nevertheless finding themselves victims of male sexism.[1] They had been exposed to the same revolutionary and reformist ideologists of the times as the young men had been exposed to. Antiwar activism had trained them for their own new role. In the 1960s and early 1970s they had been members of Students for a Democratic Society (SDS) and, along with college men, were learning the skills and the vocabulary of civil rights activism and of antiwar demonstrations. They had envied the protesting men who had had draft registration cards to burn before the television cameras. They identified with all the liberation movements, felt themselves to be as much a part of them as were the men with whom they were working. They thought of themselves as belonging in the protesting groups. They thought of themselves as "in." When enough had been achieved by this activism and new paths were being planned to carry on, they assumed that they would continue participating as equals when the antiwar movements abated. They expected to participate as equals in the planning of new activities, in discussions of strategy, in clarification of ideology . . .

They certainly did not expect the sexism of their male co-members. It was, therefore, with shocked amazement that they learned that the men did not accept them as their equals. After participating as equals in a decade of activism, they certainly did not relish being ousted from sharing the prestigious work of developing strategies for reform—or revolution, as the case might be—and being asked instead to do female kinds of menial chores—typing, copying, serving coffee, office work—which, however essential, were uninfluential, even down-putting, low in prestige. Now, suddenly, they were face-to-face with the sexism the men felt and displayed toward them, the same men for whom racial equality had been such a taken-for-granted goal of activism in the civil rights movement. The women were dumbfounded to discover this exclusion from leadership positions, infuriated at the blatant, casual, taken-for-granted, unrecognized, hypocritical sexism of the men.[2] Their eyes were opened to the real nature of their relationships with the men.

For some it produced an epiphany that removed blinders from their eyes. They could now see—in male behavior[3]—what the structure of sexism was, the "invisible paradigm" that shaped it, the infrastructure, in brief, that had been so long in place that it had become normative, invisible.

It was an enlightenment whose time had come, a new kind of enlightenment: a Feminist Enlightenment. The 1970s proved to be an extraordinary and amazing decade for women and a stunning foil for men. For, in that brief period of time, the nature of the changes taking place in the thinking of young academic women were to find fluent, even eloquent, verbal expression in a spate of feminist journals launched between 1968 and the 1980s. We are indebted to them for a thoughtful record of intellectual history in action.

THE 1970s: HERS

This page in the feminist saga was written by a more academically than activist-oriented group of young women who were also highly talented and skillful writers. Under their aegis periodicals sprang up everywhere devoted to spreading the good news of women's liberation. By the 1980s there were 50 such journals, as well as floods of other publications—papers, pamphlets, reports, newsletters—circulating among seemingly insatiable readers, all powerful tools for disseminating the new feminism. The journals were especially notable. They varied among themselves and early on—Volume 1, number 1—stated their position on key feminist issues as conceptualized at that time.

Here is the story of one of the first such journals—*No More Fun and Games, A Journal of Female Liberation*—that appeared in Boston in 1969 and of others that soon followed.

> The reactions to our first journal (untitled, unstructured, without page numbers or table of contents or date of publication or copyright, and barely escaping total anonymity) have been many and varied. The most consistent criticism from those who enjoyed the journal was that we provided no structure, no solutions. They say that although we identified a whole array of problems and feelings which touched them acutely, they felt somewhat lost as to what could be done in their day-to-day dilemma. We simply knew that we had to begin somewhere, and at least speak out. So our first action was to publish a journal. (p. 4)

Most of the other journals started in that decade were produced by university women. Their first issues—Volume 1, number 1—constitute a feminist diary of the 1970s, a documentation of what these young women were hoping for. Here they are—

1972, *Feminist Studies* (p. 1):

> Statement of Purpose. *Feminist Studies* has been founded for the purpose of encouraging analytic responses to feminist issues and analyses that open new areas of feminist research and critique. The editors are committed to providing a forum for feminist analysis, debate and exchange. The approach and conclusions of any given article do not necessarily reflect the opinions of the editors.

1972, *Women's Studies;* Wendy Martin, editor. Editorial, "Why *Women's Studies*?" (pp. 1–2):

. . . artistic and cultural values as well as the social and economic structure of patriarchal societies ensure male dominance by inculcating the myth of female inferiority. Since the university mirrors larger social structure, teaching and scholarship often reinforce male dominance, and academic disciplines such as history, literary criticism, psychology, political science and even anthropology, sociology and biology become bastions of male supremacy. Although sexism in academia is often unconscious, it is important to understand that the university, along with other major institutions, is often hostile to women.

In spite of, or perhaps, because of, this hostility, feminist thought and scholarship are rapidly advancing. The conviction that men and women should have equal political, economic, and social rights, which constitutes the core of feminism, makes it obvious that extensive research into past beliefs and practices as well as considerable rethinking of our present values is necessary in order to reverse the effects of male chauvinism and the internalization of patriarchal values by women.

1974, *Quest: A Feminist Quarterly:*

Quest: a Feminist Quarterly is seeking long-term, in-depth feminist political analysis and ideological development. *Quest* is not an end in itself, but a process leading to new directions for the women's movement possibly including such concrete forms as regional or national conferences, a national organization or a political party. We, the editors, are all women who have been in the movement for several years and have reached a point where each answer leads us to more questions. We have been through various ideological and activist metamorphoses and end up feeling that our overall perspective is still not adequate. Where has the struggle brought us? Closer to real economic, political, and social power for women? Closer to self-determination for all women? We do not have all the answers ourselves and expect that feminists across the country and the world will contribute to this process of seeking. (Inside cover of first issue, Summer, 1974)

1976, *Women's Agenda.* Editorial, "A Women's Voice" (p. 2):

A national women's voice is in the making. It is the voice of women who are able and willing to act upon the major social issues of our times. It speaks for women who are concerned about reforms that will affect not only themselves but all members of the society. It has become a catalytic force for social change on the broadest scale. This powerful new voice directly confronts the old myths that women are divided and that the goals of the women's movement are supported by a small majority. The creation of this voice was made necessary by this nation's lack of commitment to humanism. . . .

The purpose of *Women's Agenda* is to keep alive the dialogue within this greatly expanded women's movement by facilitating the interchange of information and ideas.

1976, *Psychology of Women Quarterly;* Georgia Babladelis. Editorial (Vol. 1, no. 1, 1976, pp. 3–4):

Recently concerned critics have pointed out that . . . most of our information about behavior is based on the study of men only. Once more scientists are responding effectively and a new literature on the psychology of women is emerging. A paramount purpose of this journal is to make that literature readily available. In the publication of this journal there is the intent to redress past shortcomings by filling the gaps in our understanding of women's behavior. It is time to ask hard questions about established facts and to explore new questions and find new facts.

1977, *Chrysalis.* Editorial (p. 3):

Chrysalis: A Magazine of Women's Culture . . . takes its form and content from the women's movement itself. Feminism is not a monolithic movement, but rather includes the experiences, values, priorities, agendas of women of all lifestyles, ages, and cultural and economic backgrounds. Women building practical alternatives to patriarchal institutions, women developing new theories and feminist perspectives on events and ideas, women expressing their visions in verbal or visual art forms— women's culture includes all of this, and *Chrysalis* exists to give expression to the spectrum of opinion and creativity that originates in this diversity.

1976, *Signs;* Catharine R. Stimpson, Joan N. Burstyn, Donna C. Stanton, Sandra M. Whistler. Editorial (pp. v, vii):

Journals should have an animating purpose. For *Signs: Journal of Women in Culture and Society* that purpose is to publish the new scholarship about women from both the United States and other countries. The form the work will take may be reports of original research, contemplative essays, or a synthesis of report and essay. . . . Like any decent scholarship, the study of women must avoid the luxury of narcissism. It must be neither limited nor self-reflexive. It is a means to the end of an accurate understanding of men and women, of sex and gender, of large patterns of human behavior, institutions, ideologies, and art. . . . [The consciousness of such scholarship] respects many of the concepts, tools, and techniques of modern study. It uses them to compensate for old intellectual evasions and errors, to amass fresh data, and to generate new concepts, tools, and techniques. It also tends to question the social, political, economic, cultural, and physical arrangements that have governed relations between females and males, that have defined femininity and masculinity. It even suspects that those arrangements have been a source of the errors that must be corrected. . . . Scholarship should map the consequences of specific actions. Its discoveries and conclusions should then be used to improve the material conditions of the lives of women.[4]

All this was radical enough for many young women, even for the 1980s. But not for avant-garde young women coming along. In the late 1980s—1988—a paper was submitted to an educational journal dealing with the goals of sex equity and sexuality in sex education. Beginning with a fairly moderate opening statement, it argued for underplaying sex differences and emphasizing sex similarities. Wherever possible—except for sex differences in biological determinants of behavior—socially constituted factors should be played up. Still moderately conservative was a recommendation that there should be education against violence and that female sexual desire should be defined from the female point of view. It should be recognized that intercourse—which was only one form of sexual expression—is differently valued by males and females. Among other moderately radical ideas were these: choice of life-style—living without any partner, with a same-sex partner, or any other substitute for heterosexual monogamy—was to be respected. This working model was proposed merely as a starting point, to be modified in the direction of support for diversity and full potential for students (Whatley forthcoming).[5]

A HOSTILE WAKE

As sociological theory came, little by little, to recognize feminism as intrinsically worthy of incorporation into the discipline—as these Young Turks did—the same was not true for all students of the subject. If among theorists the 1960s were His and the 1970s, Hers, among others the 1980s were a decade in which two steps forward toward feminism often led to one step backward, away from it. To them, feminism was sick, sick, sick. Feminists became the butt of hostile jokes. The wish being father to the thought, the term *postfeminism* was being used to imply that its elimination was already a fait accompli. They reported its wake.

The charges against feminists and feminism were numerous and scathing.[6] Pressures on women to embrace traditional self-effacing female values increased, as also did advice for dealing with the feminist temptation, such as, for example, protect your femininity from the Amazon in women; let men supply the motor and women provide the "emotional glue" of society; marry and be supported by your husband; depend on your own gender's traits for power to change society

(Wenzel 1988, p. 12). Some women were more susceptible than others to these blandishments. For them it was hard to be feminists. They needed jacking up.

Nor was it only from outsiders that challenges came, and drains on energy. Many feminists were disoriented on the issues, and, even more serious, "deeply divided over the future. Even within the ranks, bickering factions attack[ed] one another's ideological positions, each accusing the others of insensitivity to causes outside their own special interests" (Stasie 1988, p. 263). They had lost their feeling of unity. And unless they could get that "core of power back soon, many feminists feared that the impulse for united political action may be forever lost" (Stasie 1988, p. 263). Whether wake or terminal illness, the climate was not a healthy one for attracting fresh recruits.

Was the Sisterhood, therefore, sunk? Was the fate of Her movement to suffer the same humiliating collapse as His had? It was clear that "the rift within the women's movement" was keenly felt by all the women. Those who were committed to female bonding on common issues suffered "the trauma of separation from their sisters" and even those who publicly claimed their satisfaction within their independence, admitted, in private, to feelings of guilt. In any event, the wake was premature.

THE FEASIBILITY OF EQUALITY

Among the tasks of sociological theory today, we need a conceptual tool kit for research on the feasibility of male-female equality. Without a convincing sociological theory to justify the settlement of an issue, it may run its course to violence and destructiveness as in the story of the Civil War. And history has shown us that acceptable solutions are often hard to come by. How many issues lie buried in any society or segment of a society is hard to know, but we know that there are some observers or agitators or victims who devote their lives to making them visible.

If slavery was the great issue in the Civil War, sex-gender issues may be said to be so today. And just as an enormous volume of sociological theory was generated to deal with slavery, so is an enormous volume of sociological theory being generated today to deal with sex-gender issues. The task of encompassing such an undertaking is well-nigh incalculable.

In 1972, *Women's Studies* had stated that equality was the core of feminism. For almost two decades there had been consensus on this principle of egalitarian feminism. Until, however, in the 1980s, the new social feminists arrived at the conclusion that "being [merely] equal wasn't equal enough, wasn't fair" (Stasie 1988, p. 263). There could, in fact, be no true equality because women were already expected to do more than men. "Given the unequal distribution of their caretaker work within society, women who claim the right to such assistance as affirmative job action, pay equity, family-support social programs and reformed divorce laws do not feel that these claims are preferential at all—just fair" (Stasie 1988, p. 263). And, in fact, denying them to women "threatened the basic concept of their human equality and may eventually erode even their rights under the law" (Stasie 1988, p. 263). Such were the painfully familiar paradoxes that were plaguing modern feminism (Rosen 1987, p. 3).

The crucial questions were raised by Nancy Cott (1987, p. 3):

How can women obtain an equality that takes into account fundamental differences between the sexes? How can feminism reconcile the promise of individualistic achievement in the first place? How can feminists achieve a necessary unity that incorporates women's vast diversity of interests? And finally, how can feminism resolve the contradiction that gender consciousness is necessary to demand an end to prescribed gender roles?

How, indeed?

L'ENVOI

Now, finally, I take advantage of the privilege of *l'envoi*, which granted authors the opportunity to talk personally to their readers. I hope I have adequately expressed my admiration for the achievements of feminists in the 1960s and 1970s. I would like those years to find a niche of their own in American history. As a member of a cohort that has participated in almost nine decades of this century's history—not a few of them world-shaking—I am eager that the 1960s and 1970s not become mere dates or even just data. I believe the raised consciousness women experienced in those years—and in those following—was as epochal as any battle fought, election won, or scientific insight achieved. I am not thinking in terms of annual celebrations with fireworks. Just something characteristically feminist in the sense that the common hostile figures of speech that are often applied to such celebrations—battles, struggles, even wars—will cease to be needed in memorials to the "female liberation movement," as we no longer need "fifty-four forty or fight" or other male-type battle cries to honor the achievements of the women who have led us so far. And, as the contributors to this book make clear, we are still going strong.

NOTES

1. The 1960s are increasingly becoming recognized for the revolutionary convulsions in American society that took place at that time. A bourgeoning literature on this decade has been accumulating in recent years, but it has been defective in a major way. It makes only incidental recognition of women's contributions and makes the common error of dealing with them incidentally, as merely one of numerous minority groups. Actually, women differ from minority groups in that they constitute half of the human species. For an important discussion of the sociological significance of the 1960s, see the symposium, "The Sixties in Retrospect: Searching for the Structure of the Sixties, Journey into All-or-Nothing Politics, Political Troubles and Personal Passions," by Randall Collins, Richard G. Braungart, and Irving Louis Horowitz (in *Contemporary Sociology*, Vol. 17, no. 6, 1988, 729–39). This is a three-part review of *The Sixties: Years of Hope, Days of Rage*, by Todd Gitlin.

2. A blatant, but especially alienating, form of disparaging sexism was expressed by Stokeley Carmichael, a civil rights activist, in his obiter dictum: "The position of women in the revolutionary movements is prone." An incredulous gasp from women activists followed and then a puzzled question: Was there some subtle message in the description of the proper position of women as prone instead of supine?

3. "Although most nascent feminists at first discussed their complaints in private, a few were willing to state them in public. Feminists had already spoken publicly at the December SDS national convention; despite the ridicule with which their remarks were then received, they returned the following year with the demand that the convention members accept a plank supporting women's liberation. The women who made this proposal were 'pelted with tomatoes and thrown out of the convention.' A year later, in 1967, at the New Left 'National Conference for New Politics,' the issue was treated more gingerly though still unsympathetically. . . . During the next year most of the New Left men disregarded the women's movement growing within their ranks—but many of the women did not. Gradually they began to take sides on the issue. Some identified themselves as primarily feminists; others as primarily members of the New Left" (Evans 1979, pp. 60–61). This downgrading of women proved to be an expensive error on the part of the men. Many of the women left the male-run organization and organized their own meetings.

4. Four years later (in Vol. 6, 2, Winter, 1980), the last issue of the Stimpson editorial term, the following update occurred: "Before and during the years that we were developing *Signs*, the new scholarship about women itself changed. It started with the urgent need to document women's sufferings, their invisibility and subordination. There was disagreement about the universality of women's secondary status, but not about its existence . . . . Intelligence and passion have helped to map . . . the female world, and in the process, the

notion of woman herself has become less passive, more active; more that of a primary force than of the marginal flesh" (p. 188).

5. The only major sex-related issue not yet specified in this model was recognition of the threat to human health in the AIDS epidemic.

6. "Jokes are being made about it [feminism]. Academics are pontificating over it. Preachers are pounding it out from the pulpit. It's the idea that feminism has somehow failed women, sold them down the river for thirty thousand a year to start, and a seat in a corporate boardroom. That it has 'defeminized' women, taken away their choices and . . . fed [them] the 'big lie' of liberation" (Wenzel 1988, p. 12). Much male antifeminism was a protest against competition from women in the work force. Wenzel's article, "Feminist Failure: The Big Lie," from which the above quotation is taken, was a review of several current antifeminist books: Toni Grant, *Being a Woman: Fulfilling Your Femininity and Finding Love*; Nicholas Davidson, *The Failures of Feminism*; Sylvia Ann Hewlett, *A Lesser Life: The Myth of Women's Liberation in America*; and George Gilder, *Men and Marriage*.

REFERENCES

Alexander, J. C. and J. Turner, eds. 1985. "Key Issues in Sociological Theory" (editorial statment). P. 2 in *Neofunctionalism*, edited by J. C. Alexander. Beverly Hills, CA: Sage.

Cott, Nancy. 1987. "A Serious Case of Deja Vu." *Women's Review of Books* (December):3.

Daniels, A. K. 1975. "Feminist Perspectives in Sociological Research." Pp. 340–80 in *Another Voice*, edited by M. Millman and R. M. Kanter. New York: Anchor.

Evans, S. M. 1979. *Personal Politics: The Roots of Women's Liberation*. New York: Knopf.

Parsons, Talcott. 1959. "The Social Structure of the Family." Chapter 13 in *The Family: Its Function and Destiny*, edited by R. N. Anshen. New York: Harper.

Rosen, R. A. 1987. "A Serious Case of Deja Vu." *Women's Review of Books* (December).

Stasio, Marilyn. "The Feminist Movement: Where We Stand Today." *Cosmopolitan* 204(5):262–65.

Truehart, C. 1988. "Science and the Feminist Critique." *Washington Post* (January 19).

Viann-Ponte, 1978. "Feminism: The Road Ahead." Interview with Simone de Beauvoir, *Le Monde*. (Paris).

Wenzel, L. 1988. "Feminist Failure: The Big Lie." *New Directions for Women* (November-December):12.

Whatley, M. Forthcoming. "Sex Equity and Sexuality in Sex Education." *Peabody Journal of Education*.

Chapter 2

SOCIOLOGICAL THEORY
Methods of Writing Patriarchy

DOROTHY E. SMITH
Ontario Institute for
Studies in Education

As I was going up the stair
I met a man who wasn't there
he wasn't there again today
I wish to god he'd go away. (Anonymous)

I HAVE EMPHASIZED in my work a distinctive standpoint for women, not necessarily as a general attribute of women as a class of persons, but as a mode of experience that is distinctive to women and in important ways an experience that has marked us off from men and still continues to do so (Smith 1987). This is an experience of work around particular individuals, particularly children; it is an experience grounded in a biological difference—our bodies give birth and men's do not—but through complex institutional mediations organized as caring and serving work directed toward *particular* others or groups of others. Locating the knowing subject of a sociology in this site locates a subject *outside* the textually mediated discourse[1] of sociology; it locates her in her own life, in her self as a unitary being, as a body active, imagining, thinking, *as a subject situated in her local and particular actualities.*

Designing a sociology for a knower situated in the everyday/ everynight world of her actual lived experience means proceeding differently from the standard practice of sociology. It means, among other things, turning the established enterprise on its head: Rather than explaining how and why people act (or behave) as they do, we would seek from particular experience situated in the matrix of the everyday/ everynight world to explore and display the relations, powers, and forces that organize and shape it.

Many women have called for a sociology based on women's experience (DeVault 1986, 1987; Kasper 1986; McRobbie 1982; Oakley 1981; Paget 1987; Reinharz 1983; Stacey 1988; Stanley and Wise 1983). There has been great unanimity on this score. Though we have worked from this beginning in somewhat different ways, we share this critical stance. Here I am concerned with a problem arising when we try to carry this enterprise beyond the careful and loving listening with which women sociologists have been attending to what women have to tell us of their lives.

A central problem for a feminist sociology is the continual and powerful translation back of our beginnings in women's experience, whether our own or others, into the textual forms of the discourse placing the reading (and writing) subject outside the experience from which she starts. I hold this to be a major issue for feminists. For while we have developed methods of working with women that are fully consultative and open, a moment comes after talk has been inscribed as texts and become data when it must be worked up as sociology.

This chapter explores and unfolds this contradiction.[2] It suggests that a feminist critical consciousness, grounded in experiencing and insisting on knowing from where women are, is reconstructed into the older paths of a patriarchal organization of knowledge as we work within the conventions of sociological discourse. So long as we work within the objectifying frame that organizes the discursive consciousness, we will find ourselves reinscribing the moment of discovery of women's experience, as women talk with women, into the conceptual order that locates the reader's and writer's consciousness outside the experience of that talk.[3]

The objectified and objectifying modes of organizing the systematic consciousness of society developed by sociology (and other social sciences) set up a standpoint within relations of ruling that have class, gender, and racial subtexts. Objectivity in the social sciences is a form of social organization in and through which those who rule transliterate the relevances, experiences, and dialogues going on among them into the universalized forms they must have if they are to be effectively part of the relations of ruling. I will argue here that conventions of objectivity have been laid down as constitutive conventions of sociology, that is, as methods of writing the social into texts, making them recognizable to readers *as* sociology and generating the phenomenal worlds that organize the multiple theoretical enclaves of the discourse.

I'm not addressing the issue of positivism or the related issue of quantitative versus qualitative methods in sociology. The constitutive conventions I am addressing in this chapter are more general and pervasive in the discipline than these special sites. They present special problems for feminists trying to find ways of working from women's experience for two reasons: First, they remorselessly undo our attempts to write a sociology from a standpoint in actual women's experience so that imperceptibly we are returned to just that way of looking we have tried to avoid; second, they organize the construction of a phenomenal world, as the world known to sociology, that incorporates through and through a world known from within the relations of ruling, presupposing the relations of gender, race, and class that are already there. As we work within these conventions, we are returned, I suggest, to the standpoint in the relations of ruling that they carry and transmit, much as a gene carries and transmits particular properties from one generation to the next.

The particular version of the standpoint of women that I've worked with comes out of my own experience. Feminism taught me the freedom to see the significance of working in two worlds for developing an alternative consciousness of society than that I had practiced. When my children were small I was working at the University of California at Berkeley. I went back and forth between doing the work of mothering in all its particularities and demands, and the sociological world-in-texts that I taught and contributed to in my research. Becoming a feminist taught me to see the latter as an integral part of the abstracted, extralocal relations of ruling, so characteristic of the extraordinary societies we live. The work of mothering gave me a site of knowing prior to those relations; it located a knowing within the actualities, the particularities of our being, where knowing is always embodied and where the lifting-up that the abstracted organization of ruling requires is itself a material, actual, work organization, carried on in particular sites, by particular actual people. And, of course, having myself been for several years a secretary, I could add to my understanding of a knowing situated in the actualities of people's worlds, my experience of being among those workers who directly produced for others, for men, the abstract character of texts as mere meaning, purified from the dross of their materiality by she who did the typing (in those days).

In learning feminism, not as a discourse, but as a personal practice, I discovered that I had to discard a practice of being that had involved me in situating myself as subject in the objectified discourses and relations that I now identify as the relations of ruling. I realized slowly that as a member of a department and a university I had participated in decisions and upheld practices that often I had either no personal interest in or at some other level loathed. I had learned to be "responsible."[4] I became conscious that I had learned how to be a subject alienated in an objectified mode. I had learned how to teach sociology as it was embodied in the texts of the discourse and to teach the different perspectives and theories as they were written and authorized. Sociological discourse was something outside me that it was my business to reproduce for students, and I did that pretty well. But feminism called that into question because it called into question the ways in which I had become simply a means through which these objectified modes of ruling were passed on, through which, therefore, ruling got done. I was the medium through which a systematically developed consciousness of society governed by formulations developed at the imperial center were transmitted uncontaminated and unmarred to the provinces.

The critical consciousness of feminism was more than the perception that women were not part of this, it was also a search for a consciousness in myself that had been present (in the anxieties, the tension, the headaches, the feelings of nausea accompanying my work, departmental meetings, trying to write sociology, and so forth) but impotent. It was the learning of how to be a subject in my body, in the actualities of my life, and working from a grounding in experience and an ongoing sensitivity to "where I am." It was the learning and practice of a subject to whom the alienated practice of a subject in the relations of ruling was no longer tolerable.

Of course, this meant doing sociology differently; and it meant too a desire to explore how the relations of ruling were put together, how our lives were shaped and determined from outside us. These have indeed turned out to be aspects of the same enterprise, for to explore alternatives is also to explore how normal sociology is done, and to explore normal sociology has led me to an exploration of the social organization of knowledge in the relations of ruling of which sociology is part. This enterprise has been ruled by a commitment to taking the standpoint of women as I've spelled it out above. This doesn't mean trying to find an experience that is general to all women and setting that up to govern our relevances. It does mean that the knower is always situated in the particular actualities of her everyday world; it means that she's always embodied. That constrains the method of inquiry and analysis. It declares that from a particular standpoint, generalizing relations, objectified knowledge, universalized forms, and so forth are always to be made problematic. There is always a question about how the knower thus situated is enabled to transcend the particular site of her knowing to enter an objectified realm. How does she do it? What are the actual practices of the social organization and relations that she herself knows how to do, and does? What are the material conditions enabling her to neglect her particular local existence, as Alfred Schutz (1962) tells us we must do, to enter the cognitive domain of scientific theory?

I am making use here of just that approach I have been developing elsewhere in my work as a feminist sociologist.[5] It proposes an insider's sociology, that is, a systematically developed consciousness of society from within, renouncing the artifice that stands us outside what we can never stand outside of. Beginning from where the subject is actually located returns us to a social world arising in and known in and through the ongoing actual activities of actual people. Here there is no contrast between thought and practice. Thought, the social forms of consciousness, belief, knowledge, ideology, is as much actual socially organized practice as cutting the grass in the front yard,[6] taking place in real time, in real places, using definite material means and under definite material conditions.

This doesn't mean working subjectively; rather it means working from that site of knowing that is prior to the differentiation of subjective and objective. It means an explication of the actual practices in which we are active. It means attending to the primary materiality of the text as an essential moment in the transition from the locally embodied to the discursive. Hence in exploring how sociology is assembled and organized as actual practices in which we too participate and by which our practices too are organized, we are also engaged in a reflexive examination and critique of what we know how to do and do.

THE OBJECTIFIED ORGANIZATION OF RULING

By the "relations of ruling," I mean that internally coordinated complex of administrative, managerial, professional, and discursive organization that regulates, organizes, governs, and otherwise controls our societies. It is not monolithic,[7] but it is pervasive and pervasively interconnected. It is a *mode* of organizing society that is truly new for it is organized in abstraction from local settings, extralocally, and its textually mediated character is essential (it couldn't operate without texts whether written, printed, televised, or computerized) and characteristic (its distinctive forms of organizing and its capacity to create relations both independent and regulative of local setting depend on texts). This is a world we enter every day when we go to work as sociologists; we enter this world organized in and through texts as we sit down to the computer to write, as we work our way through a stack of papers to grade, as we roam the bookstore looking for ideas for teaching an old course in a new way, as we wrestle with problems of data analysis, as we write a memo to the administration complaining about the arbitrary and unjust intervention they have made into our affairs. We don't even think of it as a world of relations and ourselves as insiders, as its practitioners. It has an ordinary existence for us, the ordinary existence the means, objects, practices, of our coordinated work creates. It has a kind of thickness, a solidity, a taken-for-grantedness for us that is suprising when we consider its primarily textual ground; these are created as we participate with others in the work that orients to and actively accomplishes the features of that reality.

An objectified world-in-common vested in texts is the essential coordinator of activities, decisions, policies, and plans produced by actual subjects as the acts, decisions, policies, and plans of large-scale organizations of various kinds. The primary mode of action and decision in the superstructures of business, government, the professions, and the scientific, professional, literary, and artistic discourses is symbolic and on paper or in computers. The realities to which action and decision are oriented are symbolically constructed *virtual* realities, accomplished in distinctive practices of reading and writing. Their objectification creates the necessary separations between what we know as individuals, located in our particular places in the world, and what we come to know as trained readers of the textual realities, actively implicated in the constitution of a textual world as the same for us as for any other trained reader, a world-in-common and hence a world.

Let me clarify the difference between knowing, arising directly in local historical experience of a subject, and a factual account, a property of the externalized and objectified relations, with an example. In 1968, in Berkeley, California, there was a confrontation between police and street people (Smith 1981). An account of what one witness to the events saw was published in the form of a letter in an underground newspaper. It accused the police of trying to provoke a reaction from the crowd that would justify harassing and arresting them. The story is told from the perspective of someone who was there. It begins when he comes on the scene, ends when he leaves, and is told in terms of what he could see from where he was.

The second story is a rebuttal. It was published from the mayor's office and contains the story as told to the mayor by the chief of police after an internal investigation. The mayor's story, of course, denies the accusation of improper police behavior. But what is of relevance here is that the standpoint built into the mayor's story is quite different from that as told by the witness to the events. The second account is represented as the product of an official inquiry. It is produced in an institutional process using its distinctive methodologies for producing an objectified account. It is not located in the perspective and experience of any particular individual; police officers—presumably the source of the account—appear as interchangeable with one another and have no narrative continuity. Which individual saw what, and was involved in what, cannot be determined.

The reading subject is placed quite differently with respect to the original events by the two accounts. The witness is enraged; he seeks to enliven the reader's anger by sharing his experience with her. The mayor's account in its objectification sets us at a distance, detaches us from the immediacy of the events; it has a different temporal structure setting the events in an institutional order. The methodology of the positionless account[8] relates us differently to what happened than the engaged, involved account given by the witness.

Further, the positionless account both depends upon and transmits the institutional order in which it originates. The witness's account describes one young man being roughly searched by the police and then sent on up the street. The mayor's version is put together quite differently. It is not bounded by the situation of observation. We are told that the young man is a "juvenile" already known to the police. We are told that, far from being sent on up the street, the young man was arrested and later pleaded guilty to the charge of being a minor in possession of alcoholic beverages. A complex division of labor among police, court, probation officers, and the law and legal process provides for the possibility of a description of events beyond the present of observation in which the young man has been charged and found guilty.

Such a social organization of knowledge is integral and essential to the organization of large-scale enterprise, government, and profession and to the organization of a discourse. Objectified worlds-known-in-common are also integral to the organization of sociology as a discourse. It is argued here that the methods of accomplishing its worlds-known-in-common are conventions originating in sociological theories that have had a constitutive force in the organization of the discourse. The conven-

tions provide general procedures for "transliterating" interests and experience of readers and writers of sociological discourse located in particular social relational sites into the objectified forms that entitle them to
treatment as presences in the textual world-in-common of sociological
discourse (and hence subduing individual subjectivity to the authority of
the objectified). They provide methods of writing (and reading) the
social as external to the particularities of people's lives, organizing in that
mode relations among reading subjects and of reading subjects to those
others of whom the text does—or, as we shall see, does not—speak.

THE OBJECTIFICATION OF SOCIETY
IN THE SOCIOLOGICAL TEXT

Shoshana Felman (1987) in her marvelous explication of Jacques
Lacan makes use of Austin's notion of "performative" to contrast the
making of statements with writing (or talk) that *organizes* relations
(Felman 1987). Here we are adopting a similar strategy. It is to attend to
(some) theoretical texts of sociology with respect not to their content or
substance as theoretical statements, or in terms of what they have to say
about "society" or the "social." Rather we will focus here on theories as
organizers of the relations between the textual world created by such
methods in the text and the actual local world of she who writes and
reads sociology. Some, although not all, sociological theory provides
the ground rules or conventions for generating the virtual realities of
sociological discourse.

Of course, society is always and forever through and through brought
into being precisely in such particularities, in actual local settings, at
particular times. Sociology thus has had to struggle with an essential
problem, that of constructing a suprapersonal consciousness out of a
whole stuff that is ineluctably and actually, as I've emphasized above,
known only from within.

From the distinctive site of women's consciousness in the place of our
bodies and in the actualities of our lives, the text is not disembodied
meaning as it is in the theorizing of contemporary literary and philosophical theorists of the text. The text is an actual material presence; it is the
book, the pixilated letters that come up on my computer screen, the
paper, or in whatever form it enters the actual present site of my reading. The text occurs in the actual local historical settings of our reading

and writing. Sitting just where we are, we enter through the text into relations of a different order, the relations mediated by texts that organize our participation as we read. We are raised, in our reading, from the narrow localities of lived actuality into the textual world with its marvelous capacity to launch us as subjects into looking-glass land. From where we are at a particular moment of reading (sitting as I am now in a midsummer café under a colorful umbrella), we haven't already entered the magic of time-space freedom that entry to the textual world gives us; we haven't stepped outside time or outside ourselves. So taking up the material text and reading (or sitting down at the keyboard with the monitor before us and writing) is an actual practice, something I do, you do, and know how to. The text is there as given; it defines a subject or subjects; it calls for and enables methods of reading. We know how, we know partially how, or we may not know how. But in any case our reading is a practical activity in time and as in conversation we are not the same at the end as we were at the beginning. Even though text enables us to escape the local historical constraints of lived actuality, it does so as an ongoing sequence of living in that very actuality. Reading too is living and lived; reading too is practical activity; escaping the constraints of local time and place as lived is a practical activity located in a particular time and place, accomplished by a particular subject.

So here I am, and there you are, my reader. Here I am writing this in a third-floor room looking out at the large old maple tree (now dying from the effects of acid rain) that shades my attic in summer and half-hearing in the background on the radio the latest figures on unemployment in the United States. The linear text conceals my transition from café lunch to workroom. And you, wherever you are, are reading. There is a movement in time, I writing now, you are reading then. I writing then and you reading now. The text lies between us, organizing our relation.

This is the sense of the text I want to hang on to. I want to see texts as occurring in time and as organizing relations between people. I want somehow to move away from the notion of texts as existing as meaning, and see them as occurrences in time (partly captured in Derrida's notion of *différance*) and as organizing, through time, relations between people considered as *sequences of action* in which more than one is involved.

In Alfred Schutz's paper "On Multiple Realities," he writes of different cognitive domains. To each such domain, or "reality," corresponds a specific tension of consciousness, a specific *attention à la vie*. In the domain of scientific theorizing, the subject (knower) sets aside (brackets) his personal life, his pragmatic relevances, the localized time-space coordinates that exist for him as body. He enters as subject the temporal-spatial order of the domain of scientific theorizing according it, during his occupancy, the "accent of reality" (Schutz 1962b). But Schutz's ethnography of consciousness sees the process from one side only. He does not see the essential complement to this work of consciousness, the social organization of that domain, nor its character as a discourse or its essential textuality. For if Schutz's knower is to set aside his personal and local life, what is it about the world he enters that enables that forgetting, that gives him a mode of being and activity in which his personal and local existence has no place, which takes him out of himself? This separation, unproblematic perhaps in the context of natural science, comes to have a peculiar extension in the context of sociology, for it constitutes there a separation between the subject's actual life and the textually mediated discourse that claims to speak of the same world she lives.

Reading sociology, we are reading about a world we are part of and active in, a world that situates exactly the actualities that we live. We are also, of course, reading in that world and being related to the same world as that in which our reading is going on. Sociology then has this peculiarity; it organizes our relations not only to other members of the sociological discourse but also to ourselves and others known and unknown.

What then are the characteristic ways in which sociological texts organize those relations, entering us through them into relations that stand us outside the actualities in which we read, locating us in the objectified modes of the relations of ruling? How do the texts of sociology organize relations between subjects reading and the others of whom they speak, do not speak, or speak only by indirection? In examining these questions, we are examining the properties of what I shall call, for short, "the sociological relation" to emphasize again that analytic attention here is on sociological texts as organizers of reader/writer relations rather than on the substantive propositions of theory. The constitutional theories of sociology have provided methods of writing society into texts. The conventions established construct an objectified standpoint situating their readers and writers in the relations of ruling and subduing particular local positions, perspectives, and experiences. This is *an organization of relations* that we enter in reading.

DESIGNING OBJECTIVITY: ÉMILE DURKHEIM AND OTHERS

(Some) sociological theories have been constitutional for the discourse in providing rules and conventions organizing a standpoint-within-the-text detaching the social-in-the-text from society as it is lived and experienced by those who write and read.[9] Such methods of writing and reading texts create positionless accounts (White 1976), versions of the world in which subject is relegated to no place in particular and before which, therefore, all subjects are equal and equally absent. The construction of an absence of position both enables and is constituted by the writing of accounts of society as if it could be embraced in its totality, the writing of a social system as if indeed there were a position outside, a no place in which totality could be brought into view. At one time, I thought of such positionless accounts as a bird's-eye view, but indeed there is no bird, no place in flight from which a city appears laid out before the subject. The great imaginary constructions are brought before us as if we could participate in that odd mode of knowing that has been attributed to god alone, the capacity to see all aspects at once without taking a particular view or perspective upon them. We can roam then through the corridors and hallways of the text untrammeled by constraints of space and time. There is no now or then, there is no distance, nearness.

Such organization is realized in the textual practice accomplishing the appropriate, proper formation of discursive entities and objects (Foucault 1974), the proper attributions of capacities such as subject, agency, causal efficacy, and so forth, and hence the proper calling of syntactic relations among discursive entities. Sociological theories providing "constitutional" rules and conventions can be thought of as governing these textual practices, selecting of language forms and syntax in the writing of society into the text.[10]

In exploring theory as an organization of sociological discourse, I turn first to the rules of sociological method developed by Émile Durkheim. These have, of course, been subsequently challenged, improved upon, modified, and discarded. I shall suggest, however, that they are of particular significance because they enunciate conventions that have become standard, normal practices of writing sociological texts. I am not making a historical argument here in the sense of what or who came first. I am making the claim that these, among other early sociological texts, were foundational and that in them we can identify a set of constitutive conventions that, stripped of their vulgar positivism, can be identified as normal practices of writing sociological texts and hence of producing the world in texts organizing sociology as discourse.

Durkheim's *The Rules of Sociological Method* are designed cumulatively. He goes through a series of steps, each building upon its predecessor and enabling its succesor. These steps (1) suspend the presence of the subject; (2) posit social phenomena (or social facts) as existing externally to particular individuals; (3) reattribute agency from subject to social phenomena; (4) require explanations of social phenomena to be in terms of social phenomena (without reference to other orders of being such as biology or psychology); and (5) substitute for goals, purposes, and so on the conception of function as a procedure for expressing relations among social phenomena. We try then to see these steps in the performative mode, that is, imagining how the reader learns from the text a practice of thinking society into texts.

Durkheim's first step is teaching us to "see" an objectified order of presence that is independent of particular subjectivities:

> There is in every society a certain group of phenomena which may be differentiated from those studied by the other natural sciences. When I fulfil my obligations as brother, husband, or citizen, when I execute my contracts, I perform duties which are defined, externally to myself and my acts, in law and in custom. Even if they conform to my own sentiments and I feel their reality subjectively, such reality is still objective, for I did not create them; I merely inherited them through my education. (Durkheim 1964, p.1)

We learn the externality of law and custom in learning to ignore the testimony of experience. The issue here is not the social efficacy of law and custom. It is rather the procedure the reader learns from this text, which is to exclude what subjects might feel of duty, guilt, or the like as a component of the social-in-the-text. What subjects feel or think is declared as simply irrelevant to the constitution of the sociological phenomenon. The objectification of law or custom is *to be accomplished* by following a procedure something like this: Find ways of writing about law or custom (or whatever) to exclude reference to subjectivities.

And having been instructed in a preliminary, simple procedure for constructing social facts, agency can be transferred from actual subjects to the virtual entities of the sociological text.

These types of conduct or thought are not only external to the individual but are, moreover, endowed with coercive power, by virtue of which they impose themselves upon him, independent of his individual will. Of course, when I fully consent and conform to them, this constraint is felt only slightly, if at all, and is therefore unnecessary. But it is, nonetheless, an intrinsic characteristic of these facts, the proof thereof being that it asserts itself as soon as I attempt to resist it. If I attempt to violate the law, it reacts against me so as to prevent my act before its accomplishment, or to nullify my violation by restoring the damage, if it is accomplished and reparable, or to make me expiate it if it cannot be compensated for otherwise. (Durkheim 1964, p. 2)

The first step that objectifies has already laid the basis entitling us to ascribe agency to law or custom. Law assumes the function of agent; "it" reacts.

This ground achieved, Durkheim is able to make a move that would otherwise be incredible. Thinking and feeling can now be treated as objectified agents acting on and controlling individuals: "Here, then, is a category of facts with very distinctive characteristics: it consists of ways of acting, thinking, and feeling, external to the individual, and endowed with a power of coercion, by reason of which they control" (Durkheim 1964, p. 4).

Through steps such as these Durkheim sets up procedures for constituting an object world that is the proper object of sociology. It is a self-contained world, explicity independent of biology and psychology. A new variety of phenomena is constituted and it is to this exclusively that the term *social* ought to be applied (Durkheim 1964, p. 3).

The introduction of functional reasoning is the final step: *"When, then, the explanation of a social phenomenon is undertaken, we must seek separately the efficient cause which produces it and the function it fulfils"* (Durkheim 1964, p. 95).[11]

This has two effects; one of introducing a final cause that grounds and governs the attribution of agency to "social facts," transferring telos from subjects to society;[12] more important is the creation of a self-contained explanatory space in which social facts are explained socially (in Durkheim, with reference to a reified conception of society). Sociology is thereby insulated from the claims of other disciplines to its empirical.

We could, I think, trace the history of these constitutive conventions as they are rewritten, modified, and their awkward and sometimes incoherent postulates refined and even discarded. But, of course, that isn't possible or indeed relevant here. The interest here is in isolating some of the steps that have brought us to the conventions with which we now work. Here the constitutional work of Talcott Parsons has been of major significance. He does away with the prima facie problems arising from Durkheim's impetous and unconvincing elimination of the subject. He overcomes the problem of Durkheim's declaration-by-fiat of the externality of a normative and representational order vis-à-vis the individual, first, by building his theoretical structure upon an abstraction of the actor, disembodied, and assigned just those properties that are concordant with the theoretical order (Parsons 1968),[13] and, second, by adapting psychoanalysis as a theory of the internalization of practically everything (Parsons 1982) so that subjects are in effect treated as *expressions* of a sociocultural system.

Equally important is Parsons's establishment of conceptual procedures in which the virtual reality of society, as an essential organizing constituent of the emerging discourse, is vested. He set up an array of concepts defining the parameters of the field, role, role-expectations, social system, norms, values, order, and so forth, perhaps even introducing the importance of such concepts as organizers of sociological discourse. As procedures for ordering transliterations from actuality to sciological text, they hold and carry, as constituents of their "genetic" material, the objectification of the social. They govern the narrative practices of sociology, producing society as an emergent that can be stripped away from individual actors who can then be reconstituted in the text as "bearers"[14] of structure or system. The actualities of a world created in the actual activities of actual individuals are transliterated to a textual order in which those actualities can be read as properties of *system* or *structure* (other such term with a different provenance are *class, stratification, status, power,* and so forth). As concepts such as these become ordinary sociological currency, they vest objectifying practices in the discourse. We don't have to go back to Durkheim any longer or even to Parsons to find out how to accomplish the proper objectifications of sociology; we learn to use its concepts.

Subsequent developments have stripped sociology of the global theorizing that characterized the foundational work of theorists such as Durkheim and Parsons. But the framework organizing the discourse that their and similar work founded has remained. Subsequent steps have detached the principles and conventions organizing an objectification of the same world that sociologists live from inside. The founding theories are no longer needed. Robert Merton argued for "theories of the middle-range" in contrast to the global theorizing of his predecessors

(Merton 1967). In proposing a strategy of building cumulatively toward the grand theoretical synthesis, he in effect stripped away the grand theoretical enterprise while preserving the "logic" of the relations grand theory had put in place. Discarding functionalism on the grand scale, he preserved it as a device for isolating sociological knowledge from what anyone might know by distinguishing between manifest and latent function, between functions of which people are or may be aware and that may indeed be planfully organized and produced, and latent functions, the unseen interrelations of social phenomena. Later Kingsley Davis declared the demise of functionalism, arguing that the interrelations among elements of social structure were now fully established as normal sociological practice (Davis 1967). Davis was announcing publicly a shift that had already taken place in sociological practice. The ad hoc "theorizing" of the relations among variables, the increasingly sophisticated methods of theorizing variables and of developing and testing hypotheses, the technically sophisticated methods of sampling, of developing "instruments," and of measurement give practical substance to the organization set in place by theorists such as Durkheim.

Such methods operate within and give technical substance to the parameters of the discursive space organized by the founding fathers. They realize as sociological practice (1) a discursive universe vis-à-vis which the reading subject is positionless—she cannot locate its presences in relation to the actual site and situation of her reading; (2) the suppression of the presence of subjects as others whose presence defines the reader, who are related to the reader in and through the text; (3) the constitution of boundaries demarcating sociology from other disciplines and establishing an internally referential universe of entitites; (4) the constitution of a self-contained discursive world that does not require (let alone insist on) a reflexive grounding in actualities for its sense[15] or, while dependent on actual individuals to produce what it recognizes as phenomena, require that their active presence be registered in the text.

ORDINARY SOCIOLOGICAL
PRACTICES OF OBJECTIFICATION

The world as we know it in our everyday/everynight direct experience of it doesn't "naturally" yield up the properties and organization of the virtual realities of sociological discourse. The foundational conventions of sociology provide a general set of instructions for selecting and shaping concepts and categories, grammatical forms expressing relations among them, and methods of representation.[16] Here are examples of how they work in practice.

Suspending the Presence of the Subject

Positing social phenomena (or social facts) as existing externally to particular individuals has been developed through the development of specialized conceptual and categorial forms that operate as objectifying devices. Characteristic are methods of representing people's activities, talk, relations, thinking, without the subjects who act, talk, relate, think. A common practice is the use of nominalization, where a verb expressing the action of a subject is given the form of a noun. For example, *aggression, depression, suicide, family violence.* Related are terms construing subjective states of individuals, as entities in and of themselves, capable of entering into relations with other such entities. Examples are *attitude, opinion* (as in *opinion poll*), *motivation, belief, alienation, interests;* also reliance on terms originating in "institutional" forms such as *law, education, medicine.*

Reattributing Agency from Subject to Social Phenomena

An example is useful to show that agency is reattributed from subject to social phenomena. There's a considerable body of studies focusing on the relations among family, class, and school achievement. Here is a passage from Maurice Craft's (1970) introduction to a British collection of papers on the topic:

> Demographic calculations tell us little of the subcultural processes (social class attitudes), or of the more intricate psychosocial processes of the individual family which together provides the motivation to excel and the implementary values which can turn school achievement into career success. (Craft 1970, p. 7)

This passage is almost overloaded with terms of the kind described above. Here too we can see how this enables a shift of agency from people to the sociologically constituted entity. Behind the veil of such formulations are women and men whose work in the home is directly oriented toward a child's work in school. People take time, think and plan, and work under definite material conditions within constraints placed on them by the exigencies of providing the economic basis of the family. They also work within constraints and under standards imposed on them by the schools that for the most part they have little control over. The term "intricate psychosocial processes" collects the work and thought of actual people into a sociological entity that is the agent in the text, providing "the motivation to excel and the implementary values" turning school achievement to career success. In an analogous version, homes provide varying levels and kinds of the cultural capital that determines school achievement (Bourdieu and Passeron 1977).

The relations among sociologically constituted phenomena explain sociologically constituted phenomena. The drama of sociological texts is the active relations among phenomena (dependent variables ruled by independent variables, structures ruling history, culture ruling consciousness) transliterated from human lives and activities.

Detaching the Sociological from the Actual

Various methodological moves have deprived the dominant sociological discourse of accountability to the actual. Parsons's conception of the analytic status of theory, categories, and concepts vis-à-vis the actual removes theory from the requirement that it recover properties or features of the actualities of people's lives.

> Analytical theory in the sense in which I mean the term here. is a body of logically interrelated generalized concepts (logical universals) the specific facts corresponding to which (particulars) constitute statements describing empirical phenomena. (Parsons 1982a, p. 72)

Facts themselves are conceptually ordered. It is a procedure that privileges the order of the discourse over the order of the actual. Analysis, for Parsons, isn't dissection, isn't exploring the anatomy of a social world, but the conceptual carving out from "the concrete phenomena" (Parsons 1982a, p. 73) those aspects constituting (and constituted by) the values of variables. Such thinking has been foundational to the later positivism of quantitative research, developments to which the philosophical positivism of Carl Hempel has written the conceptual architecture.

In different ways, such moves privilege the textual order of discourse and its textually constituted realities as the object of sociological work. A peculiar distance between the discursive world and the actual world is created. Theory, concepts, categories, of discourse aren't accountable to the actual; theories may be tested through hypotheses generated from them, but the *existence* and privileging of the discursive world itself is never called into question. The universe created within sociological texts by such methods realizes in its research practices the actual as an expression of the discursive. It is a peculiarity of sociological discourse that its constitutional procedures deny it any common ground *outside the text* to which sociologists can refer in settling disputes. Common ground must be constructed within the text and is always held in place by prior agreement about and commitment to the conventions that sustain it.

Reconstructing Subjects as Figments of Discourse

The practices evolved from constitutional principles privilege socio-logical interpretations. It is normal practice to treat our interpretations as the attributes, properties, interpretations of subjects of study. The originals are entered into the sociological texts as pseudosubjects, categories of personages, such as parents, children, to whom the objectified attributes and properties can be assigned, sometimes producing the appearance of action, but action fully regulated by the sociological theorizing of relations. Here is a story about how the school performance of children is influenced by the attitudes of parents (Douglas 1970, p. 151).

> The middle-class parents take more interest in their children's progress at school than the normal working-class parents do, and they become relatively more interested as their children grow older. They visit the schools more frequently to find out how their children are getting on with their work, and when they do so are more likely to ask to see the Head as well as the class teacher, whereas the manual working-class parents are usually content to see the class teacher only. (Douglas 1970, p. 152)

Actual subjects are entered into the text as actors in the sociologist's narrative. We can imagine the methodological techniques providing for this transition. The sociologist can begin with a concept that will organize the transposition of what subjects say, and say about what they do, as a variable. Concepts of parental attitudes or interests make use of theoreti-cal work already completed that provides for the treatment of subjective states as an objectified entity, "attitude." In using such a concept to organize inquiry, sociologists develop "indicators" (numbers of visits to school, whether parents see head or class teacher, and so on), that is, have specified what interviewed subjects might say and report of what they do as expressions of the discursively constructed object.

The actual then becomes an indicator of the discursively constructed phenomena. For example, numbers of parental visits to school and to school principal are used as an indication of "parental interest" (Musgrove 1970). Such elaborate, technical, and artful practices produce from the actualities of people's lives readings that are expressed in terms that are not theirs and from a standpoint that is no one in particular's. They also enable properties of the social organization and relations in which people are active to be attributed to the constructed individuals who represent them in the sociologist's narrative. Even the interpretive sociologies insisting that our interpretations conform to those of our subjects still entitle the sociologist to take away what people have told us and remake it in the terms of our discourse, creating in the text the subjects who bear our interpretations (as well shall see).[17]

HOW CONSTITUTIVE CONVENTIONS SUBVERT THE FEMINIST ENTERPRISE

Feminists, myself among them, have criticized the overriding of women's local experience by the interpretive hegemony of sociology and have sought solutions. We have made a specifically feminist critique of sociology's objectifying practices. Judith Stacey (1988) writes:

> Feminist scholars evince widespread disenchantment with the dualisms, abstractions, and detachment of positivism, rejecting the separations between subject and object, thought and feeling, knower and known, and political and personal as well as their reflections in [sic] the arbitrary boundaries of traditional academic discipline. Instead most feminist scholars advocate an integrative, trans-disciplinary approach to knowledge which grounds theory contextually in the concrete realm of women's everyday lives. (Stacey 1988, p. 23)

This critique cannot be reduced, as it sometimes is, to a critique of positivism or as calling for traditional qualitative methods. Rather it searches for a sociology related quite differently to its subjects, denying the separations that refuse to admit to discursive presence subjects in the fullness of their feeling, thought, and knowing.

But in seeking an alternative, we all too often find ourselves caught in a trap created by the constitutive conventions of our discipline. We begin with attempting to establish relations with subjects that don't produce them as research objects. Shulamit Reinharz (1983), for example, has developed a conception of experiential analysis, recommending that sociologist and subjects work out interpretations together as a joint product rather than simply imposing upon subjects. Stacey (1988) sought consciously to work with her respondents by treating them as full subjects, getting to know them well, even developing friendships. Ann Oakley (1981) sought an approach that involved an interchange between herself and those she interviewed. These are only some of the many innovative approaches to the feminist researcher's relation to her respondents. The problem does not lie here, but at the next stage.

Both Reinharz and Stacey locate problems of disjuncture in the process of producing the research product. Reinharz locates these in the historical process that breaks apart the developments in the local setting and the agreed-on framework. Stacey attends to a more fundamental difficulty, one that I would like to suggest is "symptomatic" of the organizing power of the sociological relation built into discourse over the years.

> A major area of contradiction between feminist principles and ethnographic method involves the dissonance between fieldwork practice and ethnographic product. Despite the aspects of intervention and exploitation I have described, ethnographic method appears to (and often does) place the researcher and her informants in a collaborative, reciprocal quest for understanding, but the research product is ultimately that of the researcher, however, modified or influenced by informants. With very rare exceptions it is the researcher who narrates, who "authors" the ethnography. In the last instance an ethnography is a written document structured primarily by a researcher's purposes, offering a researcher's interpretations, registered in a researcher's voice. (Stacey 1988, p. 23)

Stacey individualizes the dilemma. But the protagonist of her story is a researcher producing a research product. The relations of the discourse (or discourses) within which research is conceived are already implicated. The research product will be located in the ongoing textually mediated conversation of sociology. It will, I suggest, be in some way organized by the sociological relation, even when the researcher is committed to work from the viewpoint of subjects. Even working collaboratively with subjects on the production of the interpretation of their talk does not as such exorcise the presence and power of the founding conventions of the discourse.

Here is an instance of the emergence of this contradiction at the juncture between "interviewing" and the sociological product. Ann Oakley (1981), in the paper "Interviewing Women: A Contradiction in Terms," referred to above, analyzes a "lack of fit" between the proper sociological practice of interviewing as the textbooks prescribe it, and what happens when a feminist interviews women. She describes her own experience of doing a study of women's experience of pregnancy and childbirth. It was, she found, ridiculous, if not impossible, to avoid personal involvement. The women she talked to asked her questions and were interested in her own experience. She saw no reason not to engage with them fully as a person and did so, answering their questions, responding to their interest, getting to know many of them, some as friends or long-term acquaintances.

Yet turning to an analysis of some of the interview material, we find that the switch engineered by the constitutive conventions has gone through. With Hilary Graham, Oakley wrote a paper called "Competing Ideologies of Reproduction: Medical and Material Perspectives on Pregnancy" (Graham and Oakley 1981). The title itself is indicative of the power of the founding conventions. The paper, using a wealth of interview material, describes two different perspectives on childbirth, that of obstetrician and that of women in childbirth. The two perspectives conflict:

> Specifically, our data suggest that mothers and doctors disagree on whether pregnancy is a natural or a medical process and whether, as a consequence, pregnancy should be abstracted from the woman's life-experiences and treated as an isolated medical event. (Graham and Oakley 1981, p. 52)

We've still got people here. But they are now framed as instances or expressions of a conflict that is located in ideology. The actualities explored in interviews and observation, become *illustrations* of the two frames of reference. Graham and Oakley (1981, p. 52) write, for example, of "some of the ways in which the differences between them [the two frames of reference] are displayed in antenatal consultations and women's experience of having a baby." There is a characteristic, although undramatic, shift of agency. They ask: "How do the conflicts . . .

between medical and maternal frames of reference manifest them-selves?" (Graham and Oakley 1981, p. 56). The conflicts are not conflicts directly between doctors and patients. The conception of two ideologies orders a selection of passages from interviews contrasting what women in childbirth say with what obstetricians say. The conflict is a dramatic production scripted by the sociologists in the virtual reality of the text.

The convention of explaining social phenomena in terms of social phenomena is also found, although in a relatively weak form, as conflicts between the two perspectives are "explained" "by rooting [them] in the particular frames of reference employed by the providers and users of maternity care." The displacement from subjects to discourse is decisively characteristic. Although multiple citations from interview material are used and no causal attributions are made, the "constitutional" move shifts agency from people to discursively constructed entities. The relationships are not between pregnant women and doctors but (as the title indicates) between medical and maternal perspectives.

My second example is not a feminist text.[18] I came across it in investigating the ways in which the constitutive conventions can be seen to be at work in qualitative sociologies and use it because it exemplifies the contradiction between commitment to the viewpoint of subjects and the capacity of the constitutive conventions to subvert it. In this instance the researchers were explicit in intending to work from the subjects' point of view. A work by Peter March, Elizabeth Rosser, and Rom Harré (1978), *The Rules of Disorder,* claims to do a study that expresses the standpoint of young men[19] involved in the notorious football gangs of British soccer.

> We have come to see it through the eyes of the people who take part in it [what is happening]. They see their social life as a struggle for personal dignity in a general social framework that daily denies them this dignity. Far from valuing disorder, they are engaged in the genesis of significance for their lives and an order in their action that is their own. The struggle begins when they see many of the things that seem routine to the rest of us as ways of devaluing them. (March et al. 1978, p. 2)

However the researchers may have begun their project, in the analysis and writing they create a structure subduing the voices of those with whom they talked to just that organization of relations in the text that I am exploring. They begin with a critical view of how these young men and their activities are presented in the press and in the pronouncements of a British intelligentsia. Their own strategy will diverge; they will work differently; they will look at things "through the eyes of the people who take part in [them]." They are also specifically critical of Parsons's theorizing of school as integrating young people into the larger social order. From the point of view of the playground, they argue, school is to be seen as generating an alternative order in the playground, deviant in terms of the official norms. Notions of order, deviance, and so on are, of course, familiar vesting devices entering the constitutive conventions of sociology into the text. Inverting the standard application of these concepts doesn't change the standpoint built into them; the latter is carried in the concepts like a virus hidden in computer software.

The researchers' interviewing and analysis is organized by the notion of rule. Rule has become one of those "vesting" concepts referred to above in my discussion of Parsons. For these researchers, "rule" will bridge the "view through their [informants'] eyes" and the sociologists' interpretation of these young men as participating in an alternative order. The concept of rule runs a line through the interviews and other ethnographic material linking artfully selected passages as expressions of the sociologically known. Working within the constitutive conventions, almost as a discursive habit, the viewpoint written into the text shifts imperceptibly to the standard sociological standpoint. The young men's view is supplanted.

Much theoretical and methodological work is done to transfer the constructs of discourse to the subjects, producing them as "figments" of discourse. This has the effect, as so many such devices do, of making the transition from subjects' viewpoint to researchers' invisible by attributing the latter to the former.[20] The researchers want to interpret the behavior of the young men on the football ground as governed by rules. They also want to be able to treat such rules as the sociological expression of the views and actions of the young men. They hold that they are entitled to use the concept of rule in this way if they can show that in fact their subjects do use rules in guiding their actions. This can be established if respondents talk rules.[21] Thus what the young men do can be interpreted as an expression of "rule" if the subjects themselves will tell or talk about rules. And indeed they do, in interviews, if the extracts are any indication, in which respondents produce "rule like" statements in response to questions about the reasons why they did such and such. The interviewer is complicit in producing the rules.

At the beginning of the book, they describe the young men they studied as the "dramatis personae." The metaphor expresses exactly the sociological relation created in the text. Respondents have the appearance of free agents. They have the appearance of speaking with their own voices. But in fact the sociologists' script prescribes how they appear and what they say. The sociologists speak through their dramatis personae.[22] Standpoint has in effect been conceptually shifted from that of the young men with whom they talked, and whose viewpoint they had wanted to make central, back to the standpoint of the discourse locating the reading subject in the relations of ruling.

FEMINIST RESISTANCE

Sociology as a discipline arises in and never manages to leave behind a struggle with the problem of how to extricate its discursive self from the society in which that discursive being is always necessarily embedded. Unlike the natural sciences, it has never developed technologies of encounter with reality that fully and as a practical matter constitute it as other. Its objectifications are always at odds with the lived actuality in which they are accomplished. The essential fracture continually breaks through as each next attempt to resolve the contradiction re-creates it. Sociological discourse is marked with constant breaks and discontinuities as we are nudged once again by our own life experience to make it somehow say what it will not say, or will say only partially; there is a constant struggle going on to remake the discourse so that finally what is unsatisfactory, missing, unclaimed, unspoken, will somehow find its discursive vehicle (Stinchcombe 1983).

But the problem we have confronted is more than simply a disjuncture between the world and the discourse that knows it. The feminist critique has questioned the standpoint from which sociology is written. Sociological discourse builds in a standpoint in the relations of ruling that have been occupied almost exclusively by White men, and the phenomenal world it has created has been the view from their site. Here is Pat Hill Collins's 1986 critique of the categories vesting the sociological representation of the family that absent the experience and consciousness of Black women.

> Sociological generalizations about families that do not account for Black women's experience will fail to see how the public/private split shaping household composition varies across social and class groupings, how racial/ethnic family members are differentially integrated into wage labor, and how families alter their household structure in response to changing political economies (e.g., adding more people

> and becoming extended, fragmenting family and becoming female-headed, and
> migrating to locate better opportunities). Black women's family experiences repre-
> sent a clear case of the workings of race, gender, and class oppression in shaping
> family life. Bringing undistorted observations of Afro-American women's family
> experiences into the center of analysis again raises the question of how other
> families are affected by these same forces. (Collins 1986, p. S29)

Indeed, bringing undistorted observations of African American women's family experiences into the center of analysis does more than raise questions about the effect of these forces on other families;[23] it subverts the sociological relation that has written into sociology the exclusion of Black women and continues to write in other exclusions whose representatives have still to be heard. As Sandra Harding (1986) has pointed out, the opening of public discourse to mulitple voices and perspectives calls into question the very notion of a single standpoint from which a final overriding version of the world can be written. Indeed the constitution of society as *object* accomplished by conformity to the founding conventions of sociology also constitutes the singular omni-present Archimedean subject that feminism calls into question. The specific competence of the founding conventions is the resolution of multiplicity into one.

Of course, sociology has back doors through which the local histori-cal actualities of sociologist's experience leak into the sociological text, as Arthur Stinchcombe has described, but as he also describes, the end product is a reworking of the object.[24] At each historical point the society objectified in sociological discourse crystallizes the invisible presences and concerns of its makers; at each historical point, it sanctifies through such objectification the institutionalized exclusions, as *subjects,* from the discourses of power, of women as a social category, of people of color, and of members of nondominant classes. Sociology's constitutive con-ventions are organizers of those relations among ourselves and among ourselves in relation to others. They have their political effect. They subdue people's ordinary everyday/everynight knowledge of society; they seal off sociology, as a systematically developed consciousness of society, from modes of knowing beginning where people are, in their lives, who are not among the makers of discourse or participants in ruling.

To seek alternatives is also to revise our relations, to seek a sociology that, as systematic consciousness of society, learns it from inside, from precisely the multiple standpoints from which the social relations in which we are active and that determine our lives are known, creating accounts of their organization and dynamics that are constantly enriched as they are explored again from a new site.

Susan Sherwin (1988) writes about the differences between how masculinist and feminist philosophers proceed. She proposes a feminist transformation of the relations of knowing, contrasting a feminist ideal of "cooperative, collective work" with the competition for certainties, the zero-sum approach to truth, characteristic of traditional masculinist philosophy.[25] Feminist ideals call for very different social relations of knowledge:

> Scholarship in pursuit of a shared goal is to be undertaken as a collective enterprise where different people do piece-work on different aspects of the problem. . . . Each contribution is related to the larger system of ideas, the larger project, and is not offered as a private theory then to bear one's name. (Sherwin 1988, p. 23)

Of course, a sociology for women, for people, seeking a knowledge of how our lives and relations (direct and indirect) are shaped, directs us toward a knowledge community beyond our discipline. Discovering and uncovering how our societies are put together must embrace in its cooperative growing those who have formerly been the objects of our study and must now be, in a new sense, its subjects, its knowers.

We do not despise our knowledge and our skills. It is not these as such that divide sociologists from those to whom we would be responsible and responsive. A revolution must also have a division of labor. And others have skills and knowledge we do not have. But we are hampered by methods of writing the social into texts that seal in a knowledge divorced from the lively part it might play in coming with others to know, *together,* our relations and society differently, from within yet not subjectively, knowing them as we actively participate in them and as they are brought into being in the actual practices of actual people in the multiple sites from which they are experienced.

NOTES

1. I use the term *discourse* somewhat differently from other writers. I want to encompass more than statements or the concepts, frameworks, methodologies of a discipline. We are talking about the same world as we inhabit and our knowledge of it; our share in its ongoing accomplishment is the basis on which we can claim to know and speak of it. Sociology known in this way isn't just ideas in people's heads but a complex of sites,

communications, printed texts, teaching in classrooms; a work of reading and writing from and to reading; of the practices of inquiry, thinking, ideas, concepts; of multiple settings of organized talk—workshops, conferences, annual meetings—all of which imply, involve, are accomplished by, and exist only in people's actual activities of which thinking is one moment. I use the term *discourse* to identify these socially organized complexes of actions and material conditions, of course, including the texts and statements they bear. I've adapted my use of the term from Michel Foucault's use (Foucault 1974) to describe the actual organization of social relations coordinating multiple sites through the reading and writing of texts, without compression within a single budgetary jurisdiction and hence single system of accountability (business, government agency, university, or the like). As I use it, the term *discourse* refers exclusively to what I have distinguished here as "textually mediated discourse."

2. I've worked in a preliminary way on this topic first in a presentation to Judith Baker's course in philosophy at Glendon College, York University, in the spring of 1988, and then in a paper called "Writing Sociology: The Feminist Contradiction" presented at a conference, the Feminist Transformations of the Social Sciences, at Hamilton College, Clinton, New York, in April 1988 (Smith 1988). I am very appreciative of these opportunities to work out and try out a rather complex argument.

3. Note that this is *not* an epistemological issue. It is not an issue of realism, positivism, interpretive sociology, or the like. Sociological epistemologies for the most part presuppose the sociological relations that I've attempted to delineate here.

4. Indeed my dissertation supervisor compared me favorably to other women who had dropped out of the Ph.D. program at Berkeley (largely, I believe, because of the systematic but impalpable discouragement they experienced), telling me that the difference between myself and other women graduate students was that I was "responsible."

5. Of course, this approach has an intellectual history, even though its break with "normal" sociology is sharp in at least one major respect that will be clearer later. But I should acknowledge my intellectual debts to men from whom I have learned a great deal about how to do it. These are Karl Marx, George Herbert Mead, and Maurice Merleau-Ponty.

6. For a fuller exposition of this approach, see Chapter 3 of my *The Everyday World as Problematic: A Feminist Sociology* (Smith 1987). It is a method developed from a conjunction of the materialist method developed by Marx and Engels (Marx and Engels 1970) and Garfinkel's ethnomethodology (Garfinkel 1967). Both of these ground inquiry in the actual ongoing activities of actual individuals. For Marx and Engels, society and history come into being only as the ongoing actual activities of individuals and the material conditions of those activities and not otherwise. Although there are, of course, important divergences, notably in the siting of Marxist materialism in the labor, the ongoing productive work that both produces and is the very form of social existence, as contrasted with the siting of ethnomethodology in micro-social contexts, in which activities in language are the differentiated and virtually exclusive mode. In particular Garfinkel's work opens up the site of concerted social activities and practices in the textually mediated organization of management, professional work, government agencies, and so on to inquiry conforming to the stipulations of a materialist method, which requires a focus on actual ongoing practices in definite actual settings. It is this aspect of his method and thinking that I have brought into relation to Marxist materialism as I have interpreted it and that I have developed in my work in the social organization of knowledge.

7. Although it currently has quite a strong monolithic tendency.

8. See Hayden White's analysis of this form (White 1976).

9. Indeed, it could be argued that sociology has been peculiarly subject to theorizing that makes primarily constitutional claims.

10. My interest here is in the constitutional dimensions of theories that organize the objectification of society in the discourse and in so doing organize the discourse. I am not concerned with epistemological issues such as positivism. This is not a critique of positivism but an exploration of the social organization of discourse.

11. Italicized in the original.

12. Thus Durkheim: "We use the word 'function,' in preference to 'end' or 'purpose,' precisely because social phenomena do not generally exist for the useful results they produce. We must determine whether there is a correspondence between the fact under consideration and the general needs of the social organism, and in what this correspondence consists, without occupying ourselves with whether it has been intentional or not. All these questions of intention are too subjective to allow of scientific treatment" (Durkheim 1964, p. 95).

13. Thus Parsons in *The Structure of Social Action:* "The unit of reference which we are considering as the actor is not this organism ['a spatially distinguishable separate unit in the world' as studied by the biologist or 'behavioristic' psychologist], but an 'ego' or 'self.' The principal importance of this consideration is that the body of the actor forms, for him, just as much part of the situation of action as does the 'external environment'"(Parsons 1968, p. 47).

14. To use a term from Marx that has been given central theoretical weight in the work of Louis Althusser.

15. That, as Garfinkel has instructed us (Garfinkel 1967), such a universe of discourse is always necessarily indexical does not preclude the existence of conventions that constitute a claim to self-subsistence.

16. I was recently reading Peter Gay's collection of "Enlightenment" texts and was struck by the absence of many of the devices I'm describing here in the writings of the Scottish philosophers (represented here by Hume, Ferguson, and Smith). The possibility of producing the social as agent independent of actual individuals seemed in general not available to them. Typically generalized properties of societies were handled by treating larger units as collectivities resolvable into individual members replicating properties assigned to the collectivity (this would seem to be the origin of the "national character" type of thinking that was still popular up to 20 years ago), or as typifications or personifications (the use of typal concepts such as Man, species concepts such as Mankind, or personifications such as Nature). Collective terms were handled pronominally in the plural so that at the point of action they were resolved into individual actors. These devices were most prominent in the excerpts from Adam Ferguson's *A History of Civil Society.* It is interesting that excerpts from Adam Smith's *The Wealth of Nations* showed more instances of causal relations posited between abstract properties of economy and society, notably quantifiable (in principle) entities such as wealth and population growth. Obviously, this is an area that would be worth an investigation, which I don't have time for at this point. For excerpts from David Hume, Adam Ferguson, and Adam Smith, see Gay (1973).

17. Schutz, a major proponent of such commitment to keeping faith with subject nonetheless destined subjects' constructs to form the motivations of homunculi representing those motivations and their effects in pure form—presumably after the model of

economic reasoning (Schutz 1962). See also my comments on Max Weber's method of *verstehen* in Chapter 3 of *The Everyday World as Problematic* (Smith 1987).

18. It is perhaps even masculinist. I have cleaned up the account a bit so that this dimension is subdued because it is not my main point.

19. Note that a major problem in this study is the treatment of a story about young men as a story about youth. I wondered as I read about the relations of young women to these groups and in the situations described. I thought that an account from *their* view-point might result in an account that was considerably less sympathetic. I think the same of Paul Willis's *Learning to Labour* (Paul Willis 1977). Apart from these issues, the formula-tion of general statements as statements about youth in general and a youth subculture is extremely problematic in the textual suppression of young women.

20. This is the "cultural dopes" procedure that Harold Garfinkel has criticized though on other grounds. It is also a procedure foundational to contemporary cultural theory, one put in place in part by structuralism, but more strikingly by the constitutional procedures developed by Jacques Lacan to treat the subject as a property of discourse (in a sense inclusive of but broader than by usage here).

21. Contrast the extraordinary ethnographic clarity of Laurence Wieder's work in insisting that the notion of rules in ethnographic contexts be restricted to situations in which "rules" are actually talked about by members of the setting in the ordinary course of its and their business (Wieder 1974). Much of ethnomethodology avoids the constitutive conventions, although as it develops on from its startling and revolutionary founding impetus, some of it has reassumed them as its concealed working practices.

22. Paul Willis's *Learning to Labour* is again an example. He was close to the young men whose lives in school and out were the source of his ethnography, but strikingly when he asked them to read it, as he reports honorably in an appendix, they could only read the bits about themselves, although they tried (Willis 1977, p. 195). Perhaps this was simply a problem of the language in which it is written, but as we have seen, in sociology, the language is precisely the problem that is the concern here and Marxist sociology has been quite as much governed by the founding conventions of sociology as any other.

23. Indeed, Pat Hill Collins may be skipping over a textually concealed contradiction between *observing* African American women and their experience—as they tell it.

24. Stinchcombe (1983, p. 10) writes: "As a discipline, sociology as a social structure leads toward scholasticism. But fortunately scholars are not allowed to construct monaster-ies, so there is a constant stream of empirical pollutants that threaten the scholastic structure. The reason we go to such effort and have some venom behind our pejoratives for those who upset the cultural system of the discipline by letting in undisciplined facts is because they are serious threats. There are enough general intellectuals, enough people who deal with problems in their own lives through intellectualization, enough people who take what they say about sex and ambition in the classroom seriously in their scholarly life, to supply the materials for a constant tension within the sociological community. The thing that keeps our scholastic structure from being perfect and eternal is that we keep having our attention called to social facts that we cannot yet manage without it turning into 'high class journalism' or 'catering to the students' interest'. This threatens discipline, yet it keeps it alive. The disorganized flow of empirical social reality is the only thing that creates problems difficult enough to make it worthwhile to have a discipline trying to tame the flow into theoretically and methodologically unimpeachable sociology."

25. "Philosophers," she writes, in contrast to feminists "continue to hope to find the

pure, general, universal point of view. Thus, feminists readily admit to bias in their perspective, while philosophers continue to assume bias should and *can* be avoided" (Sherwin 1988, p. 20; italics in original).

REFERENCES

Bourdieu, P. and J. P. Passeron. 1977. *Reproduction in Education, Society and Culture.* Beverly Hills, CA: Sage.

Collins, Pat Hill. 1986. "Learning from the Outsider Within: The Sociological Significance of Black Feminist Thought." *Social Problems,* 33(October/December):S14-S32.

Craft, Maurice, ed. 1970. *Family, Class and Education: A Reader.* London: Longman.

———. 1970. "Family, Class and Education: Changing Perspectives." Pp. 3–27 in *Family, Class and Education: A Reader,* edited by M. Craft. London: Longman.

Davis, Kingsley. 1967. "The Myth of Functional Analysis as a Special Method in Sociology and Anthropology." Pp. 379–402 in *System, Change and Conflict,* edited by N. J. Demerath and R. A. Peterson. Glencoe, IL: Free Press.

DeVault, M. L. 1986. "Talking and Listening from Women's Standpoint, Feminist Strategies for Analyzing Interview Data." Paper prepared for the annual meeting of the Society for the Study of Symbolic Interaction, New York.

———. 1987. "Writing Women's Experience/Writing Sociology." Paper presented at the annual meeting of the Society for the Study of Social Problems, Chicago.

Douglas, J. W. B. 1970. "Parental Encouragement." Pp. 151–57 in *Family, Class and Education: A Reader,* edited by M. Craft. London: Longman.

Durkheim, Émile. 1964. *The Rules of Sociological Method.* New York: Free Press.

Felman, Shoshana. 1987. *Jacques Lacan and the Adventure of Insight: Psychoanalysis in Contemporary Culture.* Cambridge, MA: Harvard University Press.

Foucault, Michel. 1967. *The Archaeology of Knowledge.* London: Tavistock.

Garfinkel, H. 1967. *Studies in Ethnomethodology.* Englewood Cliffs, NJ: Prentice-Hall.

Gay, P., ed. 1973. *The Enlightenment: A Comprehensive Anthology.* New York: Simon & Schuster.

Graham, Hilary and Ann Oakley. 1981. "Competing Ideologies of Reproduction: Medical and Maternal Perspectives on Pregnancy." Pp. 50–74 in *Women, Health and Reproduction,* edited by H. Roberts. London: Routledge & Kegan Paul.

Harding, Sandra. 1986. *The Science Question in Feminism.* Ithaca, NY: Cornell University Press.

Kasper, A. S. 1986. "Women's Consciousness and a Feminist Methodology." Washington, DC: George Washington University, Department of Sociology.

Marx, Karl and Friedrich Engels. 1970. *The German Ideology,* part I. New York: International Publishers.

March, Peter, Elizabeth Rosser, and Rom Harré. 1978. *The Rules of Disorder.* London: Routledge & Kegan Paul.

Merton, Robert K. 1967. *On Theoretical Sociology.* London: Collier-Macmillan.

Musgrove, F. 1970. "The 'Good Home.'" Pp. 184–202 in *Family, Class and Education: A Reader,* edited by M. Craft. London: Longman.

Oakley, Ann. 1981. "Interviewing Women: A Contradiction in Terms." Pp. 30–61 in *Doing Feminist Research*, edited by H. Roberts. London: Routledge & Kegan Paul.

Paget, M. A. 1987. "Unlearning to Not Speak." Paper presented at the meetings of the Society for the Study of Social Problems, Chicago.

Parsons, Talcott. 1968. *The Structure of Social Action*. Vol. 1, *Marshall, Pareto, Durkheim*. New York: Free Press.

———. 1982a. "The Role of Theory in Social Research." Pp. 65–75 in *Talcott Parsons on Institutions and Social Evolution*, edited by L. H. Mayhew. Chicago: University of Chicago Press.

———. 1982b. "The Superego and the Theory of Social Systems." Pp. 129–44 in *Talcott Parsons on Institutions and Social Evolution*, edited by L. Mayhew. Chicago: University of Chicago Press

Reinharz, Shulamit. 1983. "Experiential Analysis: A Contribution to Feminist Research." Pp. 162–91 in *Theories of Women's Studies*, edited by G. Bowles and R. Duelli Klein. London: Routledge & Kegan Paul.

Schutz, Alfred. 1962a. "Commonsense and Scientific Interpretations of Human Action." Pp. 3–47 in *Collected Papers*. Vol. 1. The Hague, the Netherlands: Martinus Nijhoff.

———. 1962b. "On Multiple Realities." Pp. 207–59 in *Collected Papers*. Vol. 1. The Hague, the Netherlands: Martinus Nijhoff.

Sherwin, Susan. 1988. "Philosophical Methodology and Feminist Methodology." Pp. 13–28 in *Feminist Perspectives: Philosophical Essays on Method and Morals*, edited by L. Code et al. Toronto: University of Toronto Press.

Smith, Dorothy E. 1981. "The Active Text." Paper presented at the meetings of the World Congress of Sociology, Mexico City.

———. 1987. *The Everyday World as Problematic: A Feminist Sociology*. Boston: Northeastern University Press.

———. 1988. "Writing Sociology: The Feminist Contradiction." Paper presented at the conference, Feminist Transformations of the Social Sciences, Hamilton College, Clinton, NY.

Stacey, Judith. 1988. "Can there Be a Feminist Ethnography." *Women's Studies International Forum* 11:21–27.

Stanley, L. and S. Wise. 1983. *Breaking out: Feminist Consciousness and Feminist Research*. London: Routledge & Kegan Paul.

Stinchcombe, A. 1983. "The Origins of Sociology as a Discipline." *Ars Sociologica* 27:1–11.

White, Hayden. 1976. "The Fictions of Factual Representation." Pp. 21–44 in *Selected Papers from the English Institute*, edited by A. Fletcher. New York: Columbia Univesity Press.

Wieder, D. Lawrence. 1974. *Language Social Reality: The Case of Telling the Convict Code*. The Hague, the Netherlands: Mouton.

Willis, Paul. 1977. *Learning to Labour: How Working Class Kids Get Working Class Jobs*. New York: Columbia University Press.

Chapter 3

MAKING GENDER VISIBLE

JOAN ACKER

Swedish Center for Working Life and University of Oregon

IN "THE MISSING FEMINIST REVOLUTION in Sociology," Judith Stacey and Barrie Thorne (1985) argue that feminist theory has made little impact on the core theoretical perspectives in sociology. On the contrary, they contend, feminist thought has been co-opted and ghetto-ized within sociology, and the paradigm shift that feminist scholars pre-dicted in the early 1970s has not occurred. I believe that the general situation they describe continues—a vast accumulation of new empirical and theoretical work about women existing in relative isolation from a world of sociological theory that continues in a prefeminist mode.[1]

This new research has revealed many anomalies, findings that cannot be accounted for in the old theoretical frameworks, that according to Kuhn (1964),[2] are precursors to fundamental change. Perhaps a para-digm shift is in process but simply has not yet been fully achieved. In any case, producing sociological theory that incorporates the understanding that social life is deeply gendered has been far more difficult than we thought a number of years ago, and the new understandings that we have developed neither have been integrated into, nor have they trans-formed, the old, "general" theories of society. Thus Stacey and Thorne's question about why this has occurred is still an important one.

In this chapter, I hope to contribute to the discussion initiated by Stacey and Thorne. First, I examine the concept of paradigm, asking what must change, and how, if we are to claim such a shift. Second, I develop the explanations offered by Stacey and Thorne, taking up some sociological dimensions of the question that they noted but did not elaborate. I suggest that an additional reason dominant sociological paradigms have not been transformed lies in their success, which is

AUTHOR'S NOTE: I want to thank Joke Esseveld for her helpful comments on this chapter. To the work of Dorothy Smith, I also owe a large debt that goes beyond my references to her in this chapter.

rooted in their relationship to the structuring of power. Further, I argue, again extending Stacey and Thorne's critique, that the feminist alternative has not yet been sufficiently well developed to present a clear challenge to the dominant paradigms because of the way that gender is already incorporated within their fundamental terms. However, at the same time, the outlines of such an alternative are emerging within feminist sociology, particularly in the work of Dorothy Smith (1987a, 1987b), and, in certain areas of empirical and theoretical work outside the main domain of feminist sociology, one can also see the emerging impact of feminist thought. Finally, I question whether the acceptance of a new paradigm, the achievement of a paradigm shift, is possible within the present structure of social relations.

WHAT IS A PARADIGM AND WHAT SHALL WE CHANGE?

A paradigm consists of the "orienting assumptions and conceptual frameworks which are basic to a discipline" (Stacey and Thorne 1985, p. 302). Although Stacey and Thorne, noting that Kuhn uses the word *paradigm* in many different ways, only implicitly elaborate this definition, the word has additional meanings that can help us to identify more precisely in what ways a paradigm shift has not occurred. I want to emphasize two of these: First, a paradigm includes the central questions of a discipline and the concepts used to pose, think about, and answer those questions. Second, a paradigm can also be defined as the model for the critical investigation or experiment that illustrates to students and others how to do "science." This notion of paradigm implies assumptions about methodology and epistemology,[3] even if these are not always clearly formulated and articulated in the models. As Stacey and Thorne observe, although sociology today is a confusion of competing paradigms, a paradigm in this second meaning still has a predominant place in American sociology in the positivist model of the natural science investigation that produces quantifiable data organized as variables manipulated to test hypotheses. This dominant methodological paradigm cuts across different paradigms in the other sense, adapted to competing conceptual frameworks as different as Marxism and structural-functionalism. Alternative interpretive methodologies, developed by feminist theorists using—but going beyond—existing male-defined critical approaches (Stanley and Wise, 1984) have also been melded to a variety of conceptual frameworks. When feminist sociologists discuss a paradigm shift, I take it that they are talking about paradigms in, at least, these two meanings, both of which include competing and contradictory forms (see also Saarinen 1988).

A new paradigm would mean, then, a new methodological-epistemological approach and a new or altered conceptual framework depicting the empirical world. A new conceptual paradigm would encompass, probably redefine, at least some of the questions dealt with in the old paradigm; it would provide more adequate accounts of the phenomena covered by the old paradigm as well as including ways of understanding issues that were not dealt with in the old mode of thought. Thus, as Stacey and Thorne recognize (1985, p. 311), a gendered paradigm would provide a better understanding than we now have of, for example, class structure, the state, social revolution, and militarism, as well as a better understanding of the sex segregation of labor, male dominance in the family, and sexual violence. A new feminist paradigm would place women and their lives, and gender, in a central place in understanding social relations as a whole. Such paradigm would not only pose new questions about women and gender but also help to create a more complex and adequate account of industrial, capitalist society. A feminist paradigm would also contain a methodology that produces knowledge *for* rather that *of* women in their many varieties and situations (see, e.g., Harding 1987).

The task of creating both a new methodological paradigm and a new substantive conceptual framework and, at the same time, working out what one implies for the other, is huge in a field that aspires to include everything about human social life.[4] Perhaps we should be amazed at the progress that feminist sociologists have made rather than distressed at how far we have to go. However, the size and complexity of the undertaking is not the only problem. There are more serious difficulties that at least partly account for the failure to achieve a paradigm shift.

WHY HAS THERE BEEN NO PARADIGM SHIFT?

Stacey and Thorne (1985, p. 306) discuss several reasons for the lack of a feminist transformation of sociology, including the "limiting assumptions of functionalist conceptualizations of gender, the inclusion of gender as a variable rather than as a central theoretical concept, and the ghettoization of feminist insights, especially within Marxist sociology." Additional reasons, they also note, have to do with the dominance of positivism in sociology, the social organization of the discipline, and the underdevelpment of feminist theory. The strength of positivism in sociology has been, I agree, one of the factors inhibiting a feminist transformation. However, this strength needs explaining, as does the resistance to feminist insights that we find in substantive conceptual paradigms. I will look at these problems by further examining the social organization of the discipline, particularly its relation to the structuring of power in the society, and look again at the problem of developing an adequate alternative feminist theory.

Power and the Organization of the Discipline

Sociology, like political science and economics, has an underlying resistance, deeply embedded in the organization of the discipline, to acceptance of the feminist critique and possible new feminist frameworks. This resistence is also related to problems of constructing new feminist paradigms.

An academic discipline is an organized set of acitivities that define a discourse and who may participate in the discourse. We may look at sociology both as ongoing activities that maintain a variety of organizations and produce a discourse, and as the discourse itself. These two ways of viewing sociology reveal different facets of power.

Sociology as a discourse, produced within organizational processes that define and redefine its content and arguments (here I draw on the work of Smith—1979, 1987a, 1987b), has, in common with other academic fields, a particular connection to power in society as a whole or to the relations of ruling; the almost exclusively male domain of academic thought is associated with abstract, intellectual, textually mediated processes through which organizing, managing, and governing are carried out (see also MacKinnon 1982). These processes constitute a particular location in our societies and it is from the perspective of that location that objective, rational, scientifc sociology looks out upon society and defines its contours and what is significant about it. As Smith (1979, 1987a, 1987b) argues, the concepts and definitions of the problematic in sociology have their origins in the issues of interest to those involved in the business of organizing and ruling the dominant socioeconomic structures. Thus the standpoint of the knowledge creator is not outside the social relations she studies, not objective, but deeply embedded within them. The argument that the standpoint of the sociologist or any other knowledge worker is not objective in the sense of being value free is well known (for a discussion of several feminist versions of the. argument, see Harding 1987), but we less often explicitly talk about another obvious fact: The perspectives that develop their concepts and problematics from within what is relevant to the relations of ruling are successful. Their success continues, even though disputed by those such as feminists who stand outside the limits of that domain and see very well that they are wrong, or at least incomplete, in their claims. This success of the dominant paradigms—and I include here the versions of Marxism that exclude the embodied and gendered human being and have adopted the natural science model of research—is one of the reasons that there has been no paradigm shift.

These paradigms are successful to the extent that they make sense of a world in which what is relevant has been decided from the perspective of the processes of ruling. Social science, in attemping to describe and explain the world as it is, often adopts the taken-for-granted categories of ruling and thus makes sense of the world as seen from the perspective of the location of the creation of those categories. For example, the idea of position or "empty slot" used in some theories of class is almost identical to—one might think adopted from—managerial categories that are used in organizing and controlling work organizations. (Acker 1987; Smith 1987b). Even oppositional and critical theories, such as Marxism, often work within the boundaries of the problematic as defined in the institutions that structure the broad relations of power. For example, the Marxist definition of the sphere of the economic covers much the same territory as that covered by neoclassical economic theory (Thompson 1978).

The discourses, spoken and written, of the processes of ruling help to organize and shape the world they describe. That is what they are intended to do. Sociological frameworks not only use the concepts of that sphere but also often provide conceptualizations of the way the world works for managers and administrators, politicians, reformers, and political movements. This is another reason that the established paradigms have some success: They participate in the creation and re-creation of the very structures they are meant to study. As Giddens (1987) argues, ideas about how societies work have a reflexive relation-

ship with the social processes they seek to describe and explain. Sociological ideas are taken up by and inform the practice of those formulating social policy or those seeking to manage more effectively. I am not
arguing that policies work, that management is effective, or that reform
efforts are successful, but that, for example, policies get formulated, to
some degree, in the terms invented by social science, which then is able
to discover the same phenomena. Social science does not create fiction,
it creates concepts anchored in the organization and problems of ruling.

For example, the recently popular concept of an underclass, which
includes mothers on welfare, addicts, homeless mentally ill, and others
with extreme problems of survival, groups together people defined as
troublesome who might be dealt with through similar administrative
means. The idea of an underclass makes some sense from the perspective of ruling, although it may make little sense from the perspective of,
for example, welfare mothers. What is problematic to them is probably
not what is problematic to the authorities. How women receiving public
aid experience and think about their situations is probably quite distinct
from the experiences of addicts, nor are all welfare mothers alike. Although this is not a a new argument, it points to the ways that old
paradigms are successful: They do provide concepts to understand,
locate, and organize aspects of ongoing societal processes that are problematic from a certain standpoint, that of the relations of ruling.

Sociological concepts may also give form to the experiences of ordinary people within bureaucratized, institutionally differentiated and com-
plicated societies, organized and coordinated through abstract textually
mediated means. I think that this helps to explain the continuing pervasive use of the concept of role. As Stacey and Thorne (1985, p. 307)
point out, "Early on, contemporary feminists recognized the influence
and limitations of functionalism as a framework for understanding gender." But, as they also say, "Much of feminist sociology is cast in the
language of roles" with all its attendant functionalist assumptions. The
language of roles is well adapted to the processes of ruling in which
people, in multiple ways, are instructed, cajoled, and coerced into
proper performance according to the demands of various organizations
and institutions. Although an individual's experience is, feminists have
argued, seamless, she is approached as a mother by the schools, as a
debtor by the credit company, and as a female worker by the boss. The
concept of role may help to make sense out of this reality, even while
helping to perpetuate that reality by defining its personal consequences
as a depoliticized role conflict or a psychological problem rather than,

for example, the consequences of unequal power. In sum, I suggest that to understand better the persisting liveliness, even in the work of feminist researchers, of concepts that have been widely criticized as either androcentric or as inadequate for the development of feminist theory, we need to recognize their contradictory character. Many concepts both reflect recognizable reality and, at the same time, mystify the underlying relations, which include the complex connections between the discourse and the organization of power.

Existing paradigms are also supported by the system of universities, departments, associations, journals, and funding agencies—almost all still dominated by men at the top—that organize the power to allot money, job security, and status. To be a sociologist meant and still means to learn and to use the skills of survival within this complex (Smith 1979), which includes learning how to think within a discipline that had already excluded women and their concerns in the process of becoming a separate discipline.[5]

Survival involves much more than learning the proper ways of thinking. This was illustrated to me in a recent conversation with another sociologist, a man, who told me about a colleague who had never learned "how to package a career." The colleague, who was quite competent, had failed to understand that "a career" demands publication in the right places and a deemphasis on teaching and community service. Because of the colleague's failure, others in the department had the unwelcome task of ending his appointment. A familiar story, it is also a cautionary tale understood in some form by all those who intend to survive. What we are about, at some level, is the packaging of careers, rather than the doing of intellectual work. A safe, easy, and quick way to package a career is by using old paradigms. Indeed, no other way may be visible, because to do sociology still means emersion in the established ways. The heavy prestige of the natural science model recommends it as the pattern to follow. The fact that this model has been elaborated to specify how to proceed is important, for sociology is about concrete societies and people, and demands the collection and analysis of empirical data. One of the attractions of the natural science model is that one can get on with the work without having to think through its epistemological underpinnings—without, in other words, having to confront questions raised by the feminist critique of sociology. The result is perpetuation of an atheoretical sociology that Stacey and Thorne identify as one of the barriers to further feminist theoretical development. Much of the mass of new work on women and gender has been done within this implicit understanding of sociology. Thus women and gender have opened new topics around which to package careers and new avenues to survival, but with far less impressive theoretical results than we might wish.

The imperatives of survival in academia derive from the organization of power within the discipline that is integral to the maintenance of sociology as a "discipline" with boundaries that distinguish it from other disciplines. I think that we should not underestimate how much this organization of power acts as a barrier to the introduction of new ways of thinking. Sometimes men also feel such pressures, both subtle and direct, to get on with the career by doing "normal science." However, men are, I think, unlikely to propose changes as potentially radical as that of the feminist critique because they have not been excluded as part of the prior conditions upon which the discipline was erected. From their standpoint, the gendered nature of social relations is not so clearly problematic.[6]

The success of the old paradigms—evident in both their congruence with the taken-for-granted ways that things are organized and their continuing power within the discipline as ongoing activity—is one of the reasons that feminist inroads have been so few. Why should sociologists abandon whatever version of sociology they are using if it seems to work, if it answers, or even only deals with, questions they and the discipline as an organization of resources and power define as the relevant ones?

The Underdevelopment of Feminist Theory

Although feminist social theory has developed rapidly, we have run into formidable problems that have prevented us, so far, from realizing the goal of theory that fully comprehends the gendered nature of social relations. We have not, as yet, been able to suggest new ways of looking at things that are obviously better than the old ways for comprehending a whole range of problems—from how organizations function to how capital accumulation processes alter class structure. We know a great deal more about how such things affect women, but are only beginning to know how gender is fundamentally involved in the processes.

We began, necessarily, looking for ways to conceptualize and explain female subordination. These efforts produced, in the main, new conceptual frameworks that were dual systems theories, innovative theorizing about women, male dominance, and patriarchy that still leave the old structural conceptualizations of the political-economic-social system essentially intact. Such theorizing goes part of the way, but is ultimately unsatisfactory because the very theories we have identified as part of the relations of male domination are unaltered, unaffected by the feminist insight that all social relations are gendered. This is, of course, a very summary assessment that skips over much complexity, but as a summary, I think it is still fair. In addition, we have had difficulties developing a methodology that deals satisfactorily with the criticisms we ourselves have made (Acker et al. 1983) and, with a few exceptions (Smith 1979, 1987; Esseveld 1988), proposals for a feminist methodology in sociology have not gone beyond proposals previously made by male critics of positivism.

The question is this: Why have we had this difficulty? The answer, I think, is at least partly that we have to use—start with—the successful, as I have argued, conceptual frameworks that exist. Even if we consciously attempt to start "in the work and practical reasoning of actual individuals," rather than in the received discourse, as Dorothy Smith (1987a, p. 165) suggests, we cannot avoid framing our interpretations in some conceptualization of the broader social context if we wish to go beyond description or beyond local experience to comprehend the constraints and possibilities that set the conditions for that experience.

The problem is, no doubt, different with different theoretical starting points; some of the existing perspectives are better, I believe, than others as a place to begin.[7] Given a beginning in a Marxist framework concerned with understanding oppression, which seems to be most reasonable for a feminist theory, we have to talk about class, the state, capitalism, politics, even though we talk about them as gendered. There is no other way.

However, the ways of thinking at hand, which we want to transform but that still are where we start, appear to be gender neutral, but are deeply gendered. The discourse that excludes the female speaks from a male situation, but conceptualizes itself as gender neutral. Moreover, this is a discourse that shares a common conceptual ground with the rational, objective, organizing practices and principles of an increasingly abstract mode of managing and governing (Smith 1987a, 1987b).[8] This gives the gender-neutral stance its authority, its appearance of accounting for and accurately reflecting reality.

Although we have realized, since the beginning of the contemporary feminist critique that the dominant theoretical voice is a masculine one, we are only now understanding how fundamental to central sociological conceptualizations is their gendered substructure, and how difficult this is to penetrate. It seems that, having assumed the masculine, but then framed conceptualizations of the human and of society in genderless terms, there is no easy way to bring the feminine or gender back into the framework in an explicit and conscious way. To talk about gender, too often meaning women, is to take the theorizing from the general to the specific, and this appears to undermine the theorizing about the abstract and the general. Consequently, talking about gender and women can be seen as trivializing serious theoretical questions, or it can be seen as beside the point. All of this rests upon obscuring of the gendered nature of fundamental concepts under the cloak of gender neutrality (Acker 1988).

Recent work of Carole Pateman (1983a, 1983b) on theories of democracy illustrates an attempt to deal with this problem. She analyzes the idea of the individual in liberal democratic theory and the importance of the disembodied abstract individual for the development of a general theory of liberal democracy. This individual must be disembodied, because if he were not it would be clear that he is a man and does not represent all humanity: thus there would be no general theory that applies to all people. Giving a body to the abstract individual also reveals that women cannot have the same standing in the theory of democracy as men because, as a human category, they do not have the same access to political participation and power as men. To argue that women should demand and seize the rights and responsibilities of the abstract individual is to argue that they should become like men, which ignores the fact that their lives are different from those of men and most women must be different until there is a fundamental change in the lives of men and the overall structure of our societies. This, of course, is the radical potential of liberal feminism (Eisenstein 1981). In the meantime, the abstract and disembodied individual is still present in a great deal of theorizing in the social sciences, not only in theories of liberal democracy.

Feminist efforts to develop a theory of gender and class provide another example of the difficulties in transforming concepts that contain a gendered substructure beneath an apparently gender-neutral surface. In spite of the long attention of numerous theorists, an adequate feminist theory of class has proved to be elusive (e.g., Acker 1980, 1988; Beechey 1987). Feminist thinkers now commonly recognize the importance of class and race as well as gender and argue that these are all interconnected (e.g., Lewis 1985). However, although many theorists now accept the need for one theory incorporating both gender and class, in practice we keep on talking about class and gender (and race) as separate (Cockburn 1986).

The unsolved problem for Marxist class theory is partly, as Stacey and Thorne (1985, p. 308) point out, that "the central Marxist categories which focus on production, labor, and class—as defined through men's relationship to production and labor—are ... obviously androcentric." The development of a nonandrocentric concept of class may be so difficult because of the way that class has been conceptualized at a level of abstraction that erases the body and women and makes gender invisible. Contemporary U.S. academic neo-Marxists, for example, often use a structural notion of class that embeds it within an abstract mode of production, the domain of economic relations that constitutes the process of capital accumulation. The abstract worker in this domain is just as disembodied as the abstract individual of liberal theory, and just as fundamentally male. Theoretical treatment of capitalist processes remains indifferent to the gender-based organization of labor markets and to the unpaid work of women in spite of feminist efforts to insert this labor into the abstract theory.[9] In this version of Marxist class theory, gender becomes visible only with a move to a lower level of abstraction, from the mode of production to the social formation, where actual, concrete societies are the object of analysis. However, the labor of men is still privileged because only that labor, conceptualized as gender neutral, is theorized in the concepts that allow us to understand the system as a whole.

Feminists often implicitly ignore these theoretical twistings, perhaps wisely, and work with a general and somewhat vague notion of class, emphasizing processes and the linkages between employment and work in the home. However, this does not result in a new way of understanding the nature of class processes,[10] which is what a feminist paradigm that could challenge the existing Marxist theories of class would do. The problem resides in the gendered substructure of the definition of the territory of the problematic, "the economy," seen from the perspective of the system of ruling (the male-defined and dominated ruling of capitalist societies). The solution must be to redefine the economic, to redefine the relations of class, not simply to add reproduction to production.[11] However, this is difficult because the old frameworks, linked to the relations of ruling in various and complex ways, still "work," for feminists as well as others, even though, at the same time, they are inadequate. Thus the problems facing feminist sociological theorizing that starts from and uses a Marxist understanding lead back to the resistances of the old structural paradigm to feminist critique and to the contradictory nature of the old concepts—they *do* illuminate capitalist processes but cannot take into account their own gendered substructure. Their inadequacy becomes more and more evident as the contradictions of women's situations in contemporary societies become more evident and politically more problematic.

EMERGING ALTERNATIVES

The possibilities for a new feminist paradigm are better with some of the competing existing sociological frameworks than with others, as I have already argued. Structural functionalist assumptions, as Stacey and Thorne (1985, p. 307) also argue, "have posed significant obstacles to feminist rethinking of basic orienting assumptions within sociology." Feminist theory, which is about transformation and liberation, must start elsewhere, I believe, in ways of thinking that pose change and the elimination of oppression as central questions. Marxist theory, with all the problems and more noted above, is still an obvious place to start.

A number of developments in feminist-socialist-Marxist thinking provide some grounds for optimism. One promising direction is the discussion of a feminist standpoint, or taking the perspective of women, particularly the work of Dorothy Smith (1979, 1987a, 1987b). Smith proposes investigating the relations of ruling from the standpoint of women concretely located in a variety of places within societal structures. She avoids, I think, some of the problems of other "standpoint theories" (Harding 1986), which move either to a relativistic position or to an inter- and intrapsychic—often Freudian—analysis. Smith's approach remains anchored in the lives of actual—rather than textually created—people and focused on the processes and relations outside their immediate daily lives that help to create the conditions for those lives. She is also able to include the actions of women, and men, as they deal with and sometimes oppose the relations of ruling. Thus she is proposing a method to understand the relations of ruling from the perspective of women who themselves define the problematic, rather than from the perspective of the problematics of those who manage and organize those relations.

The assumption that all social relations are gendered is another relatively new development that promises to contribute significantly to a new paradigm. This assumption, only recently made explicit in much work (see, for example, Smith 1987; Flax 1987), changes the nature of the debate from an exclusive focus on women to a focus on how gender shapes and is implicated in all kinds of social phenomena (see also Scott 1986). I think that we are only at the beginning of working out what we mean, in concrete terms, when we say that social relations and processes are gendered. The reshaping of the meaning of gender is under way in all disciplines, but it could have a particularly profound effect in sociology in helping us move toward a more penetrating critique of our concepts and frameworks than we have yet had.

The development of the concept of reproduction as the hidden substructure upon which production relations depend—not in the rather narrow terms of a political economy of domestic labor or a theory of the reproduction of labor power, or even of nurturing and caring activities, but as the organization of activities and relations that make possible human survival—is also a promising direction. Studies of Third World societies and developing areas make visible how daily life and reproduction are shattered and sometimes reconstituted by capitalist transformation, moving reproduction to the center of the analysis (for example, Redclift and Mingione 1985). At the other end of affluence, feminist analyses of the welfare state focus on reproduction, increasingly seeing contradictions around reproduction as indications of a deep crisis in capitalism (see, for example, Sassoon 1987). Even a nonfeminist male Marxist such as Therborn (1986) recognizes that the welfare state has to do with reproduction, although he fails to make the obvious links to gender and the subordination of women.

CONCLUSION: IS A PARADIGM SHIFT POSSIBLE?

A paradigm shift means not only the transformation of existing conceptual frameworks, but also the acceptance of the new framework in the field (Stacey and Thorne 1985, p. 302). Historically, as Kuhn (1964) observed, a shift does not come about simply because the new perspective is more persuasive and provides "better" knowledge than the old one, but also as a result of a struggle for organizational power and intellectual dominance. Moreover, previous paradigm shifts have always occurred within societal structures dominated by men. This suggests a problem for feminists and their theories. If a paradigm shift can only occur with a shift in power, and if that means taking power in institutions that are already structured within the historical context of gendered relations of domination, what are the chances for the survival of critical feminist theories? Can a shift occur at all, at the fundamental level about which we have been talking, within some reasonable short run? Or is a paradigm shift part of the process of transforming those relations of domination, probably a very long-run project? What will new theory look like? Will it be a new *grand theory* with the totalizing aims that term implies? How do we put together the myriad standpoints of women? Must that lead us to the end of theory and out of the mode of thinking that posits competing paradigms, as some feminists suggest? That is, do we expect too much, or the wrong thing, when we search for a paradigm shift as an accomplished transformation?

NOTES

1. See, for example, Giddens and Turner (1987), which is a large collection of articles on state-of-the-art social theory. Feminist thinking does not appear in any of the chapters and the volume does not even contain a chapter on feminist theory.

2. Following Stacey and Thorne (1985), I am not trying to apply Kuhn's (1964) ideas about paradigms and paradigm shifts with any precision. However, his ideas are a fruitful beginning point. The feminist critique in sociology, as in other fields, constitutes a long list of anomalies. One outstanding example is the finding of persistent sex segregation of the labor force, which cannot be explained with human capital theory or labor market segmentation theories. Most versions of Marxist theory do not do much better.

3. Sandra Harding (1987) discusses the differences between research methods, methodology, and epistemology, arguing that there is no distinctive feminist method although feminist research has distinctive methodological features. In this chapter, I use *methodology* to mean both the paradigmatic models of how to do research and the epistemological implications of such models, excluding the question of the method of data gathering.

4. Stacey and Thorne claim that feminist theory has had a greater impact on core concepts in anthropology, history, and literature than in sociology, political science, economics, and psychology. Opinions on this question differ. For example, in regard to anthropology, Louis Lamphere (1987, p. 25) states that "this new scholarship has had limited impact on the field as a whole," obviously differing with Stacey and Thorne's assessment of the situation in anthropology. For this reason I have not tried to compare sociology with other disciplines. However, I think it is probable that entrenched modes of conceptualization are more difficult to challenge in fields such as sociology that deal with

the present structure of power than those that look to the past or to powerless and disappearing nonindustrial societies.

5. Sociology was constituted partly through a process of separation from women intellectuals and reformers interested in social problems often involving women (Bernard 1987, p. 200). In the process, large areas of society as well as women in general were placed outside the boundaries. For example, social welfare was consigned to the area of the applied, and was not an object of serious study in sociology until the "crisis of the welfare state" began to emerge. (There were some exceptions, for example, Wilensky and LeBeaux, *Industrial Society and Social Welfare*, 1958). As Bernard points out, the struggle to become a rational, objective, respectable science—that is, an academic discipline with standing within the institutional powers of higher education—included the active rejection of women and their interests. Women were also absent, as Dorothy Smith observes (1979, 1987), in that the domain of abstract intellectual work was made possible by the invisible daily labor of women who created the material conditions for that work. See Dorothy Smith (1979) for a complex discussion of the connections between the creation of sociological knowledge and the "abstract, intellectual domain of ruling" in capitalist societies.

6. A number of male sociologists are now making gender problematic. It will be interesting to see the extent to which their ideas are integrated into non-gender-sensitive work (see, for example, Connell 1987; Morgan 1981).

7. In my view, the most creative feminist theorizing has come from the many attempts to bring together Marxism and feminism. As an example of recent work in the critical Marxist tradition, see Benhabib and Cornell (1987).

8. In a recent as yet unpublished paper, Smith develops the idea of "the main business," "'ruling, servicing, regulating, planning, criticizing, managing, organizing, the process of capital accumulation." These processes, she argues, set the boundaries of the problematic for Marxist political economist as well as non-Marxist theorists. Although most of the ideas I present were developed before reading this paper, I have clearly been influenced by it in many ways (see Dorothy E. Smith, "Feminist Reflections on Political Economy," 1987b).

9. Feminists, of course, are not the only social analysts who have recognized difficulties with a structural Marxist interpretation of class (e.g., Thompson 1963, 1978; Giddens 1987; Connell 1983).

10. See my article "Class, Gender and the Relations of Distribution" (Acker 1988) for one attempt to deal with the problem.

11. Jaggar and McBride (1985) suggest, for example, that the concept of reproduction should be dropped on the grounds that it is male ideology and that thinking of reproductive activities as production might help us to reconceptualize societal processes.

REFERENCES

Acker, Joan. 1980 "Women and Stratification: A Review of Recent Literature." *Contemporary Sociology* 9:25–39.

———. 1987. "Hierarchies and Jobs: Notes for a Theory of Gendered Organizations." Working Paper. Stockholm: Arbetslivcentrum.

————. 1988. "Class, Gender and the Relations of Distribution." *Signs* 13(3):473–97.
————. Forthcoming. *Doing Comparable Worth: Gender, Class and Pay Equity.* Philadelphia: Temple University Press.
Acker, Joan, Kate Barry, and Joke Esseveld. 1983. "Objectivity and Truth: Problems in Doing Feminist Research." *Women's Studies International Forum* 6(4):423–35.
Beechey, Veronica. 1987. *Unequal Work.* London: Verso
Benhabib, Seyla and Drucilla Cornell, eds. 1987. *Feminism as Critique.* Minneapolis: University of Minnesota Press.
Bernard, Jessie. 1987. "Re-viewing the Impact of Women's Studies in Sociology." Pp. 193–216 in *The Impact of Feminist Research in the Academy,* edited by C. Farnham. Bloomington: Indiana University Press.
Cockburn, Cynthia. 1986. "The Relations of Technology: What Implications for Theories of Sex and Class." Pp. 74–85 in *Gender and Stratification,* edited by R. Crompton and M. Mann. Cambridge, MA: Polity.
Connell, R. W. 1983. *Which Way Is? Essays on Class, Sex, and Culture.* Sydney: Allen & Unwin.
————. 1987. *Gender and Power.* Stanford, CA: Stanford University Press.
Eisenstein, Zillah. 1981. *The Radical Future of Liberal Feminism.* New York: Longman.
Esseveld, Johanna. 1988. "Beyond Silence: Middle-Aged Women in the 1970s." Ph.D. dissertation, University of Lund.
Flax, Jane. 1987. "Postmodernism and Gender Relations in Feminist Theory." *Signs.* 12(4):621–43.
Giddens, Anthony. 1987. *Social Theory and Modern Sociology.* Cambridge, MA: Polity.
Giddens, Anthony and Jonathan Turner. 1987. *Social Theory Today.* Oxford: Basil Blackwell
Harding, Sandra. 1986. *The Science Question in Feminism.* Ithaca, NY: Cornell University Press.
————. 1987. "Introduction: Is There a Feminist Method." Pp. 1–14 in *Feminism and Methodology,* edited by S. Harding. Bloomington: Indiana University Press.
Hartsock, Nancy. 1983. *Money, Sex, and Power.* New York: Longman.
Jaggar, Alison and William I. McBride. 1985. "Reproduction as Male Ideology." *Women's Studies International Forum* 8(3):185–96.
Kuhn, Thomas. 1964. *The Structure of Scientific Revolutions.* Chicago: University of Chicago Press.
Lamphere, Louise. 1987. "Feminism and Anthropology: The Struggle to Reshape Our Thinking About Gender." Pp. 11–33 in *The Impact of Feminist Research in the Academy,* edited by C. Farnham. Bloomington: Indiana University Press.
Lewis, Jane. 1985. "The Debate on Sex and Class." *New Left Review* 149:108–20.
MacKinnon, Catherine. 1982. "Feminism, Marxism, Method, and the State." *Signs* 7(3):515–44.
Morgan, David. 1981. "Men, Masculinity, and the Process of Sociological Enquiry." Pp. 83–113 in *Doing Feminist Research,* edited by H. Roberts. London: Routledge & Kegan Paul.
Pateman, Carole. 1983. "Feminist Critiques of the Public/Private Dichotomy." Pp. 281–303 in *Public and Private in Social Life,* edited by S. I. Benn and G. F. Gaus. Bechenham, Kent: Croom Helm.
————. 1983. "Feminism and Democracy." Pp. 204–17 in *Democratic Theory and Practice,* edited by G. Duncan. Cambridge: Cambridge University Press.

Redclift, Nanneke and Enzo Mingione, eds. 1985. *Beyond Employment: Household, Gender, and Subsistence*. Oxford: Basil Blackwell.

Saarinen, Aino. 1988. "Feminist Research: In Search of a New Paradigm?" *Acta Sociologica* 31(1):35–51.

Sassoon, Anne Showstack. 1987. "Women's New Social Role: Contradictions of the Welfare State." Pp. 158–88 in *Women and the State*, edited by A. S. Sassoon. London: Hutchinson.

Scott, Joan. 1986. "Gender: A Useful Category of Historical Analysis." *American Historical Review* 91:1053–75.

Smith, Dorothy E. 1979. "A Sociology for Women." Pp. 135–87 in *The Prism of Sex: Essays in the Sociology of Knowledge*, edited by J. A. Sherman and E. Torton Beck. Madison: University of Wisconsin Press.

———. 1987a. *The Everyday World as Problematic*. Boston: Northeastern University Press.

———. 1987b. "Feminist Reflections on Political Economy." Unpublished manuscript.

Stacey, Judith and Barrie Thorne. 1985. "The Missing Feminist Revolution in Sociology." *Social Problems* 32(4):301–16.

Stanley, Liz and Sue Wise. 1984. " 'Back into the Personal' or: Our Attempt to Construct 'Feminist Research'." Pp. 129–209 in *Theories of Women's Studies*, edited by G. Bowles and R. Duelli Klein. London: Routledge & Kegan Paul.

Therborn, Göran. 1987. "Welfare States and Capitalist Markets." *Acta Sociologica* 30(3/4):237–54.

Thompson, E. P. 1963. *The Making of the English Working Class*. Hardmondsworth: Penguin.

———. 1978. *The Poverty of Theory*. London: Merlin.

Wilensky, Harold L. and Charles N. LeBeaux. 1958. *Industrial Society and Social Welfare*. New York: Russell Sage.

Chapter 4

PSYCHOANALYTIC FEMINISM
Implications for Sociological Theory

EDITH KURZWEIL
Rutgers University

AMERICAN FEMINISTS, AND the sociologists among them, have been slow in exploring psychoanalytic theory for their own ends. This reluctance, primarily, stemmed from the fact that earlier applications had been connected to "conservative" sociology and ideas. We recall, for instance, that in the 1940s Talcott Parsons used psychoanalysis as the framework for his personality system—which he subordinated to his social system. (That was one reason why the Freudians ultimately did not accept his theory; that he played down what to Freud was the "gold" of psychoanalysis—that is, the unconscious.) In the 1950s, David Riesman (1964, p. 44) found that individuals had responded to mounting social pressures by moving from inner-directedness to outer-directedness. (Freudians refused to accept this watered-down version of "the superego as a socializing agency incorporated into the child and accompanying him throughout life with ever renewed injunctions.") And in the mid-1960s, Phillip Reiff (1966), concerned with the interaction between individual and culture, relied on Freud's concept of sublimation as the means of apprehending cultural shifts and changes.

By then, Marxist sociologists already had debated the viability of Wilhelm Reich's and Erich Fromm's Freudo-Marxisms, and Herbert Marcuse had criticized them for having abandoned Freud's instinct theory. According to Marcuse (1955, p. 218), Reich's notion of sexual repression had remained too undifferentiated; he had minimized issues of sublimation and had not distinguished between its repressive and nonrepressive components; and Fromm had underplayed the role of sexuality, had shifted emphasis from the unconscious to consciousness, from id to ego, and from presublimated to sublimated expressions of human existence (Marcuse 1955, p. 242). Marcuse himself had envisioned a society without "surplus repression"—without societal domination and individual alienation.

None of these radical, theoretical approaches had addressed the repression of women by men. Hence they were as unacceptable to feminists as all the others. But, beginning with Karen Horney in the 1920s, a number of women psychoanalysts had been elaborating on Freud's theories in order to do away with the repression of women. They had taken issue with details of his views while fully embracing psychoanalysis. Freud, in turn, incorporated some of their findings, particularly in the *New Introductory Lectures* ([1933] 1965), and debated with them about the origins of femininity. These debates were renewed in France in the 1960s, and to a lesser extent in Germany, so that in recent years feminist theory and psychoanalytic theory again were being "married."

EARLY THEORETICAL ASSUMPTIONS

Essentially, Freud had pointed out that because the male sex-cell searches out the (passive) female ovum, and because the male pursues the female, masculinity erroneously had been equated with aggressiveness; and that "the suppression of women's aggressiveness (which is constitutionally prescribed and socially imposed) favors the development of masochistic impulses." For these reasons, Freud ([1933] (1965), pp. 113–18) rooted masochism in early erotic experience—in the turning inward of destructive impulses that are incorporated into personality structure. He demonstrated that little girls at play can be as aggressive as little boys; and that they use the clitoris as the penis-equivalent for masturbation. This was proof to Freud that femininity was being developed during the oedipal phase, and that it coincided with a shift of erotic sensitivity from the clitoris to the vagina—a necessary maturational task.

According to Freud ([1933] 1965, p. 129), the normal boy passes through the Oedipus complex "naturally," by identifying with his father and by renouncing incestuous, infantile claims on his mother. By avoiding castration, he manages to set up a strong sexual identity as well as a strong superego. The normal girl, however, must give up her early erotic attachment to her mother, must deal with her envy of the penis, and thus enters the Oedipus situation as though "into a haven of refuge." Unafraid of castration, Freud continued, she tends to remain in the oedipal complex for an indeterminate length of time and often does not

completely overcome it. As a result, girls never develop as strong a
superego as boys do—a factor said to determine character development. Thus Freud did not correlate biology and psychology; and he
considered neither of the sexes as totally "active" or "passive."

His follower, Karl Abraham, found that the preoedipal girl, upon
realizing that she will never have a penis but will be able to have a child,
envies her mother not because she has masculine tendencies but because she fears and resents her for thwarting her true feminine needs:
She wishes for a child by her father, although also shuddering at the
thought of congress with him (Grosskurth 1986, p. 204). Melanie Klein
disagreed. She held that the girl's anxiety is due to her unconscious
knowledge of her primordial infantile feminine sexuality. Ultimately,
maintained Klein, the lack of a penis puts the oedipal girl at a real
disadvantage: She identifies with her mother and then is pushed back
into the preoedipal phase by her father's inevitable rejection. This experience colors all future relationships with men: She reacts with revenge
and dissapointment, becomes rebellious rather than passive and submis-
sive, and tends to adopt a fictitious male role. Helene Deutsch went
along with Freud about the roots of the girl's Oedipus complex, but
chided him for "equating" the clitoris with the much larger penis.
Horney, on the other hand, maintained that the girl's so-called masculine phase was a defense against anxiety about the prospective violation
by her father—resulting from the "biological principle" of her own sexual attraction to him. She believed that psychoanalysts ought to recognize the male counterpart of the masculinity complex in women—the
womb envy in boys—and she concluded that social factors might be as
important as biological ones in the perception and subsequent socialization of all children. Ernest Jones, who had agreed that penis envy was
the girl's basic defense, thought that the denial of her femininity was her
protection from both attack by her mother and from the man's danger-
ous penis. Jones (1933, pp. 1–33) allegedly considered this to be the
little girl's only possible response to her anxiety and, therefore, backed
Klein's view that the girl's hate of her mother does not come from her
lack of a penis but from rivalry over her father's.

FEMINIST THEORY IN ANGLO-SAXON COUNTRIES

These were the major thrusts in the psychoanalytic discussions of femininity that were available to feminist theorists in the late 1960s. American feminists, however, shunned them. They tended to denounce psychoanalysis, often starting their papers by blaming Freud for women's lot, or by stating that he "was wrong."

This situation began to change after Juliet Mitchell (1974, p. xv) argued that "the rejection of psychoanalysis and of Freud's work is fatal to feminism." Mitchell, of course, was au courant with what was going on in both France and America. And she had been indignant that her Marxist friends agreed with Frantz Fanon—who had argued that women (in the Third World) should be emancipated only after a revolution. Leaning on Althusser's critique of ideology, she found that women had been kept out of the labor force not because they were physically weak but because they were needed in the family for reproduction, to please men sexually, and to socialize the children (1966, pp. 17–18). Thus she criticized the feminists' automatic denunciations of Freud, and showed that their adaptation of the views of Wilhelm Reich and R. D. Laing on sexuality were lacking a broader theoretical and ideological context; that they took Freud's texts too literally; that they tended to ignore that, to Freud, penis envy referred to unconscious mental processes and not to conscious decisions and perceptions. She reminded them also that Freud always used the term *normal* relatively—in contrast to *neurotic, pathogenic,* or *psychotic.* To prove her point, she quoted from Freud's "Case of Dora," where he had said that "so-called sexual perversions are very widely diffused among the whole population," and from a letter he had written to the mother of a homosexual—stating that "it is cruel and injust to persecute homosexuality as a crime" (Mitchell 1974, pp. 8, 11).

When she began to explain narcissism, Mitchell betrayed the fact that she had been influenced by the French psychoanalytic discussions, and by French feminists; and that she was conversant with Lacanian and other so-called structuralist notions. She pointed, for instance, to Octave Mannoni's distinction between Freud's *Three Essays,* "the book of the drive," and his *Interpretation of Dreams,* "the book of desire." And she reminded feminists that Freud had explicitly denounced the inadequacy of biologically based instinct theories (Mitchell 1974, p. 3), just as they did. She also expanded on the infant's "megalomanic moment" of narcissism, its search for itself in the mother's expressions, and the beginnings of the self. Relying on the British psychoanalyst D. W. Winnicott, she blamed confusions on the inadequate language available to Freud; and she echoed Jacques Lacan's criticism of the neglect of language in psychoanalysis. In fact, she maintained that the paucity of vocabulary led to the muddled meanings of such words as *masculinity, femininity,* and *bisexuality.*

After discussing preoedipal sexuality and the Oedipus complex, castration anxieties and penis envy, the preoedipal mother and the oedipal father, Mitchell went on to dissect prevalent applications of psychoanalysis to the liberation of the family. She showed that Wilhelm Reich, by blaming mass neurosis for sexual repression, had failed to examine the intricate dynamics of family life, and instead had extrapolated and generalized from psychoanalytic theory to politics. This led him, for instance, to brand jealousy as pathological (women are treated as possessions); to find that parents love their children to compensate for other deprivations; and to postulate the superiority of the vagina over the clitoris. His sexual revolution failed, concluded Mitchell, because the so-called dialectical unity of the sexes was unachievable, even with the help of his orgone box—the mechanic device that was to liberate repressed sexuality (Mitchell 1974, p. 223).

R. D. Laing's radical psychoanalysis, Mitchell demonstrated, had not eradicated the social causes of schizophrenia by treating "people as people." In fact, Mitchell (1974, p. 290) illustrated that Laing became increasingly hostile to the mother in his view of the family. For, "if psychosis is of pre-Oedipal formation, it is *bound* to have a great deal to do with the pre-Oedipal mother and with the absence of the Oedipal father." Finally, Mitchell (1974, p. 416) investigated the relation of psychoanalysis to "the second wave of feminism" (represented by Simone de Beauvoir, Betty Friedan, Eva Figes, Germaine Greer, Shulamith Firestone, and Kate Millett), and located women's problems in patriarchy and in "our specific ideology of a natural, biological family [which] re-expresses as a repressed Oedipal saga the kinship structure to which it is in contradiction."

By 1982, Mitchell had become a psychoanalyst. Now, she noted the intimate relationship between psychoanalysis and femininity, and their shifting orientations. This had *not* been Freud's task. As befits a member of the Independent Group of the British Psycho-Analytical Society, Mitchell (1984, p. 307) mediated between Freud's splitting and Klein's "split off parts": In Kleinian analysis the split off parts can be communicated to the analyst by projection, but in its Freudian counterpart the splitting does not get into the transference, although it may be witnessed in fetishism. And she contrasted their views on femininity (Mitchell 1984, p. 310):

> The boy and the girl have both the same and different drives: where their biology is different, their urges must differ. For Klein the instinct is biological; for Freud it is "our main mythology." The boy and the girl have the same objects. In Klein's theory, the object they first take in is predominantly part of the mother, then the whole mother. . . . For Freud it is the attachment to what you have had to abandon that you take in.

Thus Mitchell provided a bridge not only between Freudian and Kleinian views on feminism and between feminism and psychoanalysis but between French and Anglo-Saxon feminists.[1]

FRENCH FEMINIST THEORIES

In many ways, Mitchell's career is similar to Julia Kristeva's: Both women began as literary critics, became political activists, were drawn to Lacan's ideas, and then turned into Freudian psychoanalysts. But Kristeva belonged to a group of feminists who argued (Marks and de Courtivron 1980, p. 4) that "feminism exists because women are, and have been, everywhere oppressed at every level of existence, from the simplest social intercourse to the most elaborate discourse." She worked with Roland Barthes and listened to Lacan, who insisted that only through *mis*understanding, that is, through interpreting what is said along with what is left unsaid, could we ever understand anything. Yet, when she became a psychoanalyst, Kristeva chose the classical Société Psychanalytique de Paris.

The French, of course, are accustomed to Lacan's philosophical allusions and to the peculiarities of French discourse, which made for the gap between French and Anglo-Saxon psychoanalysis and between feminists in the two countries. Except for an occasional contribution in *Signs* and in deconstructionist publications such as *Sub-Stance*, few French feminist works have reached the United States (Marks and de Courtivron 1980, p. ix), even though French women had raised feminist questions soon after the student uprisings in 1968. But unlike their American counterparts, they grounded their arguments in theory and in history, and they embraced psychoanalysis because they found Lacan's ideas useful.

Helence Cixous, one of the most effective of these feminists, developed Lacan's criticism of Jones's differences with Freud (in "Early Feminine Sexuality") and then maintained that "sexual difference is not determined merely by the fantasized relationship to anatomy . . . [and thus] to exteriority and to the specular in the elaboration of sexuality—a voyeur's theory" (Marks and de Courtivron 1980, p. 95). And Cixous argued that woman must be asked what *she* wants, how *she* experiences sexual pleasure (*jouissance*), and how this pleasure is inscribed at the level of her body and her unconscious. For Cixous, there were no such things as destiny, nature, or essence, only structural conditions that must be fought at every level, and especially at the unconscious one.[2]

Cixous's colleague Luce Irigaray was yet more militant. She held that sexuality has always been placed within masculine parameters, whether "virile" clitoral activity is contrasted to "feminine" vaginal passivity, or the clitoris is perceived as a little penis. Because her pleasures are never considered, woman has to find them however she can: "By her somewhat servile love of the father-husband; by her desire of a penis-child, preferably male; [and] by gaining access to those cultural values which are still 'by right' reserved for males alone" (Irigaray 1986, p. 99). For this reason, woman's autoeroticism had become more central than man's. In fact, stated Irigaray (1986, p. 103), woman's self-stimulation, unlike the man's, needs no instrument (such as the hand); and she may even experience the sex act as an intrusion, especially when the man takes her only as the object of *his* pleasure. Still, because the "woman has sex organs just about everywhere, . . . the geography of her pleasure is much more diversified, more multiple in its differences, more complex, more subtle, than [men may] imagine."

Both Cixous and Irigaray, by adapting the Lacanian discourse to feminist ends, provided a sweeping social critique.[3] In one of the American deconstructions of their (and other) feminist texts, Gallop (1982) went even further in her "Lacanian" reading but ignored the fact that psychoanalysis deals with the unconscious of individuals. This is always a problem, however, with writing *about* psychoanalysis and with its application to politics. Actually, both Kristeva and Mitchell kept their liberation politics rather private after becoming practicing psychoanalysts—because an analyst's political stances are thought to interfere in the transference. Now, says Kristeva, her engagement is with individual patients, and it replaces her former political engagement—

though not her politics (Kurzweil 1986, p. 222). In introducing their translation of Lacan, Mitchell and Jacqueline Rose (1982) were careful to stay with the *psychoanalytic* debates of the feminists. In fact, Mitchell started out by stating that there is a difference between pointing to contradictions in Freud's work and extrapolating from one part or another (Mitchell and Rose 1982, p. 1). Mitchell and Rose heralded Lacan for being the "legitimate" critic par excellence, and for extending psychoanalysis. And they considered his focus on *desire* and on the *process* of the drive (the subject's specific means of relating to others) as central to feminine sexuality (Mitchell and Rose 1982, p. 34). Focusing on Lacan's reading of Melanie Klein, Mitchell and Rose (1982, p. 37) agreed that

> the relationship to the mother [is] a mirrored [one]: the maternal body becomes the receptacle of the drives which the child projects onto it, drives motivated by aggression born of a fundamental disappointment. This is to neglect the fact that the outside . . . is the place where he or she will encounter the third [person] the father.[4]

Because the father is synonymous with the law and, therefore, with the concept of castration, Lacan had addressed the symbolic meaning of castration in the family "triangle" rather than in the mythic past—in the phallus (as the symbol of unity and fertility belonging to and joining both sexes), which also doubles as the paternal metaphor. Woman was found to be excluded from this phallic definition because she is *not* man (1982, p. 49). But, because to Lacan there was no feminine outside language, and the "feminine" in language was produced as a negative term, Mitchell and Rose (1982, p. 56) concluded that Lacan too "was implicated in the phallocentrism he described, just as his own utterance constantly rejoined the mastery which he sought to undermine."

The women in the (classical) Société Psychanalytique de Paris did not proclaim their feminism, and none of them joined a feminist group. Nevertheless, many of them have been defending feminist principles and follow in the footsteps of the early women analysts, often those of Melanie Klein. The most prominent among them are Janine Chasseguet-Smirgel and Joyce McDougall.

In 1964, Chasseguet-Smirgel published a collection on questions of femininity. Reviewing the literature on femininity and focusing on the father-daughter relationship (and the basically feminine propensity to incorporate anal-sadistic components along with the paternal penis), she connected female masochism to the accompanying guilt and to the revolt against an omnipotent mother rather than to a wish to become a man. She also extrapolated from the "basic feminine wish to separate from the mother." Like Jeanne Lampl de Groot, she considered the castration complex a secondary formation; like Ruth Mack Brunswick, she found the desire for a child to precede penis envy; and like Josine Mueller, she noted the early centrality of the vagina (Chasseguet-Smirgel 1970, pp. 1–47).[5] In a similar vein, Maria Torok suggested that the envied penis becomes idealized; Catherine Luquet-Parat thought that a "masochistic feminine move" defends against sadistic drives directed toward the father's penis; and Joyce McDougall suggested that some measure of female homosexuality must be part of every woman's psyche.

Later, Chasseguet-Smirgel (1985, p. 52) extended her "classical" focus to perversions; and she adapted some of the Lacanians' metaphoric formulations. She maintained, for example, that relinquishing the oedipal object may be tied to the child's painful recognition of his smallness, and to the inadequacy of his sexual organ. Furthermore, she (Chasseguet-Smirgel 1984, pp. 15–16) invoked reality not only as resulting from the differences between the sexes but from generational ones: "The mother has a vagina that the little boy's penis cannot satisfy . . . [and] the sight of the female genital organs is so 'traumatic,' . . . because it confronts the young male with his inadequacy."

Joyce McDougall (1985, p. 44), whose references to Lacan were even more direct, maintained that the phallus—as the symbolic function of the penis in its intra- and intersubjective dialectic—is truly significant. She also stated that the phallus is the basis for the "fundamental signifier" determining how the female genitals will be represented in an individual's unconscious. In an earlier essay on female homosexuality, McDougall (1980, p. 118) had stated that the (Lacanian) phallus is taken as the symbol of narcissistic integrity, or as the fundamental signifier of desire. These are only a few examples of the theoretical questions the women among the Parisian Freudians addressed and their relation to Lacanian concepts.

GERMAN FEMINIST THEORIES

In Germany, Margarete Mitscherlich-Nielsen (1975, p. vii) was first in addressing questions of sexuality rather directly. Identified with the Frankfurt School, and (reservedly) with Habermas, her left critical views are in line with those of feminism. Hence it is not surprising that, in the 1970s, she applied psychoanalytic theory to the liberation of women. Publicly identified with left political goals, she has upset those of her classical colleagues for whom neutrality is an essential ingredient of psychoanalytic technique.

In the introduction to her bestseller, *Die friedfertige Frau,* Mitscherlich-Nielsen (1985, p. vii) wondered why men go to war and women seem to accept men's destructive drives more or less willingly— as victims, forced accomplices, or servants. And she demonstrated that Freudian theory proves that women are better equipped than men to combat the irrationalities of modern society. Thus she went beyond the arguments in the postwar "fatherless society" she and her late husband, Alexander Mitscherlich, had so brilliantly described—in order to "re-place" the psychic legacies of the Hitler regime and to further democ-racy in the Bundesrepublik. Her younger feminist friends, however, now were denouncing the inadequacies of this democracy: She agreed with them that moral double standards were prevalent in economic and political life. For, "everywhere," Mitscherlich-Nielsen (1985, p. 172) noted, "men's associations, fraternities, and manliness are self-idealizing; and they militate against true fatherliness—which stands for humanity, civic duty and integrity."

Mitscherlich-Nielsen, who always explained psychic processes against the background of postwar German realities, also paralleled her compatriots' hatred of Turks and other "guest-workers" to the anti-Semitism of the Nazis. And she postulated that this resulted from the prevailing socialization of (unconscious) male and female ways of ex-pressing aggression—which in turn was institutionalized in the division of labor. Even German psychoanalysts, she stated (Mitscherlich-Nielsen 1985, p. 22), mostly ignored the neo-Kleinians' and Chasseguet-Smirgel's contributions on female psychology. Had her colleagues paid attention, they might have focused more on women's unconscious ha-tred of their mothers—itself rooted in patriarchal family relations. Where fathers did not assist in the child's upbringing, Mitscherlich-Nielsen often repeated, disturbances of early mother-child relations tend to be played out in later sexual disturbances or in alcohol or drug abuse. Most psycho-analysts, she held, although continuing to dispute the content and roots of women's superegos, no longer question Freud's tentative specula-tions about femininity but mistakenly consider them to be facts (Mitscherlich-Nielsen 1985, p. 47).

Because Mitscherlich-Nielsen wants to advance the emancipation of women, she rarely goes in for abstract discussions. Instead, she has advocated addressing the consequences of positions for or against, for instance, abortion or the dire consequences of overpopulation. She has pointed out that women tend to overvalue everything that is thought of as manly; and that the girl's early socialization to be considerate of others limits her later freedom of choice (Mitscherlich-Nielsen 1985, p. 145). By mediating between unconscious drives and political realities, she has come down against those who dominate the world, who decide upon war and peace: They are the same men who dominate women. That was why she has become the German-speaking feminists' idol.

The Swiss feminist Maya Nadig (1986), for instance, applied the unconscious meanings of psychic dynamics of socialization Mitscherlich-Nielsen had outlined to the ethnoanalysis of Mexican peasant women. In a similar vein, Waltraud Gölter (1983) examined the problematic socialization of female identity, especially in the works of Marguerite Duras, Christa Wolf, Anaïs Nin, Simone de Beauvoir—in order to show how an inevitably "open" identity formation may bring about freedom from compulsive habits of thinking, as well as a utopian consciousness that may induce great creativity. Yet another feminist psychoanalyst, Ellen K. Reinke-Koeberer (1978), took issue with the theses of Chasseguet-Smirgel's group, arguing that analysts' views themselves influence their drives (and drive theories) and that cultural and long-standing individual and family-specific role models lead them to con-clude (erroneously) that "culture is destiny."

CULTURAL TRANSFER OF PSYCHOANALYTIC FEMINISM

Both male and female Anglo-Saxon Freudians, however, when con-fronted with the questions raised by the presence of a strong feminist movement have countered with their own "scientific" arguments. Among them, William Grossman and Walter Stewart distinguished be-tween the early phase of penis envy (it occurs in the first two years of life and is registered as a narcissistic injury), and a later phase (it represents an effort to resolve oedipal conflicts). They then suggested (with illustra-tions from cases) that penis envy be considered the manifest content of a symptom rather than "bedrock" (Grossman and Stewart 1976). Elea-nor Galenson and Herman Roiphe, instead, focused on early genital-zone experiences as influencing subsequent sexual identity and ego functions. Their research led them to conclude that Freud had been only partially correct about the relations between penis envy, the female castration complex, and feminine development, because these occur earlier than he had thought and are related to fears of object and anal loss as well as to affective experiences with parents (Galenson and Roiphe 1976, pp. 29–57). Two years earlier, Roy Schafer (1974) had proposed that psychoanalysts who genuinely appreciate ego psychology ought to deal with issues connected to the exploitation of women. He came to think that Freud had been applying a nineteenth-century biological-medical framework, which inevitably flawed his clinical and theoretical insights about women.

Ethel Person (1980, p. 36) challenged the popular assumptions that sexuality functions best when freed of cultural repression, and that female sexuality is inhibited (hyposexual) while male sexuality represents the norm. She illustrated the differences between biological sex, gender, sexual behavior, and reproduction; between theories about the nature of sexuality and about sexual motivation. But all these theories, she went on, are expected to explain too much: the motor force behind the desire for sexual behavior, the strength of the sexual impulse as subjectively experienced, the absence, avoidance, or inhibition of sexuality and the variable intensity of sexual desire, the diversity of erotic stimuli and situations that may trigger them, the existence of a "sex print"—that is, an individual's restrictions of erotic responses, the confluence of sexual and nonsexual meanings in both sexual and nonsexual behavior, and the cultural preoccupation with sexuality (Stimpson and Person 1980, pp. 37–38). Object-relations theory, although limited by specific problems of internalization, such as affect, perception, maturational stages, and conflict, Person (1980, p. 46) maintained, best accounts for cultural influences on sexuality. Still, "culture"can explain neither how sexuality influences the development of the autonomous personality nor the variations of personality structure between one individual and another within each culture. Sexual liberation and female liberation are separate. But structures of gender and sex print, she concluded, do mediate between sexuality and identity formation. Therefore, it may be difficult to "liberate" sexuality from the contaminants of power, although female liberation might act as the midwife in the struggle (Stimpson and Person 1980, p. 61).

Male sexuality as well, Person held, might be incomplete or skewed and suffering from cultural biases.[6] By examining Alan P. Bell and

Martin S. Weinberg's *Homosexualities* (1978)—their views on sexual experience, their typologies, and the relation between homosexual life-styles and psychological adjustment—she drew attention to the fact that male and female homosexuals construct different psychodynamics, symbolic universes, and gender organization (Person 1983). Furthermore, Person thought that not only the conceptualizations of female sexuality but those of male sexuality too are incomplete: They overlook that boys' "fundamental sexual problem is the struggle to achieve phallic strength and power vis-a-vis other men," and that the fantasies accompanying the mother-son relationship have their own impact (Fogel et al. 1986, p. 72). To learn more about their dynamics, Person explored the widespread male fantasies of "the omni-available woman and lesbian sex"—as these might parallel homosexual and transvestite solutions of the oedipal conflict (Fogel et al. 1986, p. 73).[7]

Nancy Chodorow drew on much of this psychoanalytic literature. We recall that she maintained (Chodorow 1978, p. 142), among other things, that Mitchell had placed too much emphasis on women under patriarchy and too little on Freud's own "unexamined patriarchal cultural assumptions, . . . [his] blindness, contempt of women, mysogyny, [and unsubstantiated] claims about biology." Focusing primarily on sociological facts, Chodorow wanted to find out *why* women not only give birth but also take on *all* mothering functions. So, after rejecting physiological, biological, hormonal, and even sociological theories as unconvincing, she too found object-relations theory to be the best means to understand "the reproduction of mothering as a central and constituting element in the social organization and reproduction of gender" (Chodorow 1978, p. 7). In the process, as the psychoanalyst and historian Peter Loewenberg observed, "she left out the body." He and other critics chided her for ignoring biological reality, such as gestation or early bonding. Still, she demonstrated how male and female sexual differences are being reinforced in the individual's psyche at every step of socialization; and she pointed to the consequences of these practices for *all* women. In her view, and in mine, Freud's account of superego formation was plausible. The psychological consequences of women's mothering, Chodorow noted (1978, p. 169), lead to asymmetries in the relational experiences of girls and boys—which have their repercussions in the role learning replayed in every family. Thus "women mother daughters who, when they become women, mother" (Chodorow 1978, p. 209).

Chodorow even more than Mitchell or the French feminists helped convince American sociologists and (nonpsychoanalytic) feminists that psychoanalysis was not analogous to the plague. That she drew on object-relations theory once more brought classical analysis into the realm of sociology. Thereby, psychoanalysis was being relegitimated. Most recently, sociological questions about homosexuality, and about women's psychic mechanisms in early development, are being explored with the help of psychoanalysis.

Last but not least, I believe, sociologists now are following the feminists in departments of English and French literature—who were the first ones to pick up on French feminist theory. There, the *id* was no longer being replaced by the *ego* but by deconstructions of Freud's texts, by questions about "phallocentrism," and the language of the Lacanian *it*. In other words, psychoanalytic feminism sparked by international contacts within the women's liberation movement—for better or worse—inadvertently brought psychoanalytic thinking into academic establishments, and finally into sociology.

NOTES

1. Here, I am ignoring the fit between feminist and deconstructionist theories.
2. Cixous pursues this issue in her most recently translated book: *The Newly Born Woman* (Cixous and Clement 1986).
3. To address it here would lead me too far afield.
4. Quoted from Lacan, "L'instance de la lettre dans l'inconscient ou la raison depuis Freud" [*Ecrits*].
5. Phyllis Greenacre (1950) is also cited frequently as picking up on Abraham's notions of the possible links between vaginal and anal eroticism in infancy as possible roots of later perversions.
6. Person came to this interest after studying transsexuality (Person and Ovesey 1974).
7. The historian Henry Abelove's thesis, that Freud's own theories did not allow for the stigmatization of homosexuals but that American puritanism and prudery won out over his objections, is yet another effort to explain the biases against homosexuality during the era of liberation movements, which a number of analysts have addressed.

REFERENCES

Bell, Allen P. and Martin S. Weinberg. 1978. *Homosexualities: A Study of Diversity Among Men and Women.* New York: Simon & Schuster.

Chasseguet-Smirgel, J. 1970. *Female Sexuality*. Ann Arbor: University of Michigan Press.
———. 1984. *The Ego Ideal*. New York: Norton.
———. 1985. *Creativity and Perversion*. New York: Norton.
Chodorow, Nancy. (1978). *The Reproduction of Mothering: Psychoanalysis and the Sociology of Gender*. Berkeley: University of California Press.
Cixous, Helene and Catherine Clement, eds. 1986. *The Newly Born Woman*. Minneapolis: University of Minnesota Press.
Fogel, G. I., F. M. Lane and R. S. Liebert, eds. 1986. *The Psychology of Men: New Psychoanalytic Perspectives*. New York: Basic Books.
Freud, Sigmund. [1933] 1965. "Femininity." In *New Introductory Lectures on Psychoanalysis*. New York: Norton.
Galenson, E. and H. Roiphe. 1976. "Some Suggested Revisions Concerning Early Female Development." *Journal of the American Psychoanalytic Association* 24(Supp.):29–57.
Gallop, J. 1982. *The Daughter's Seduction: Feminism and Psychoanalysis*. Ithaca, NY: Cornell University Press.
Gölter, Waltraud. 1983. "Aspekte weiblichen Schreibens." *Psyche* 7 (July):642–68.
Greenacre, Phyllis. 1950. "Sexual Problems of Early Female Development." *Psychoanalytic Study of the Child* 5:122–38.
Grosskurth, P. 1986. *Melanie Klein: Her World and Work*. New York: Knopf.
Grossman, W. I. and W. A. Stewart. 1976. "Penis Envy: From Childhood Wish to Developmental Methaphor." *Journal of the American Psychoanalytic Association* 24 (Supp.):193–212.
Irigaray, L. 1986. "The Sex Which Is Not One." Pp. 99–106 in *The Newly Born Woman*, edited by Helene Cixous and Catherine Clement. Minneapolis: University of Minnesota Press.
Jones, Ernest. 1933. "The Phallic Phase." *International Journal of Psychoanalysis* 14 (January):1–33.
Kurzweil, Edith. 1986. "Interview with Julia Kristeva." *Partisan Review* (2):216–26.
Marcuse, Herbert. 1955. *Eros and Civilization* New York: Vintage.
Marks, E. and I. de Courtivron. 1980. *New French Feminisms*. Amherst: University of Massachussetts Press.
McDougall, Joyce. 1980. "The Homosexual Dilemma: A Study of Female Homosexuality." In *Plea for a Measure of Abnormality*. New York: International Universities Press.
———. 1985. *Theaters of the Mind*. New York: Basic Books.
Mitchell, Juliet. 1966. *Women: The Longest Revolution*. New York: Pantheon.
———. 1974. *Psychoanalysis and Feminism*. New York: Pantheon.
———. 1984. *Women: The Longest Revolution*. 2nd, rev. ed. New York: Pantheon.
Mitchell, Juliet and Jacqueline Rose, eds. 1982. *Feminine Sexuality: Jacques Lacan and the École Freudienne*. New York: Norton.
Mitscherlich-Nielsen, Margerete. 1975. "Psychoanalyse und weibliche Sexualitat." *Psyche* 9:769–88.
———. 1985. *Die friedfertige Frau*. Frankfurt: Fischer.
Nadig, Maya. 1986. "Zur Ethnoanalyse der Frau." *Psyche* 3(March): 193–219.
Person, Ethel S. 1980. "Sexuality as the Mainstay of Identity: Psychoanalytic Perspectives" In *Women: Sex and Sexuality,* edited by C. R. Stimpson and E. S. Person. Chicago: University of Chicago Press.

————. 1983. "Review of *Homosexualities: A Study of Diversity Among Men and Women*" [by A. P. Bell and M. S. Weinberg]. *Journal of the American Psychoanalytic Association* 31(1):306–15.

Person, Ethel and Lionel Ovesey. 1974. "Transsexual Syndrome in Males." *American Journal of Psychotherapy* 28:4–20.

Reinke-Koeberer, Ellen K. 1978. "Zur Diskussion der weiblichen Sexualität." *Psyche* 32:695–731.

Rieff, Phillip. 1966. *The Triumph of the Therapeutic. The Uses of Faith After Freud.* New York: Harper Torchbooks.

Riesman, David. 1964. *The Lonely Crowd.* New Haven, CT: Yale University Press.

Schafer, R. 1974. "Problems in Freud's Psychology of Women." *Journal of the American Psychoanalytic Association* 22:459–85.

Stimpson, C. K. and E. Person, eds. 1980. *Women: Sex and Sexuality.* Chicago: University of Chicago Press.

PART II

Critique and Reevaluation of Existing Theories

Chapter 5

FEMINISM AND THE
THEORIES OF TALCOTT PARSONS

MIRIAM M. JOHNSON
University of Oregon

IN THE 1960s AND 1970s, feminists joined others in various progressive movements in criticizing Talcott Parsons for his "ahistorical" and "functionalist" approach. Parsons's association with "functionalism" and especially his statements concerning the positive functions of a gender-based instrumental/expressive division of labor within the family seemed to be nothing but an attempt to justify a status quo that, for feminists, cried out for change. Moreover, Parsons's association with "grand theory," a term coined by C. Wright Mills to describe his more formalistic middle period work, made Parsons even more of an anathema to feminist critics of academic male pretentiousness.

While some feminists, including myself, have continued to work within a broadly Parsonian tradition (Giele 1978; Stockard and Johnson 1980), many turned to Marx, to Mills, to Marcuse, to phenomenology, and to interactionist approaches for theoretical guidance. Parsons's name generally came to stand for all that feminists were against—he was the bad guy, Mr. Conservative, someone to be vanquished and forgotten. How could Parsons ever have anything to say to people who were trying to change the world? Most feminists stopped reading Parsons, although he continued to write until his death in 1979.[1] But as time has passed, feminists have found problems with other theoretical approaches too, and have produced critical and corrective readings of these, discarding some ideas and developing others. The time now seems ripe for a similar project with respect to Parsons. This feminist project could become a part of the general reevaluation (and rehabilitation in a more leftist direction) of Parsons's work that has been taking place in the United States in the 1980s. (For example, see Sciulli and Gerstein 1985, and especially Alexander 1985.)

Only now, after other approaches have been tried and found lacking,

101

are we in a position to create a more balanced assessment of Parsons and to see the value in his multileveled, multicausal, and interdisciplinary approach.[2] We can also see that the early critics of Parsons often misinterpreted him and made more serious errors in their own analyses than Parsons had made in his (Alexander 1983).

I do not claim that Parsons is above criticism. He clearly must be faulted for condemning others (including feminists) for their "ideological" biases while not recognizing the ideological implications of his own "scientific" discourse. He can also be faulted for his lack of emphasis on contingent, everyday practice and for his failure to problematize power.

It is also true that Parsons was not a good writer, and that he was not a Marxist, not a feminist, and not a postmodernist. But neither was he a conservative. While clearly no radical egalitarian, it is now generally agreed that Parsons was a liberal, both in the broad sense of standing for the maximization of individual freedom and in the narrower sense of protecting individuals from the onslaughts of unbridled capitalism. He was a staunch supporter of modernity and progress and shared with Marxists the belief that the course of human history has, overall, been progressive (B. Johnson 1975, p. 60). Moreover, he disliked and feared a fundamentalist backlash.

The possibility of using Parsons's work for feminist ends, and even radical feminist ends, rests in part on the liberal assumptions guiding his work. As Zillah Eisenstein points out in her book, *The Radical Future of Liberal Feminism* (1981), twentieth-century feminism has fed on the nineteenth-century liberal tradition but gains radical potential when it moves beyond formal citizen rights and demands a radical restructuring of public and private spheres. Another reason that Parsons's work can be used for feminist ends is its interdisciplinary nature and its high level of generality. Precisely because Parsons's work is so general and open-ended, one can make creative modifications in it and put it in the service of explicitly feminist ends.

In this chapter, I will first discuss the feminist critique of Parsons's functionalism and suggest that if his early essays on kinship and the family are read as *description* and not *prescription* they seem more insightful now than they appeared to be amid the revolutionary optimism of the 1960s. I will show how the rise of feminism itself can be understood, and might even have been anticipated, in terms of the evolutionary processes he posits. Finally, I will use some of my own work as an example of how one can take Parsons's ideas about evolutionary change further and in a more radical, as opposed to liberal, feminist direction.

PARSONS'S FUNCTIONALISM VERSUS FRIEDAN'S FUNCTIONAL FREEZE

In the 1960s, Parsons's functionalist approach naturally brought criticism to the extent that functionalism was interpreted to mean that whatever exists is functional—implying that the status quo is in equilibrium, is right, is inevitable, is unchanging. Betty Friedan (1963, pp. 117 ff.) interpreted functionalism this way in *The Feminine Mystique* and labeled the era of the 1950s the "functional freeze in social science." It is true that Parsons was a functionalist in that he was consistently concerned with the conditions for the stability and ongoingness of systems of interaction, but it is also important to understand that Parsons did not consider equilibrium in a given system to be the empirical case. Rather he used the notion of equilibrium as an abstract standard by which to judge the requirements for a given social system to remain ongoing (Alexander 1987, pp. 46–47). Parsons also explicitly pointed to patterns that were dysfunctional or a point of strain in a given system. Especially in his early essays, he was far more concerned with conflict and strain than with equilibrium.

The Early Essays

It is true that Parsons failed to predict the reemergence of feminism in the twentieth century. No one else that I know of predicted it either. But he did point out that the "feminine role" expected of middle-class women was a major point of "strain" in the larger system and for women themselves. In his 1942 article, "Age and Sex in the Social Structure of the United States," he describes how the increased dependence of the family status on the husband's occupation deprives the wife of her role as a partner in a common enterprise and reduces the housewife role to a kind of pseudo-occupation (Parsons 1954, p. 95). In his 1943 essay "The Kinship System of the Contemporary United States," he concludes that "the feminine role is a conspicuous focus of the strains inherent in our social structure, and not the least of the sources of these strains is to be found in the functional difficulties in the integration of our kinship system with the rest of the social structure" (Parsons 1954, p. 194). In his 1947 essay, "Certain Primary Sources and Patterns of Aggression in the Social Structure of the Western World," he describes how strains in both male and female socialization produce aggressive motivation in both sexes, which in turn can feed into fascistic and militaristic stances. Here he describes the effects of the male's occupational role as a source of frustration for the growing girl:

> The first is the discovery of what is, in the relevant sense, "masculine superiority", the fact that her own security like that of other women is dependent on the favor— even "whim"—of a man, that she must compete for masculine favor and cannot stand on her own feet. This is a shock because in her early experience her mother was the center of the world and by identifying with her she expected to be in a similar position. (Parsons and Bales 1955, p. 308)

In the 1960s, feminists read this with anger. Why didn't he protest? He almost did when he went on to say that this reversal of expectations would produce "much insecurity" and hence "aggression" . . . "directed against men" for causing the problem "and against women" for deceiving them (Parsons 1947, p. 308, 1954). In an earlier article he had predicted that insecurity in the adult feminine role would be widely manifested in "neurotic behavior" (Parsons 1942, p. 99, 1954).

We can now read these essays as a cold but accurate analysis of the situation of middle-class women in the 1940s and 1950s, the problem that Friedan brought to light as "the problem that had no name." Moreover, in contrast to Friedan, Parsons understood that women's situation was structurally induced by the mode of articulation between "family" and "occupational system" that had developed with industrialization, a mode that emphasized sex differences more rather than less.

Parsons was also aware of strains in male development related to the prominence of women as mothers. Long before Nancy Chodorow and Dorothy Dinnerstein turned Freud on his head to argue that male misogyny was a reaction formation to the early prominence of the mother in child rearing, Parsons, who had also read Freud, described this phenomenon as being particularly characteristic of urban middle-class boys. In his "Certain Primary Sources and Patterns of Aggression," he labeled it "the bad boy pattern" and saw it as a reaction formation against making a "feminine" identification and as a source of male fear of the femininity in themselves and ambivalence about the morality that had become associated with femininity in the modern family (Parsons and Bales 1955, pp. 304–8).

In my view, these early articles provide an overview of the structured strains in the nuclear family at midcentury—strains that he might well have predicted would lead to the feminist movement, especially as middle-class women's occupational participation increased.

The Instrumental-Expressive Distinction

Perhaps the most widespread feminist criticism of Parsons had to do with his assertions in the 1950s that a division of labor based on sex was functional for maintaining the integration of the family. He viewed the husband's instrumental specialization and the wife's expressive specialization as being "functional" for marital solidarity because it eliminated competition betweem husband and wife.[3] Betty Friedan (1963, p.122) used this as a prime case of Parsons's attempt to argue against careers for women *and* against the possibility of husband-wife equality.

To support her contention, she quoted the following passage from his "Age and Sex" article as follows:

> It is, of course, possible for the adult woman to follow the masculine pattern and seek a career in fields of occupational achievement in direct competition with men of her own class. It is, however, notable that in spite of the very great progress of the emancipation of women from the traditional domestic pattern only a very small fraction have gone far in this direction. *It is also clear that its generalization would only be possible with profound alterations in the structure of the family.* (Parsons and Bales 1955, p.96, italics added)

Friedan quotes this passage to prove Parsons's anti-egalitarianism, but significantly enough she ignored the last phrase of the quote, namely, that adult women having equal careers with men "would only be possible with profound alterations in the structure of the family." Friedan, the liberal feminist, was not ready for anything like a radical restructuring of the family (Eisenstein 1981). While Parsons clearly did not advocate such a radical restructuring of the family either, he leaves the future open and understands that the changes necessary to bring about equality would indeed be profound.

Parsons's statement that most middle-class women's jobs are far from equal to their husbands' is still empirically correct. It remains true that in the large majority of middle-class families, wives' working for wages has not altered the male-dominant family structure or the male-dominant occupational world. Men are not sharing work at home to any great extent and women are not paid as much as men. Moreover, as women have entered the labor force they have not relinquished major responsibility for the household but rather have added an outside job, and the public-private split remains. This seems to be true in both capitalist and socialist countries. Liberal feminists in the early 1970s were overly optimistic about the equalizing effects of women's working outside the home. Equality can only come about with more radical change.

From a radical feminist standpoint, Parsons was correct to point out the negative association between marital stability and occupational equality. Panel studies show that as the earnings or potential earnings of the wife increase relative to those of her husband, so does the likelihood of divorce (Cherlin 1981, pp.49–50, 54–55). What this may mean is that many women stay married because they cannot afford not to and that many women when they can support themselves leave. The nature of marriage itself will need restructuring.

Parsons must be faulted, however, for not understanding the degree to which women's financial dependency, rather than "role differentiation," may have been accounting for the marital stability associated with the nonemployment or underemployment of middle-class wives in the labor market. Clearly he did not see the degree to which the economic power that goes with the male provider role was used by men to legitimate male dominance in the middle-class family.

Leaving aside the question of the power imbalance and focusing only on a division of labor, it may well be that some gender-based division of labor with regard to child care is desirable. I do not say this to affirm the status quo but to suggest that we need to devise a division of labor that does not penalize women and does not reinforce the privatization and isolation of the family. Parsons would call this "a tall order," but, nevertheless, it is one that must be taken seriously.

I shall return to more recent changes in family and work after showing how the feminist movement itself and the changes associated with it can fit into Parsons's evolutionary theory of change (Parsons 1966).

PARSONS'S SOCIAL CHANGE MODEL

As we have seen, Parsons's "functionalism" did not preclude discussion of strain and dysfunction. Neither did it preclude his dealing with change, for Parsons was in fact a celebrant of progressive change. His life project, which began with *The Structure of Social Action* in 1937, was to understand "progress" in more broadly sociological terms than had been possible when it was conceived of from a narrowly utilitarian perspective (Mayhew 1984).

The Nature of Progress

Parsons's definition of progress embodied general movement away from interdependencies based on ascribed and particularistic connections toward interdependencies based on achieved statuses and universalistic standards. Thus individuals came to depend on the law, the state, the market, and, later, public schools and unions, rather than on more limited and personalized relationships established on the basis of birth. This idea of progress also involved increasing autonomy for the individual. But this freedom for the individual was not a freedom to do anything one wanted. Parsons used the concept of institutionalized individualism to stress that individual autonomy was always normatively defined and regulated. Marxists have pointed out that this freedom more often than not when applied to workers turned out to be only the freedom to sell their labor to capitalist exploiters; and historians have chronicled the human misery accompanying so-called progress. Nevertheless, if one looks at "the big picture" as Parsons usually does, it is difficult to contend that "progress" has not been made, even though the idea of continued progress is increasingly under attack in postmodernist circles.

Admittedly, the ideological implications of Parsons's view of evolution fit with the beliefs of middle-class people in positions of relative privilege in Western society. But then Western feminism itself arose among the relatively privileged middle class and comes out of this same basic ideological tradition. Feminism is a logical next step in terms of this scheme, which involves freeing the individual from dependencies on particularistic ascribed relationships.

Parsons's Four Evolutionary Processes and Feminism

Parsons's four evolutionary processes are differentiation, inclusion, adaptive upgrading, and value generalization. These processes parallel his four system functions: goal attainment, integration, adaptation, and latency. I will discuss each process briefly in relation to feminism.

Differentiation. Parsons (1966, p. 22) defines *differentiation* as occurring when "a unit, sub-system, or category of units or subsystems, having a single relatively well defined place in the society divides into units or subsystems (usually two) which differ in terms of both structure and functional significance for the wider system." The most familiar example of evolutionary differentiation as it relates to women and the family is the breakup of the agricultural household, which was both a unit of residence and a unit of production. As productive functions were removed to factories for greater efficiency, household functions also become more specialized. I will return to this aspect of differentiation later when I examine adaptive upgrading, but for now I am concerned with another meaning of *differentiation*.

Parsons used *differentiation* also to refer to an increasing distinction between culture, social organization, personality, and the biological organism. With modernization, a clearer differentiation between personality and society occurs that is related to the increasing autonomy of individuals (Parsons 1966, p.24), that is, individuals come to see themselves as being increasingly separable from the social matrix. I believe that the perception of gender inequality itself depended in part on a process of differentiation by which people's identities and sense of self-worth became separable from the roles they played and the activities they pursued. This process preceded and made possible the understandings that have characterized Western feminism.

As women began to perceive themselves more as individuals, it became obvious that women did not share in the same rights that men as individuals did. Nineteenth-century feminism was based on this perception. The same perceptions fueled the more recent feminism also, but the structural situation was different with married women increasingly working outside the home. The main tendency of feminism in the 1970s (which has liberal and radical versions) sought to eradicate gender difference itself, leaving only the individual. How far this process can go or whether it is desirable remains to be seen, but certainly feminists in the 1970s usually minimized those gender-differentiated characteristics that could be ascribed to biology and condemned biological rationalizations for gender inequality. "Woman" came to be understood as a social construction rather than a biological given. Gender itself was problematized (Flax 1987). Another aspect of this was that feminists began to value their own subjective experience and their own definition of what was going on. This fed into the feminist critique of the family and its "functions" as they were usually described by males from a male perspective.

All of these changes, those that rested on a perception of similarity with men and those that rested on a recognition of women's different perspective, were made possible when gender itself was problematized. My point is that this problematizing of gender was made possible by processes of differentiation by which self could be seen as separate from biology and social structure. This form of subjectivity was most fully embodied among middle-class Whites.[4]

Inclusion. In introducing the concept of inclusion, Parsons (1966, p. 22) says, "Differentiation and upgrading processes may require the *inclusion* in a status of full membership in the relevant general community system of previously excluded groups which have developed legitimate capacities to 'contribute' to the functioning of the system." Thus in the course of societal evolution more and more people who had been excluded from such things as education and political participation gradually attained the privileges of citizenship and full personhood. He was thinking particularly of the inclusion of lower classes that had previously been excluded from full membership into the wider system.

However, the ideology that prevailed until the mid-twentieth century, which decreed that married women do not work, coupled with the radical separation of work and family, of public from private, created a situation for middle-class women in the United States that excluded them from the dominant activities of the society even more than lower-class men. The feminism that developed in the 1960s represented a new push for inclusion, this time by middle-class women seeking occupational opportunities commensurate with men of their class. Again the impetus came from middle-class women because it was here that the occupational disparity between husband and wife was most apparent.

In the United States, the reactivation of efforts to get the states to ratify the Equal Rights Amendment epitomized the push for inclusion. Feminists hoped that passing this amendment would affirm and enhance equal access to jobs for women, equal pay, and equal opportunity for advancement. Women also sought inclusion in the political arena as elected officials, culminating in Geraldine Ferraro's selection as the Democratic party's vice-presidential candidate in 1984. Women's entrance into graduate and professional schools is another step toward inclusion, albeit again it was generally middle-class women who profited.

In the sphere of personal relations, the so-called sexual revolution (not to be confused with a revolution in gender roles) legitimated nonmarital sex for "respectable" women and emphasized the lack of difference between male and female sexuality. This is another aspect of the process of inclusion—in this case, the definition of what constitutes human sexuality.

Unfortunately, this inclusion of women as sexual beings has been accompanied by an increase in rape. It then becomes even more important that women be included as individuals under the protection of the law. Women are deserving of the protection of the law not because they are good and faithful wives but because they are citizens with rights to protection. Another example of inclusion is the remarkable success of shelters for women who are the victims of domestic violence. Within less than 10 years' time, a grass-roots movement to provide shelter for battered women has become "respectable" and in many cases these shelters and their staffs are partially supported by marriage license fees. Thus women who were literally at the mercy of a particularistic relationship—namely, marriage—now have protection as individuals. Another example of this is the increasing number of states that have outlawed "marital rape."

Adaptive upgrading. Adaptive upgrading refers to the increased efficiency and effectiveness resulting from differentiation and inclusion. According to Parsons (1966, p.22), adaptive upgrading "applies to both role and collectivity levels; the participating people, as well as the collectivity as a whole, must become more productive than before, as measured by some kind of output-cost relationship." In his works specifically on the family written in the 1950s, Parsons seemed especially sanguine about the effectiveness of the "specialized" nuclear family in modern society. He clearly thought that the family, which had become differentiated from farm production, performed its core functions of early socialization (for achievement) and adult tension management better than it had been able to do in the past (Parsons and Bales 1955, pp. 16 ff.). Feminists questioned the adaptiveness of this family type on the grounds that, while the family may have been relieving tensions for men, it was creating tensions for women. By the time Parsons codified his ideas on evolution in the 1960s, however, he had begun to hedge on the adaptiveness of all the differentiated units and thus implied that it was an empirical question whether the family had been upgraded (1966, p. 22).

But Parsons would see not only the process of differentiation but also the process of inclusion as contributing toward adaptive upgrading of the collectivity as a whole. One of the most powerful arguments feminists have used to gain access to jobs and so on has been to point to the waste of talent caused by exclusionary practices. I think Parsons would have to agree that the inclusion of educated women into the occupational world outside the home has indeed led to adaptive upgrading by releasing more trained capacity into the system.

Value generalization. According to Parsons (1966, p. 23),

> The final component of the change process pertains to its relation to the value system of the society. Any given value system is characterized by a particular type of *pattern* so that, when it is institutionalized, it establishes the desirability of a *general type of social system.* . . . A system or sub-system undergoing a process of differentiation, however, encounters a functional problem . . . its value pattern must be couched at a higher level of *generality* in order to legitimate the wider variety of goals and functions of its sub-units.

Thus for Parsons, all of the foregoing processes result in and necessitate changes in the overall value system of society, changes in values that can incorporate a wider variety of goals, activities and types of people. Indeed, now, it does seem that overall societal values themselves are changing in ways that give more emphasis to perspectives that have been more typical of women than men.

At first feminists used a highly generalized set of instrumental values to legitimate their push for inclusion. These values included economic rationality, rational utilization of human talents and resources, and equal opportunity. But from the very beginning there has been another strain within feminism that warned against this approach and argued instead that the aim of feminism was not to integrate women into a man-made competitive society but rather to critique such a society and the male paradigm it represents. Beyond this, the aim was to make these more typically female values a part of the mainstream.

Much feminist writing can be taken as an effort to bring about a redefinition of dominant societal values. For example, Carol Gilligan's (1982) description of gender differences in the moral sphere is significant not as a documentation of difference but as an effort to integrate women's perspectives into a more generally shared definition of morality. The result of such efforts is likely to be what Parsons would call "value generalization at a higher level."

Summary and Assessment of Parsons's Model

I have tried to show how the ideology of feminism itself can be fit within Parsons's views of progress. This is because feminism is very much a part of the same liberal tradition of which Parsons's work itself is a part. Moreover, the successes of feminist ideas do seem from one standpoint to be a validation of Parsons's evolutionary views of progress. Middle-class women are being included in the world of work outside the home, and in politics. Values have been or are being generalized. Male-female interaction rules are changing toward more gender-neutral forms. Physical and sexual violence against women has been "discovered" and condemned. While abuse has not been eradicated, it is notable that the moral legitimacy of the inclusion of women as equals of men in the public sphere has made great progress.

Why did Parsons not explicitly include the emancipation of women in his evolutionary scheme? My guess is that what kept him from "going further" was his resistance to the idea of "unisex," that is, something like complete role dedifferentiation. I share this resistance, and complete role assimilation or dedifferentiation no longer seems the aim of most feminists. While minimizing difference remains the larger goal, achievement of equality cannot be accomplished by ignoring difference. Rather the aim is to achieve gender equality in the presence of difference by restructuring both work and family. As I pointed out earlier, Parsons never said women should not work outside the home or that equality was impossible. He simply said this would be difficult without profound changes.

Parsons did not try to envision what these changes might be like and he probably did think feminists were "going too far" in their demands. Moreover, his insistence on taking the stance of the rational, objective, outside observer made it difficult for him to listen to the subjective experiences of women, especially when he himself was under attack.

In the next section I discuss the current status of the family and suggest ways to carry the foregoing analysis forward.

GOING FURTHER—FUTURE DIRECTIONS

While the gains women have made are real and important, from the standpoint of gender equality the millennium is hardly here. Women's working has not brought on a "symmetrical" family envisioned by some in which husband and wife work equal time for equal wages and share equally in child care. Women's wages are still far below those of men; and working outside or not, women continue to take major responsibility for the home. Far more prominent than the equal sharing of child care by fathers and mothers is family breakup. Single parenting, and especially single mothering, continues to increase. Nonmarriage is increasing.

Further Structural Differentiation

In my view it is possible to conceptualize these changes in terms of a further process of structural differentiation in which the husband-wife axis of the nuclear family is becoming increasingly separable from the parent-child axis. This separation has been implicit in previous analyses (e.g., Bane 1976) and has become more salient in analyses of divorce law whereby no-fault divorce assumes that the couple relationship is dissolvable by consent but responsibility for children is expected to continue (Weitzman 1985; Blumberg 1985). One often reads explicit statements to the effect that the couple relationship may readily be dissolved but the parent-child relationship must (somehow) remain intact. Practically speaking, what this usually means is that the mother-child bond remains and the father-child bond is broken or sharply attenuated when the father remarries.

This separation of couple relationships from parent-child relationships is obviously not the empirical case with most families and may never be, but then (as Parsons's critics delighted in pointing out) neither was the nuclear family of husband, wife, and small children the empirically dominant form. The point is, however, that these partially descriptive analytical classifications can help us make sense of a great deal of complexity. Breaking the nuclear family up in terms of these two distinct systems allows us to ask how these systems intermesh with other relationships to form new kinds of kin and quasi-kin solidarities. Most important, making this distinction between couple and parent-child relationships helps to pinpoint the causes of the gender inequality that feminists are seeking to eliminate. Much can be learned from examining mother roles and wife roles separately.

Marriage and Inequality

In my view, an important source of gender inequality is the structure of the marriage relationship or the heterosexual couple relationship. Most analyses of gender inequality that focus directly on the family have attributed women's secondary status and relative lack of occupational achievement to the handicaps that mothering imposes on women. Marriage and the structure of the marriage relationship has been less analyzed, except in terms of the handicaps imposed on women by housework. In my book, *Strong Mothers, Weak Wives* (M. Johnson 1988), I argue that the status of wife itself as defined by the marriage contract and our informal expectations concerning husband superiority lie behind women's secondary status in the wider society.

Although the current context and organization of marriage is a barrier to gender equality in this society, until very recently, marriage has been made to be by far the most desirable choice for women, especially women with children. But this is the paradox: The relationship that the structure of society causes women to need is precisely the relationship in which women are also defined as and expected to be secondary.

In my view, neither nonmarriage nor a perfectly symmetrical family involving husband and wife sharing child care equally and participating equally in paid labor is a realistic solution. In the 1980s, some feminist analyses began to back off a bit from this total assimilationist position and began to reassert the importance of women's family involvement. Other feminists feared this was a step toward a new conservatism. (For a summary, see Stacey 1983.) More recently the strain of feminism that emphasizes and celebrates the noninstrumental, noncompetitive, humane and expressive values with which women have been associated has gained more ascendancy. Because of other structural changes that have occured, not the least of which is women's greater involvement in the occupational world and public life in general, I do not believe that this emphasis on expressiveness is regressive, but rather it points the way to a new synthesis.

While the general trend is toward less differentiation between male and female roles, some difference related to women's association with motherhood may remain. In order not to allow this difference to become a basis for enforcing gender inequality, it becomes even more important to analyze the implications of mother and wife roles separately. Valuing women's special strengths as mothers and the expressive and non-sex-typed values with which mothering is associated does not in itself produce inequality. Rather, inequality results from the way in which women's mothering has been organized and supported—that is, either by husbands or by the state acting as husband.

The economic downturn that divorce often means for middle-class women has brought home the degree to which marital solidarity has rested on women's economic dependence. Divorce has also brought an increasing awareness of the lack of institutionalized backup care for children and along with this, a questioning of the desirability of total parental responsibility for child care in the first place. Women have also gained new strengths as they manage on their own for longer periods before marriage and after divorce and widowhood.

New Directions

While some of these phenomena may be experienced now as dislocations, they may also presage new and better modes of articulating family and work—modes that may bring about greater gender equality and transform definitions of both family and work in ways that could erase the partially false distinction between private and public spheres.

In order to imagine directions of change that might be beneficial to women, it becomes important to study nonnuclear family types along with the changes that are occurring with regard to nuclear families. I am especially interested in examining the literature on matrifocal families characterized by a weaker intensity of the husband-wife relationship and the relative cultural prestige and economic power of women as mothers and sisters. In spite of the complexities involved with matrifocal situations, not the least of which is class underprivilege, I believe matrifocality should be examined more seriously by feminists for clues as to how greater gender equality might look, and for indications of structural situations in which the status of women vis-à-vis men is enhanced. This may provide a fruitful project for collaboration between Marxists, primarily concerned with class inequality, and radical feminists, concerned with gender inequality.

At this point I do not see any easy solution to the problem of gender inequality. My own best guess and hope is that feminism will become a part of a larger and more integrated movement that revives and revises maternal values, involving a less hierarchical approach and a concern for the preservation of the earth and its population while retaining some of the best elements of "normal" social science that can tell us what is happening and keep us grounded—perhaps a kind of merger of ecofeminism and science. The inclusion of women has made these statements and this kind of thinking possible. Parsons would understand this and call it "value generalization."

Summary and Conclusions

In this chapter, I have tried to show how Parsons's evolutionary framework as well as his early analyses of the family can serve as a useful framework to understand feminist thinking and the changes associated with it. Even though he himself tended to privilege the nuclear family of the 1950s and, more often than not, stressed positive functions rather than dysfunctions, there is nothing inherent in his categories of analysis that would prevent him or others from taking the analysis further and in different directions. There are other alternatives within his own system, some of which I have explored.

Finally, in my view, if feminism is to make a difference, we must not ignore "grand theory," because to ignore it is to give up power. Feminists must deal with major synthesizing theoretical systems within sociology, most notably Parsons and Habermas, because they are systems of rhetoric—major texts—that influence and persuade and that are not going to go away. Clearly it is important for feminists to critique these theories and their claims to objectivity. At the same time, it is important to join the game to modify and perhaps even transform these theories. We can at least test the limits of their usefulness.

NOTES

1. I was a student of Parsons in the late 1940s and early 1950s, and, certainly then, Parsons was personally less sexist than most male professors. During a period when women could not count on support in graduate school, much less in the professional world for which it was supposed to prepare us, Parsons did encourage women and always assumed that women were the intellectual equals of men. He facilitated women's entrance into the Social Relations Department at Harvard and, I think most who knew him would agree, did not disparage, condescend to, or exploit his female students or colleagues.

2. In my view, one of the most useful aspects of Parsons's overall theory of action for feminists can be his insistence on the validity of differing levels of analysis and the perspectives of different disciplines. The Social Relations Department at Harvard constituted an early experiment in interdisciplinary cooperation. Also, micro and macro perspectives were included. Feminism itself has been an interdisciplinary movement and has drawn from and changed a variety of disciplines. In this sense, Parsons's lack of disciplinary

parochialism fits well with feminism. Parsons, too, always tended to reject single-factor theories of causation, and relegated such theories to what he referred to informally as "the kindergarten school of sociology."

3. Parsons did treat "expressiveness" as a positive virtue that he did not associate with irrationality or rank emotionalism. Rather, expressiveness had to do with a sensitivity to the needs of others and concern with social integration within a given system. Elsewhere my colleagues and I have conducted research using a definition of *expressiveness* derived from Parsons that excludes the pejorative connotations that have become attached to the term. In a series of studies we show that women do see themselves as more expressive than men see themselves, but that women do not see themselves as being any less instrumental than men see themselves to be. We conclude that expressiveness is the basic orientation for both sexes and that it has been undervalued and misunderstood in this society because of the hegemony of male perspectives (Gill et al. 1987; Johnson et al. 1975).

4. The ideology and practice of individualism was strongest in the middle class. It was also in the middle class that the impediments to women's acting as individuals were most clearly perceived. One reason for this perception of inequality was the lack of support systems from other kin or friends for the wife. The nuclear family, most fully institutional-ized in the middle class, cut women off from each other and enhanced their economic dependency on husbands. These were the women Betty Friedan's book could speak to. Significantly enough, however, the women who actually fueled the feminist movement were not housewives but were professionals or radical students, and Friedan was talking about their mothers.

REFERENCES

Alexander, J. 1983. *The Modern Reconstruction of Classical Thought: Talcott Parsons.* Berkeley: University of California Press.

———. ed. 1985. *Neofunctionalism.* Beverly Hills, CA: Sage.

———. 1987. *Twenty Lectures: Sociological Theory Since World War II.* New York: Columbia University Press.

Bane, M. J. 1976. *Here to Stay: American Families in the Twentieth Century.* New York: Basic Books.

Blumberg, G. G. 1985. "New Models of Marriage and Divorce: Significant Legal Develop-ments in the Last Decade." In *Contemporary Marriage,* edited by K. Davis. New York: Russell Sage.

Cherlin, A. 1981. *Marriage, Divorce, Remarriage.* Cambridge, MA: Harvard University Press.

Chodorow, Nancy. 1978. *The Reproduction of Mothering.* Berkeley: University of Califor-nia Press.

Dinnerstein, Dorothy. 1976. *The Mermaid and the Minotaur.* New York: Harper & Row.

Eisenstein, Zillah. 1981. *The Radical Future of Liberal Feminism.* New York: Longman.

Flax, Jane. 1987. "Postmodernism and Gender Relations in Feminist Theory." *Signs* 12(4):621–43.

Friedan, Betty. 1963. *The Feminine Mystique.* New York: Dell.

Giele, J. 1978. *Women and the Future: Changing Sex Roles in Modern America.* New York: Free Press/Collier Macmillan.

Gill, S., J. Stockard, M. Johnson, and S. Williams. 1987. "Measuring Gender Differences: The Expressive Dimension and Critique of Androgyny Scales." *Sex Roles* 17:375–400.

Gilligan, Carol. 1982. *In a Different Voice.* Cambridge, MA: Harvard University Press.

Johnson, B. 1975. *Functionalism in Modern Sociology: Understanding Talcott Parsons.* Morristown, NJ: General Learning Press.

Johnson, Miriam M. 1988. *Strong Mothers, Weak Wives: The Search for Gender Equality.* Berkeley: University of California Press.

Johnson, M. M., J. Stockard, J. Acker, and C. Naffziger. 1975. "Expressiveness Re-Evaluated." *School Review* 83:617–43.

Mayhew, L. 1982. "Introduction." In *Selected Writings of Talcott Parsons: On Institutions and Social Evolution,* edited by L. Mayhew. Chicago: University of Chicago Press.

———. 1984. "In Defense of Modernity: Talcott Parsons and the Utilitarian Tradition." *American Journal of Sociology* 89(6):1273–1305.

Parsons, Talcott. 1954. *Essays in Sociological Theory* (rev. ed.). Glencoe, IL: Free Press.

———. 1966. *Societies: Evolutionary and Comparative Perspectives.* Englewood Cliffs, NJ: Prentice-Hall

Parsons, Talcott and Robert F. Bales. 1955. *Family, Socialization and Interaction Process.* Glencoe, IL: Free Press.

Sciulli, D. and D. Gerstein. 1985. "Social Theory and Talcott Parsons in the 1980s." *Annual Review of Sociology* 11:369–87.

Stacey, Judith. 1983. "The New Conservative Feminism." *Feminist Studies* 9:559–83.

Stockard, J. and M. Johnson. 1980. *Sex Roles: Sex Inequality and Sex Role Development.* Englewood Cliffs, NJ: Prentice-Hall.

Weitzman, L. 1985. *The Divorce Revolution.* New York: Free Press.

Chapter 6

HABERMAS AND FEMINISM
The Future of Critical Theory

THOMAS MEISENHELDER
California State University, San Bernardino

THE COMPLEX AND STILL-GROWING opus of Jürgen Habermas includes, at least, a theory of knowledge, a theory of social action, and a theory of society. The various parts of the total theory are grounded in a conception of the nature of human reason. It is this model that is the primary topic of this chapter.

Of course, a central subject in Habermas's version of critical theory is society, its structure and development. Here he proposes a reconstruction of historical materialism that focuses attention on the "superstructure." History, for Habermas, involves changes in the relations of production caused by the learning of new normative structures. Tied to a social formation's principle of organization, normative structures make it possible to develop and implement new forces of production (Habermas 1979, pp. 78–90). Also they are internalized through the processes of socialization and form the "inner nature" of individuals. From this reconstruction of historical materialism, Habermas formulates the idea of a legitimation crisis produced by the capitalist state's increasing intervention in the economy as a response to economic crises. Through these themes, Habermas alerts us to the significance of conceptions of rationality in society by portraying the crises of late capitalism as failures of instrumental or practical rationality within the state, economy, and individual.

Habermas's model of human reason is discussed directly in *Knowledge and Human Interests* (1971) and is stated more or less formally in Habermas's ongoing analyses of "communicative actions." In the first work, Habermas develops the sociology of knowledge by arguing that all knowledge is bound to material "interests" and social conditions. He uses this perspective to reconstruct philosophical conceptions of rationality. Each succeeding concept is studied through its connection to a particular "cognitive interest," or basic orientation, rooted in material

119

social relations (Habermas 1971, p. 196). Habermas uses this analysis to present a devastating critique of positivism as instrumental rationality.

Habermas shares with other critical theorists the position that a core characteristic of the human being is the potential to reason (Held 1980, pp. 195–196). He goes on to suggest that communicative action is the materialization of the human capacity for reason. Analyzing human speech and its presuppositions, Habermas concludes that "truth" is attainable only in a situation of free and open discourse motivated by a goal of unconstrained agreement. This leads him to his much discussed description of the counterfactual "ideal speech situation." In the ideal speech situation, individual speakers possess an equality of speaking chances and they can speak about whatever they wish to call into the play of discussion. Therefore, he concludes, reason itself is grounded in social norms like freedom, equality, and justice. This description, then, becomes the standard for proposing that modern society is irrational, alienating, and dehumanizing. It also guides Habermas's call for social change. He argues that the struggle for a just society is in the interest of all humanity as reasoning beings (Habermas 1981). This analysis has been elaborated further in Habermas's *The Theory of Communicative Action* (1984). A study in social action theory, this work also provides an in-depth look at Habermas's conception of the totality of human reason and reveals a major problem in the contemporary critical theory of Habermas. This is his nearly complete silence about the emotional aspects of social life. His orienting discussion of reason includes mention of self-expressivity as a kind of rationality but even this is dealt with only as a variety of argumentation or therapeutic discourse. In other words, he only considers expressivity as reasonable if it has passed through cognitive processes (Habermas 1984, pp. 15–22). Throughout the work Habermas uses a conception of reason premised on the centrality of argumentation to truths of all kinds. Certainly he must be given credit for adding to previous analyses a consideration of the rationality of morality, art, and identity (Habermas 1984, p. 83), but he does not question the idea of an "impartial" human reason removed from subjective particularity (Young 1987).

Habermas (1982, p. 247) accepts the idea that "compassion is the limit concept of the discourse ethic," a simple and clear declaration that emotional experience is irrelevant to his critical theory. He continues the discussion by turning to the issues of animal rights, vegetarianism, and an ethic of solidarity with the nonhuman as subjects for critical theory. These topics are conceptualized through reference to the relationship of "caring-for," which he labels "*paternalistic*" (Habermas 1984, p. 248). This discussion reveals something of crucial and subtle importance, the implicit sexism of Habermas's perspective on human reason and critical theory. When Habermas does take up emotionality, he turns to a discussion of the "paternal" relationship of human beings to the rest of nature. This he presents as an important problem for the theorist attempting to avoid "*anthropocentrism.*" It does not occur to Habermas to investigate human experiences of emotionality such as are evident in the relationships of caring, affect, and solidarity within the private sphere of the family. Instead he presumes that his conception of reason encompasses all humanity, and subjects not included therein must then be concerned with the nonhuman! Habermas equates the "nonrational" and the emotional with "nature" just as for centuries men have equated emotion, nature, and the female (Merchant 1980).

In another attempt to deal with affective experience, Habermas classifies it as one subpart of "aesthetic-practical rationality," which is an attitude one can take toward "external nature" (Habermas 1984, p. 249). Once again Habermas seems to take it for granted that emotionality is nonrational and, therefore, nonhuman. Once again these positions follow from his universalization of a "male" notion of human reason. Indeed when he attempts to diagram the "complexes of rationality," Habermas leaves empty (with the exception of the aforementioned aesthetic-practical rationality) those cells that might refer to the place of emotion and affect within reason (Habermas 1984, p. 249). Writing about one of these empty cells he states that "expressively determined forms of interaction . . . do not of themselves form any structures susceptible of rationalisation; they are rather parasitical" (Habermas 1984, p. 250).

Thus, for Habermas, reason is devoid of emotionality. In the terms of contemporary feminists such as Harding (1983), Habermas's model of reason is patriarchal. It elevates the kind of thinking learned and performed by men to a position of theoretical and practical superiority over that learned and performed by women. This conception of affectivity as nonrational leads Habermas to "correct" the emotions by declaring them a distorted form of communication that must be—through logic and analysis—invaded and destroyed or at least isolated and degraded.

In the few other places where Habermas (1979, pp. 41–43, 86–91) does write about emotionality, he reduces it to self-presentation and the problematics of sincere expressions. This focus follows from his commitment to a discourse model of reason. The only questions about feelings that are of concern to Habermas are those directly related to language. That is, he allows into the play of his theory only those emotional experiences that can be made public: "An actor has desires and feelings in the sense that he can at will express these experiences before a public" (Habermas 1984, p. 91). Here, once again, the "objective" world of the abstract mind is granted determining significance over the "subjective" experiences of the body-mind. Habermas uses his linguistic theory of reason as communicative action to explain his priorities. Until coded as language, emotions remain subjective, irrational, and suspect experiences. The public realm of discourse rules the private world of experience. Thus Habermas repeatedly denies the possibility of a place for the emotions within the totality of human reason.

Still, Habermas is to be credited for reintroducing moral-practical rationality into the modern conception of reason. However, his version of morality universalizes a kind of individual rights model of justice by arguing that justice is grounded in the possibility of a free and open discourse between individuals. This discourse seems to admit only those thoughts and opinions that can be phrased linguistically. This kind of proceduralism produces a formal notion of justice based not only in the split between individual and other but also in several parallel philosophical dualities. It pictures people as abstract objects devoid of passionate concrete content. Once again affective experience is privatized and dismissed. According to Habermas, feelings have nothing to do with justice. Justice and morality, as social processes, involve the moral and instrumental rationality of the "actor" while emotions are individual subjective experiences. Habermas develops a theory of justice that presumes instrumental individuality rather than human solidarity. It would be more sociologically accurate to start with solidarity and explain individuality. As is, Habermas adopts the position of patriarchal rationalism and universalizes the point of view of the modern male ready to argue about the truth of his own perceptions and values while at the same time declaring all feelings irrational and out-of-bounds.

It is not enough to allow reason to partake of morality if one's conception of reason remains defined by the regulation of social interaction by a set of abstract procedures. It is fine to conceptualize reason as a form of life but it also must be recognized that life contains the emotions. Further if the part of life declared unreasonable is somehow the bailiwick of a particular group of people, then one's conception of reason is not only formal and idealistic but also oppressive. This kind of approach to morality has been carefully and critically analyzed by Carol Gilligan

(1982). In describing "male morality" as emphasizing position, rights, equality, strategy, hierarchy, mastery, individuation, and abstraction, Gilligan (1982, pp. 58–63) is also describing Habermas.

As mentioned earlier, Habermas does discuss expressive speech acts. He begins by categorizing them as either sincere or untrustworthy and deceptive representations of inner subjectivity. He then suggests that emotions might be judged rational if they involve reflection on the relationship between subjective feelings and cultural standards. Now Habermas might tell us more about this intriguing idea, but once again he is foiled by his linguistic model and instead declares emotional discourse to refer only to "well-formed" and sincere expressive statements (Habermas 1984, pp. 41–42) and the ability to utter trustworthy presentations of oneself (Habermas 1984, p. 91).

In reconstructing the Lukácsian critique of the reified life-world of late capitalism, Habermas (1984, pp. 358–62) stresses the substitution of exchange relations and the commodity form for less strategic or instrumental communicative structures within the life-world. Yet he fails to realize that the problems of reification stretch beyond the exclusion of practical rationality and include the exclusion of emotionality from social life and social thought. Therefore, his correction—importing argumentation into the structure of the life-world—is in good part another reified position. It enlarges the substance of the abstraction from human experience to include moral claims and discourse but continues to deny emotions a place in the totality of human reason. The model of the life-world that Habermas presents remains formal for it excludes from everyday life the human world of emotionality. In Habermas's theory the life-world remains reified and individuals are still alienated from their own subjectivity.

There is still another place where Habermas begins a line of inquiry that could lead to the study of emotionality in reason and society. In his reconstruction of historical materialism, Habermas (1979, pp. 17–24) notes that the history of society begins with the emergence of the family and the integration of instrumental labor and human nuturance according to shared norms and rules. However, rather than proceeding to analyze human nurturance and its social and psychological aspects, Habermas concentrates on the study of the norms and rules that regulate and give form to family, work, and society. Once again his formalistic focus leads him to neglect emotionality. Finally, in his most direct treatment of emotions, Habermas (1984, pp. 91–92) says that they are "rooted in needs" and are either "desires" or "feelings and moods."

The former are volitional inclinations while the latter are described as intuitive "perceptions." Both are experienced in the light of need satisfaction. Although this makes a fine beginning for an empirical sociology of emotional life, Habermas again turns to language and talks about the use of linguistic expressions to communicate predilections to others by making one's own needs culturally shareable. He then goes on to formalize the dramaturgical perspective on the presentation of self that follows from his emphasis on expressive communication. Here again he seems to presume that the substance of human emotionality is either insignificant or well known. Perhaps Habermas relies too greatly on the psychology of Kohlberg[1] or it may be that his now famous "linguistic turn" has placed language and the cerebral at the core of his critical theory. Whatever the origins, Habermas often seems to have a largely negative or dismissive opinion on the role of emotion in human experience. If "communicative rationality" leaves no room for the life of the emotions, it must in the end be seen as a disembodied and abstract idealism, which is, of course, the very brand of theorizing that critical theory has always rejected. Habermas's thoughtful critique of the philosophy of reason still suffers from Western rationalism's separation of mind from body. Heller (1982, p. 22) has summarized this point and its implications: "Habermasian man has . . . no body, no feelings; the structure of his personality is identified with cognition."

Because Habermas pays little attention to emotionality, his conception of human reason remains incomplete and strikes the reader as flat and abstract. I think that Habermas's neglect of emotionality has two interrelated causes. One of these is his borrowings from the Freudian notion of the rational and the other is the universalization of the stance of the male intellectual. Habermas (1971, pp. 214–28) appears to believe that rationality is the outcome of cognition, argument, and self-reflection as performed in the psychoanalytical interpretation of dreams. The apex of rationality, it follows, is achieved in causal explanation and in-depth understanding that leads to altering what is being explained and understood. At the core of this model lies the psychoanalytical translation of the nonrational into the rational. This is how Freud, for instance, explains dreams to the dreamer; that is, by making them causally and also hermeneutically understandable. The implication here is that emotional experiences that resist logical analysis and explanation are distortions, still-undisclosed diseases, and untrue. Put another way, psychoanalytical reasoning attempts to demonstrate the grammar of experience by assuming that the nonrational can be reduced to the rational. This kind of thinking does not admit the authentic autonomy of the emotions but instead attempts to transform them into the logical. Thus Freud studied the emotions only in order to make them "medically" comprehensible. Habermas (1971, p. 228) adopts this approach and uses it as the domain or background assumption for his investigation of human reason. In the end Habermas conceives of emotionality as epiphenomenal.

The philosophical core of Habermas's critical theory—his notion of reason—is marred by errors characteristic of patriarchal thought. Habermas's description of reason shares with patriarchal rationalism an acceptance of three qualities as universal characteristics of reason (Merchant 1980). The first of these is a tendency to describe reality as a structure composed of essential dualities or divisions. Perhaps the most crucial of these divisions is that between intellect and emotion, head and heart, mind and body. The former, it is supposed, is the realm of knowledge and truth, the latter is described as an unpredictable region characterized by sentimentality, deception, and the absence of reason. The rational is objective (of the object) while the emotional is subjective (of the subject). Thus this split parallels both subject-object duality and the division between science and nature in which the former dominates and is superior to the latter. It is important to note that in each of these cases the patriarchal mind not only sees a basic duality but also posits an invidious differentiation where one element of the pair is dominant. And, of course, the argument then continues on to the historical level where the superior element is declared to be characteristic of men and the inferior is attributed to women. So in the consideration of rationality, the patriarchal mind describes it as primarily a neutral search for objective knowledge that will allow men to dominate nature in a productive way. These conceptions are projected by the male thinker into the essence of reason. This is a point of view that underlies Habermas's conception of the totality of human reason. True, he adds the realm of moral or practical thinking to more traditional instrumental versions of patriarchal thought, but there is no room for the heart in Habermas's conception of reason. Habermas admits moral and aesthetic values into the totality of human reason, but not feelings. In the end he never really frees himself from the presumptive dualities of patriarchal thought. This is due to his failure to consider seriously the materiality of the emotions and their place within the totality of human reason. His conception of reason remains formal and fails to represent adequately the experience of really existing men *and* women. If practical and instrumental rationality must be critiqued in order to free society from a political economy of domination, a critical theory of emotional reason is also necessary to free ourselves from social repression.

FEMINISM AND EMOTIONALITY[2]

It has been left to feminist theory to explain and rectify these patriarchal errors in social theory. In doing so feminists have uncovered the connections between the denial of emotionality and the male fear of separation, death, life, and the female. This has been accomplished most notably by Dorothy Dinnerstein (1976). She explains the masculine drive to master self, other, and environment as a result of men's attempt to overcome the loss of oneness experienced within the early maternal relation (Dinnerstein 1976, p. 8). Dinnerstein suggests that this drive is in the end a product of the felt insecurity that stems from the shock of experiencing one's own individual isolation and mortality. This experience is first confronted when the child begins to see itself as a distinct human being not permanently connected to the significant other, usually a woman. This experience is frightening and men have tried to overcome it through an instrumental and practical rationality that includes the repression of emotionality. Men act to dominate their human and physical surroundings through work, science, politics, and technology without admitting their feelings about the other. Thus, Dinnerstein argues, patriarchal society is inhabited by child-men unaware of their own emotional needs (and child-women unsure of their own independent adultness).

In this way Dinnerstein draws out some connections between patriarchal social organization, instrumental rationality, and early emotional experience. It is also part of her argument that the attempt to overcome the fear of a monadic mortality through instrumental mastery of the surround is most characteristic of the male. Man's earliest experiences are of solidarity with his mother. Eventually, she argues, he must estrange himself from this first emotional relationship and constitute himself as an independent individual. Now he confronts the reality of his own death. The male is at the mercy of this confrontation in part because he is unable to hold within his biological being the possibility of life. Therefore, he is left only with an awareness of the inevitability of death. Man responds to this situation by constructing a social world in which he can dominate the sources of his nightmare—the emotions, nature, and women. As de Beauvior has said, "Death is a woman" (quoted in Dinnerstein 1976, p. 124), and man deals with his fear of death by using an unemotional rationality to dominate and control nature and woman:

> Woman acts as an intermediary, conscious and at least partly controllable, between man and unconscious, uncontrollable nature. What she helps him contact and cope with, in this capacity of intermediary, is not only brute nature as it surrounds him, but also brute nature as it exists inside him. (Dinnerstein 1976, p. 125)

Once again relying on de Beauvior, Dinnerstein (1976, p. 127) argues that the male's fear of death becomes expressed in his resentment of women: "Our resentment of mortal fleshiness . . . is aimed with special force against the flesh from which our own has emerged." In other words, man meets death when he recognizes he is not one with the other. Thus, in claiming his maleness, he sees that he cannot produce life but is only a mortal individual. His body is simply mortal. He then denies this situation by attempting to control life and gain something against death through mastery over the other. In the process he relegates women to the now-degraded roles of the natural and the maternal, imprisoning them within a world of primary relationships and charged emotionality where they are forced to subordinate their needs to his. Now he can appropriate the creative capabilities of women through controlling their bodies. Contrary to the male, oppressed though they are, women can meet death openly, secure in their ability to hold and support life.

So, recognizing—with the separation from mother—the mortality of his body and his inability to hold renewed life within himself, man attempts to deny his own mortality and his fear of death by dominating women, who are forced to represent nature in the role of mother. One of the tools men use to accomplish this is instrumental rationality. As a consequence of its success at controlling the other, instrumental rationality is elevated to the essence of reason itself. This conception of rationality is comfortable for men because it disallows the value of the emotions. The realm of the emotions is given to women, who in turn are dominated and thus pose little threat of challenging the ideology and the fundamental fears of men. Both the emotions and their carriers are degraded as inferior. To the extent that women may express emotionality and thereby reveal the fears of men, they are prospectively punished as potentially evil and irrational beings. To the extent that they represent the male's bodily impotency in the face of death, women are prospectively punished for their own sexuality.

By pronouncing a limit to the potentials and concerns of human reason that relegates the emotions to the darkness of unreason, modern social theory, including the critical theory of Habermas, reproduces this process of renunciation. Emotionality is subordinated to the instrumental and the cognitive. In the end this kind of thinking produces knowledge only useful for mastery and has brought humanity to the brink of total nuclear death. The denial of death is finally and dramatically a failure.

By repressing the female and the emotional, men demonstrate their terror and awe of women who possess the key to life and death: "What makes [the] female . . . *so formidable—so terrifying and at the same time so alluring—is the mother's life-and-death control over helpless infancy*" (Dinnerstein 1976, p. 164). Paradoxically, it is the power of the emotions that helps to account for their absence in contemporary nonfeminist social theory. It is this very condition that makes the feminist perspective crucial to the development of critical theory, for feminist theory has attempted to come to terms with the emotions and at the same time critique modern society. Forced by the rules and structures of patriarchy to experience closely the emotionality of social existence, women have transformed this experience into a powerful resource for social theory and into a forceful social movement. Women have been forced to recognize the inherent emotionality of human existence and human reason. They know only too well that the emotions must be granted their place in the totality of human reason and that this will happen when women become full participants in society. As a step toward this emancipation, feminist theorists like Dinnerstein are performing liberating critiques of male theory.

A more sociological feminist critique of male rationality is evident in the work of Nancy Chodorow. In *The Reproduction of Mothering* (1978), Chodorow demonstrates that male thinking originates in early childhood experiences within sexist society. When women mother, she argues, male children grow up with an undeveloped "relational capacity" and define themselves as independent beings separated from others. Men come to see themselves as essentially unlike the mothers with whom they have their first and most emotional relationships. Indeed, they learn to repress and deny qualities that may be "female" as they accomplish their individuated male identity. As a result, men in a sexist society tend to see the feminine as unworthy and inferior. On the other hand, female children more continously identify with the mother and the nurturing relationship with her. They develop high relational capacity, learn to reflect on their own emotions, and come to appreciate nurturant and caring relationships. As a consequence of this pattern of child development, for males,

> people are treated and experienced as things. . . . Thus the "fetishism of commodities", the *excessive rationalism* of technological thought, the rigid self-other distinctions of capitalism or of bureaucratic mass societies all have genetic and psychological roots in the structure of parenting and of male development. (Lorber et al. 1981, p. 503)

Women, on the other hand, develop a capability for relating with others and see themselves as basically existing within social relations. Empathy and care become valued skills.

A similar argument has recently been provided in Issac Balbus's *Marxism and Domination* (1982). He also proposes that male thinking, or "the instrumental mode of symbolization," elevates technical mastery over emotionality: "Male domination is rooted in and reproduced by the assumption that reason is superior to emotion and thus that reasonable men are superior to emotional women" (Balbus 1982, p. 356).

Like Chodorow and Dinnerstein, Balbus ties instrumental thinking to asymmetrical parenting in sexist society. He then applies this perspective in a critique of Marx and neo-Marxism. One of Balbus's important contributions is that he gives some needed historical background about current child-rearing arrangements and suggests how and why they might change in the future. Balbus uses a neo-Freudian perspective to suggest that the errors of social theory lie in an instrumentalist denial of affect that stems from the processes of mothering in a sexist society. He also describes an important connection between instrumental rationality and the fear of separation and denial of death that results from the end of the mothering relationship (Balbus 1982, pp. 292–302). However, more than Dinnerstein and Chodorow, Balbus seems to accept at face value the universalization of the separation experience and the resultant fear of death. He does not recognize that these specific results are rooted in the particular childhood situation of men. He simply accepts the notion that mature development requires separation and individuation from the mother. He even accepts the notion that girls shift their positive emotional attachment to the father and come to idealize men in general. In this sense, Balbus generalizes to all humanity from the specific situation of men. A major error that results from this faulty universalization is the acceptance of the dichotomy of reason and emotion; that is, Balbus does not incorporate within the totality of human reason the workings of emotionality.

Recently the need for a more impassioned theorizing has been declared by feminist philosophers like Mary Daly (1984). While much of Daly's philosophy may be of little use to sociology, her discussion of "elemental" rationality is important to the future of critical social theory. She says that she wishes to reclaim an "elemental knowing . . . that is intuitive/immediate, not mediated by the omnipresent myths of phallicism" (Daly 1984, p. ix). This "knowing" is achieved by an "elemental" rationality that results from the particular history and situation of women and that has been "buried" since the rise of the instrumental theories of Bacon and Descartes (Daly 1984, pp. 154–55). Along with Sandra Harding (1983), Daly argues that male thinkers dismember reason by repressing its emotional contents. While instrumental reasoning and even Habermas's communicative rationality are dispassionate and heartless, elemental rationality is passionate and reunites head and heart (Daly 1984, p. 280).

This new, or renewed, conception of reason can become the philosophical foundation for building a feminist critical theory. Such a project begins by jettisoning male definitions and incorporating the emotional within the totality of human reason. That is, we must formulate a dialectical conception of human reason containing both "head and heart," body and spirit. Feminist critical theory can also explain how human reason has become reduced to technique and procedure, how this can change, and what the consequences are of a feminist conception of the totality of human reason. The totality of human reason includes the emotions as a form of rationality that women have been forced to experience and respect. A new inclusive conception of reason includes the ability to empathize and feel with the other (see, also, Harding 1983, pp. 52–53). The totality of reason includes a variety of forms of human orientation—the instrumental, the practical, and the emotional—as ways to, and grounds for, knowledge.

If the emotions are repressed or ignored as inferior and irrational, they do not disappear. Rather they return in distorted forms of human destructivity such as racism, sexism, and other structures of domination. In a situation where caring and concern are denigrated or silenced, we are free to develop the powers of destruction with little empathy for our victims. Perhaps, twisted by repression, denied care becomes expressed hatred. This alone should warn us of the need to think about the emotions. We must reflect emotionally as well as intellectually. The best way to counter the distorted emotionalism of human domination is not to deny the emotions altogether but to study them in order to understand and develop positive emotional capabilities. The best defense for the distortion of the human being lies in a thorough comprehension of the totality of human reason, including emotional reason.

When experience is organized around practices of exploitation and domination, it is never enough simply to think within the current modes of thought and forms of experience. Rather, the ruling conceptions must be challenged at their very cores by a kind of thinking that strives to express the excluded. In an alienated world dominated by patriarchal reason, it is not sufficient merely to expand the existing definition of rationality. Instead, one must transform it. This is what feminist critical theory can do by challenging the very premises of social theory and constructing a new conception of human reason that includes the historical experiences of the female as well as the male.[3] We can build a feminist critical theory from that base. Such a theory will de-reify male reason by demonstrating its basis in material and ideological exclusivity. Doing so will involve challenging the institutionalized rationality of both society and profession. It will place us outside conventional science and philosophy.

In this struggle women, as the historically determined carriers of emotional rationality, are structurally placed in the role of transformational agents. By freeing emotional reason from the domination of technique and procedure, women will begin the process of freeing society from sexism and domination. The political project of critical feminism begins with the disalienation of thought by reuniting body and mind within the totality of human reason. As a revolutionary social category, women can change society only by ending their own domination in it; that is, by ending their exclusion from the public sphere and their exploitation within the private world of the family.

NOTES

1. As Thomas McCarthy (1982) has noted, Habermas has to date not adequately considered the ethnocentric and social biases of his adopted paradigm of human psychological development.

2. In this section, *male, female,* and *mother* should be read to refer to structured activities and capacities normally assigned to a particular gender. They in no way indicate biological or social identities and/or necessities.

3. An empirical road in this direction is being carved out by women in the sociology of emotional reasoning. See Gilligan (1982) and Hochschild (1983).

REFERENCES

Balbus, Issac. 1982. *Marxism and Domination.* Princeton, NJ: Princeton University Press.

Chodorow, Nancy. 1978. *The Reproduction of Mothering.* Berkeley: University of California Press.

Daly, Mary. 1984. *Pure Lust.* Boston: Beacon.

Dinnerstein, Dorothy. 1976. *The Mermaid and the Minotaur.* New York: Harper & Row.

Gilligan, Carol. 1982. *In a Different Voice.* Cambridge, MA: Harvard University Press.

Habermas, Jürgen. 1971. *Knowledge and Human Interests.* Boston: Beacon.

————. 1979. *Communication and the Evolution of Society.* Boston: Beacon.

————. 1981. "New Social Movements." *Telos* 49:33–37.

————. 1982. "A Reply to My Critics." In *Habermas,* edited by J. Thompson and D. Held. Cambridge: MIT Press.

————. 1984. *The Theory of Communicative Action.* Vol. 1. Boston: Beacon.

Harding, Sandra. 1983. "Is Gender a Variable in Conceptions of Rationality." In *Beyond Domination,* edited by C. Gould. Totowa, NJ: Rowman and Allanheld.

Held, D. 1980. *Introduction to Critical Theory.* Berkeley: University of California Press.

Heller, A. 1982. "Habermas and Marxism." In *Habermas,* edited by J. Thompson and D. Held. Cambridge: MIT Press.

Hochschild, A. 1983. "The Managed Heart." Berkeley: University of California Press.

Lorber, J., R. Coser, A. Rossi, and N. Chodorow. 1981. "On 'The Reproduction of Mothering.'" *Signs* 6:482–514.

McCarthy, Thomas. 1982. "Rationality and Relativism." In *Habermas,* edited by J. Thompson and D. Held. Cambridge, MA: MIT Press.

Merchant, C. 1980. *The Death of Nature.* New York: Harper & Row.

Young, I. 1987. "Impartiality and the Civic Public." Pp. 56–76 in *Feminism as Critique,* edited by S. Benhabib and D. Cornell. Minneapolis: University of Minnesota Press.

PART III

Emerging Feminist Theories

Chapter 7

GENDER EQUALITY
Toward a Theory of Change

JANET SALTZMAN CHAFETZ
University of Houston

ANY COMPLETE THEORY OF social change must address at least three analytically distinct issues: (1) What specific social structures and processes are most fundamental, in the sense that their change generates broad-scale systematic change? (2) How does change occur? (3) What are the effects of change on various subpopulations within a society? For activists who are ideologically committed to a specific change goal, such as feminists seeking gender equality in all areas of sociocultural life, the first issue may be seen as a question of targets of change effort (intermediate goals), and the second, as an issue of strategies and tactics (means). The third issue refers to the fact that gender system change can be expected to affect different categories of people in diverse ways, thus affecting the degree of both support and opposition to such change. In turn, this issue is directly related to the extent of, and limits to, change.

An answer to the first question assumes a theory of social stability. The choice of specific social practices or institutions as the key targets, whose change will presumably ramify into broader system change, logically rests on an explanatory system in which the "general problem" is the dependent variable, and the "targets" are critical explanatory variables. In this way, theories about what features of social life are most important to change first in order to result in general systemic change *are* theories of the maintenance and reproduction of the phenomenon in question, and vice versa. There is no paucity of such theories in the scholarly feminist literature (see Chafetz 1988a, especially Chapters 3 and 5). Recently, I have attempted to synthesize a variety of theoretical

AUTHOR'S NOTE: Helen Rose Ebaugh, A. Gary Dworkin, and Ruth Wallace read and commented on earlier drafts of this chapter. I am grateful for their helpful suggestions.

approaches into an eclectic theory of the maintenance and reproduction of systems of gender stratification (Chafetz 1988b). I will review this shortly, preparatory to a discussion of change targets.

The second issue raised above, concerning how change can and does occur, has received surprisingly little attention from feminist social scientists (see Chafetz 1988a, Chapter 5). I will devote the bulk of this chapter to outlining the major components of an eclectic theory of the process of change in systems of gender stratification. Clearly, change in any system of inequality can occur in either of two directions: increase or decrease. *In this chapter, change will be synonymous with a decrease in gender stratification.* The third issue, concerning the differential impact of change on subpopulations, will be addressed last, in a discussion that focuses on the limits to change in any one historical period.

GENDER SYSTEM STABILITY: A BRIEF REVIEW

My theory of gender system maintenance and reproduction (Chafetz 1988b) asserts that superior male power, which exists by definition in gender-stratified societies, allows men to coerce women into assuming work roles that reinforce their disadvantaged status, at both the macro and the micro levels. Moreover, male power also results in the development of social and interpersonal definitions that devalue women and femininity, and strengthen and legitimate the gender system. Yet the coercive potential of men is relatively infrequently employed or perceived. This is the result of several processes that together produce gendered personalities and gender normative choices, most importantly for women. In turn, these function to bolster male power while both hiding and futher legitimating the entire system. Undergirding both the coercive and the voluntaristic aspects of the process is a gender division of labor that provides unequal power resources to men and women.

The Division of Labor and Male Power

Gender-stratified societies are those in which males have categorically greater access than females, who are otherwise their social peers (e.g., in terms of social class, age, or race/ethnicity), to the scarce values of their society (Chafetz 1984). *By definition,* any stratification system implies that the superordinate category has superior power (and usually authority) over the subordinate, although the bases and manifestations of such power may vary extensively cross-culturally and across types of stratification systems. When using the concepts "power" and "authority," I am employing the Weberian conception: (1) authority is legitimated power; (2) power exists when a person or group is able to extract compliance from other persons or groups, even in the face of opposition. The exercise of power, in turn, requires control over resources that are needed and desired by subordinates, and not otherwise sufficiently available to them, and/or the ability to inflict harm on subordinates in the absense of a reciprocal ability. Stated otherwise, power wielders have the wherewithal to coerce or bribe compliers.

I begin by assuming superior male power, because my theory addresses the issue of how existing systems of gender stratification are perpetuated. I make one further assumption, based on extensive empirical literature in anthropology and sociology: that there exists a gender division of labor by which men and women do different work. Moreover, women's work always includes more responsibility for child rearing and family and household maintenance than does men's, regardless of what other kind of work women may do.

Using an exchange perspective, I argue that at least since the development of settled agrarian societies (that is, societies in which workers produce a surplus), and including industrial ones, the gender division of labor has functioned to place a highly disproportionate amount of the economic resources required for survival in male hands (see Sacks 1974; Vogel 1983; Lipman-Blumen 1976; Blumberg 1984). As husbands, men acquire power at the micro level of the household to the extent that women are economically dependent on them. Women grant compliance to their husbands in order to balance exchanges in which men provide more of the important resources (Parker and Parker 1979; Curtis 1986). That power, in turn, can be used by husbands to sustain the gender division of labor and household responsibility that provides relatively less access to economic rewards for women. Male power at the macro level permits elite men, in their roles as economic, educational, political, and other kinds of gatekeepers, to enforce a gender division of labor that advantages their own gender. The result is that women either work entirely within and for the household and are totally dependent on their husbands, or they work in gender-segregated, relatively low-paid jobs and remain chiefly responsible for household tasks (the double workday). In either case, they collectively lack the resources to seriously challenge male macro power (Curtis 1986; Sacks 1974; Hartmann 1984).

Definitional Power

Superior power resources permit men to exercise both macro- and micro-level definitional power. At the macro level, social definitions are created and legitimated by elite members, who control dominant social institutions (political, economic, educational, religious, cultural). Their conceptions of the valuable, good, and true become the socially accepted definitions to a substantial degree. Both historically and in the present, elite members have been overwhelmingly male. Therefore, social definitions are fundamentally androcentric, that is, they reflect a masculine perspective of the world, an assertion made by theorists from such diverse perspectives as Marxist-feminist, labeling, and symbolic interaction (Sacks 1974; Vogel 1983; Hartmann 1984; Ferguson 1980; Schur 1984). To the extent that elites create definitions that function to protect and legitimate their own advantaged status, gender-relevant social definitions will devalue women and femininity, and support traits and behaviors for both men and women that reinforce the gender division of labor and male power.

Gender ideologies, stereotypes, and norms constitute the relevant types of social definitions. Gender ideologies "explain" in terms of a broader principle (god, nature) why men and women are different and deserve different (and typically unequal) rights, obligations, responsibilities, and rewards. Gender stereotypes describe the ways in which women and men presumably differ, usually in ways that partially devalue presumed feminine traits and serve to justify the gender division of labor. Gender norms specify behaviors expected of men and women, thereby providing the basis for the stigmatization of nonconformists. They specify behaviors congruent with the gender division of labor and superior male power.

At the micro level of interpersonal interaction, superior male power resources also enable them to control the substance of interactions with women and to define the situation of the interaction (Fishman 1982; Ferguson 1980; Bell and Newby 1976). I call this "micro-definitional power." By exercising such power, men reinforce their resource-based power, especially at the micro level of the household, and help to ensure that their wives' perceptions and evaluations of reality support an androcentric view. Again, this helps to sustain the gender division of labor that disadvantages women.

Social and micro-definitional phenomena serve as a bridge between the more coerceive aspects of system maintenance available to men because of their resource power advantages, and voluntaristic compliance by women with the requirements of the status quo. To the extent that women choose to comply with gender norms, accept gender ideologies and stereotypes, and acquiesce to male definitions of situations, men need not employ their power—micro or macro—to maintain the status quo. In fact, such choices by women serve to reinforce further gender social definitions and to legitimate the gender division of labor and gender stratification.

Gender Differentiation

Why would women make choices that sustain a system that disadvantages them? Because by adulthood they are different from men in personality, priorities, values, competencies, and cognitive skills. I call this "gender differentiation." There exist three types of explanations for gender differentiation in the literature. The precise contribution of each is as yet an unaswered empirical question. For now, I posit that all three function in the same direction in gender-stratified societies and, therefore, reinforce one another.

One approach, associated chiefly with learning and cognitive development theorists, stresses the childhood socialization process by which, beginning at birth, people are taught a gender identity that incorporates substantial conformity to gender norms and that is a very central component of their self-identity (Cahill 1983; Lever 1976; Constantinople 1979). From this perspective, due to rewards, punishments, and especially modeling, children come gradually to internalize gender social definitions. As adults, everyday life sociologists argue that people actively seek confirmation of their gendered self-identity in interactions with others by behaving in gender normative ways (Goffman 1977; Cahill 1983; West and Zimmerman 1987).

A second perspective is taken by neo-Freudian feminists, who focus on the subtle but far-reaching effects of the fact that primary caretakers in infancy and early childhood are overwhelmingly female (e.g., Chodorow 1978). In turn, the structure of caretaking, which is an integral part of the gender division of labor, produces different relational capacities in males and females. Finally, the engendered personalities produced in this fashion lead to different role choices for men and women, which reproduce the gender division of labor.

The third perspective argues that the specific roles played by adults, including aspects of empowerment, advancement opportunities, and social isolation or integration, create characteristic responses in terms of attitudes, values, behaviors, and priorities. Because they are located in different types of roles, men and women become differentiated (Kanter 1977; Barron and Norris 1976; Schur 1984; Chafetz 1984). In turn, this strongly affects the probability that they will obtain (or even seek) other types of roles in the future.

Despite their differences, what these three perspectives have in common is the idea that, by some point in adulthood, men and women are really different in myriad ways that affect the choices they make concerning the kinds of work they wish to do (both at home and in the economy) and their priorities among varied roles. Women tend to make choices that reproduce the gender division of labor, and with it superior male power and gender stratification. In the process, they perceive their choices as being as unconstrained as those of men. This obviates the need for men to exercise power in order to maintain the status quo, and it functions to legitimate the entire system.

PIVOTAL CHANGE TARGETS

I have argued that systems of gender inequality are sustained, first and foremost, by a gender division of labor that reinforces superior male power at both the macro and the micro levels. It does so because, regardless of the specific tasks assigned to each gender, those assigned to men generate a greater amount of scarce and valued resources than those assigned to women. The same division of labor, and the superior male power it supports, permit elite men to create social definitions that devalue women and legitimate the gender division of labor and the entire gender system. Moreover, they permit most men to impose their definitions of situations on their own wives and other intimate females, thus further reinforcing the entire structure. Finally, the division of labor contributes in fundamental ways to the development of gendered personalities. In turn, this makes male use of power largely unnecessary, as the gender division of labor appears to result from free choice and is thereby legitimated.

The two pivotal mechanisms sustaining the gender system are superior male power and the gender division of labor, which are inextricably intertwined. I suggest that of the two, the gender division of labor is more potentially amenable to manipulation, as superior male power has sources in addition to the division of labor (see Blumberg 1984). Moreover, power advantages can only be reduced when subordinates develop substantial power resources, which women are prevented from doing in great measure precisely because of the gender division of labor.

Two other targets of change have often been stressed both in the scholarly literature and by feminist activists. The first concerns the process by which gendered personalities are constructed in childhood (e.g., Chodorow 1978; Cahill 1983; Lever 1976; Coser 1986). There is both a practical and logical problem with this. If adults have relatively stable engendered personalities that are set in childhood, how are child socializers to be changed in order to change the process of childhood engenderment? If adults are relatively easily changed, the theoretical assumption of the lifelong and fundamental importance of childhood engenderment is wrong. If adults are difficult to change, social change is all but impossible. I suggest that, in lagged fashion, to the extent that important childhood engenderment does occur, its nature will change in response to substantial change in the gender division of labor.

Other theorists and activists have stressed as a change priority those variables (normative, ideological, and stereotypical) that I term *social definitional* (e.g., Sanday 1981; Ortner 1974; Giele 1978; Kessler and McKenna 1978; Schur 1984). There is little question that definitional phenomena legitimate the status quo and male advantage. In the absence of such legitimation, however, men nonetheless possess superior power resources that can enable them to sustain the status quo by coercion. Again, it appears to me that definitional phenomena will change (and to some extent already have) in response to changes in the gender division of labor, and the resulting distribution of key power resources, more readily than the reverse. This is not to deny the importance of the development of a set of feminist counterdefinitions. Rather, I suggest that definitional phenomena should be viewed not as primary *targets* of social change, but as a central feminist *means* designed to bring about change.

Change in the division of labor would have to occur both at the household level and within the public sphere to produce greater gender equality. At the macro level, at least two separate subtargets exist. First, income equality must be achieved, which would contribute substantially to the elimination of micro power differences between husbands and wives. Second, equality in incumbency of elite, gatekeeping positions (social, political, cultural, and economic) must be achieved (see Friedl 1975). These are the positions whose incumbents establish social definitions, as well as distribute concrete opportunities and rewards. Although equality in elite incumbency is probably the most difficult of all goals to achieve, in its absence any other forms that might be achieved would be tenuous and rather easily reversed. At the household level, equality in the division of responsibility and work (which virtually presupposes substantial economic equality as a major power resource) should accomplish two things. First, it would affect the process by which new generations become engendered, presumably leading to more androgynous personalities for both genders. Second, it should equalize men's and women's ability to compete outside the household for labor force and other public sphere roles. This, in turn, should enhance the probability of achieving the two macro subtargets. The central question, then, for the remainder of this chapter is *how* change in the gender division of labor can occur.

TOWARD A THEORY OF GENDER SYSTEM CHANGE PROCESSES

There are two analytically distinct but empirically related avenues toward gender system change that reduces gender inequality. On one hand, there are general social processes that produce such change without the willful or conscious intervention of people committed to producing it. On the other hand, in specific times and places, people (mostly women) organize in a conscious attempt to bring about gender system change. The existence of two avenues to gender system change leads to at least four theoretical issues: (1) What are the important variables that produce unintentional gender system change and how do they do so? (2) What are the important variables that produce intentional change efforts, and how do they do so? (3) To what extent and how are unintentional processes linked to intentional change efforts? (4) What variables explain the outcomes (relative success in goal achievement) of intentional change efforts?

Unintentional Change

If I begin with the premise that the main support of gender inequality is to be found in the gender division of labor, then the logical place to look for the roots of unintentional gender system change is in phenomena that affect the division of labor. A variety of scholars (e.g., Martin and Voorhies 1975; O'Kelly 1980; Nielsen 1978; Blumberg 1978; Sanday 1974) have noted that the degree of gender stratification varies substantially by *type* of society, as defined by technological level and subsistence base (e.g., foraging, horticultural, pastoral, agrarian, industrial). In my theory of the causes of variation in the degree of gender stratification (Chafetz 1984), I attempted to distill from discussions of societal types the underlying variables associated with degree of gender inequality. I argued from a broadly Marxian perspective that the key set of variables are those associated with the manner in which societies structure their productive work activities. Of central importance are the extent to which (1) women, relative to men, control the means and products of production; (2) women participate in those work roles socially defined as most highly valued or centrally important; and (3) women workers are easily replaced—by other available women or by a surplus of men—in their productive roles (see also Blumberg 1984).

Although I postulated a large variety of variables that affect (and in several cases are affected by) these work organizational variables, I concluded that technological variation constitutes the primary explanation of variation in the work organization variables and is therefore, the primary independent variable for understanding the degree of gender inequality. With only slight modification in conceptualization, the same argument pertains to the issue of how change occurs. The required modification is in terms of how the critical work organization variable is defined. In the theory I am developing in this chapter, I define the gender division of labor as the central variable of interest. This concept subsumes, but is broader than, the work organizational variables enumerated in my earlier work. The question of interest here, then, is what factors produce unintended changes in the division of labor, such that women's work becomes more similar to men's (and vice versa)—within and outside the home—especially in terms of resources generated and incumbency in elite positions. I postulate that technological change, and an associated increase in economic scale, constitute the primary mechanism that alters the gender division of labor. Second, I will argue that changes in the demographic profile of a collectivity may affect the gender division of labor, although in most cases this would be temporary.

Technological change can serve to increase equality in the gender division of labor in at least two ways. First, it may function to enlarge the demand for workers in types of work roles previously monopolized by men and/or in newly emerging or expanding jobs so that a new source of labor must be found (Oppenheimer 1970; Berch 1982). For instance, in the decades since World War II, the scale of production of both goods and services has expanded dramatically in the most highly industrialized nations of the world, in fair measure because of ongoing technological innovations, especially in electronics and communication. This has resulted in an enormous increase in the demand for labor (i.e., the total size of the labor force), especially for labor produced by at least moderately well-educated people. The major pool of people available to fill this demand, who were not already members of the labor force, has been married women, including those with preschool children. The gender division of labor has thus changed, to the extent that, unlike the past, a majority of married women are now involved in the formal labor force, from which they receive some power-relevant resources. However, the division of labor *within* the labor market has changed relatively little. The genders remain largely segregated into different types of occupations and industries; women's jobs pay considerably less than men's; and elite positions are still filled overwhelmingly by men (Fox and Hesse-Biber 1984). The domestic and familial division of labor between the genders has also undergone little change as yet (Huber and Spitze 1983). However, among younger cohorts of college-educated people, there appears to be somewhat greater gender equality in terms of both pay and the job deployment in the labor force, and possibly more male participation in domestic and family work in dual-earner couples (Hertz 1986).

In the previous paragraph, the focus of discussion centered on the effect of technological change and economic expansion on the *demand* for female labor. Technological change can also affect the *supply* of such labor, to the extent that it reduces women's familial and domestic labor. Technological developments that allow women to control their fertility better constitutes one example. Research has consistently shown that women are more apt to supply their labor outside the home when they have fewer children (Stewart, Lykes, and LaFrance 1982). In turn, they choose to have smaller families when there are greater opportunities for their labor outside the household (Cramer 1980; Friedl 1975, p. 137). The development of products that may be used to reduce the time and effort required to maintain home and family can also enhance women's willingness to assume other work roles (e.g., washing machines, vacuum cleaners, refrigerators, no-iron fabrics, microwave ovens, frozen meals and other convenience foods). Whether or not women actually *use* these technologies to reduce their domestic and familial labor, as opposed to raising the standards of performance within the household, rests heavily on the options available outside that context, that is, on the demand for their labor elsewhere.

In the absence of technological change and economic expansion, an increase in the demand for female workers can also result from a shortage of male adults. There are two primary reasons why this sometimes occurs: war and migration. During wartime, women are often called upon to assume men's jobs. However, unless casualty rates are exceptionally high (e.g., the Soviet Union after World War II), the prior status quo follows hard on the heels of the end of hostilities (e.g., the United States after World War II: see Trey 1972). In the absence of technological and economic changes that significantly increase the total demand for labor, the prior status quo will tend to reemerge after a period of time, as the adult sex ratio begins to return to normal.

Migration is often highly gender-specific, especially rural-to-urban and cross-national. Where males constitute a disproportionate number of migrants, the demand for female labor may increase in the sending community or society, permitting women access to heretofore male-monopolized roles. This will only occur if there is not a problem of general overpopulation in the sending community. Given overpopulation, the migrants represent a surplus, unemployable male population, which leaves behind enough men to meet demand. This, in fact, is probably the most typical case. That is, selective male migration probably occurs primarily because of the absence of demand for their labor in the sending community or society.

In summary, I am arguing that the gender division of labor sometimes changes in the direction of increasing women's access to resource-generating work roles because technological or demographic changes create a demand for labor that men cannot fill. Technological change may also enhance women's ability and willingness to supply their work in other-than-traditional roles, but, in the absence of demand, this is all but irrelevant.

If the overall demand for women's labor remains high over a long enough period of time, then their increased access to power resources should begin to affect both the division of household labor and their entry into more highly coveted labor force roles, in an equalitarian direction. As the gender division of labor changes, cognitive dissonance theory suggests that social definitions concerning the appropriate duties and attributes of each gender should begin to change as well, to conform to an increasing reality. Given that women take on new work roles well before men's labor in the domestic and familial context increases, social definitions concerning femininity change more quickly and extensively than those concerning masculinity. The United States has experienced precisely this form of attitude change in recent decades. Between the 1950s and the 1980s, public opinion became significantly more supportive of married women assuming labor force roles, including mothers of young children; of equal employment and educational opportunity for women; of women as political leaders and elected officials; and of women's reproductive rights. Much less opinion change concerning the roles and obligations of men seems to have occurred, however (see Harris 1987). I predict that, barring economic collapse, in most highly industrialized nations, including the United States, married women will remain firmly entrenched in the labor force, and over time their occupational deployment will become more similar to that of men. The power resources generated by this will result, in time, in change in men's work and in social definitions of masculinity, in a more equalitarian and androgynous direction (which is *not* to say that I am predicting full gender equality any time soon, but more about that later).

Intentional Change Efforts: The Emergence and Growth of Women's Movements

Relative to men, for several millennia women almost everywhere have been disadvantaged in their access to societal scarce and valued resources. Yet only occasionally and in some societies have they organized and attempted as collectivities to change the gender system of their societies. Recently, A. Gary Dworkin and I developed and partially tested a theory that attempts to explain the conditions that give rise to women's movements (Chafetz and Dworkin 1986, also 1987b, forthcoming).

We define women's movements as change-oriented, grass-roots movements consciously oriented to rectifying socially rooted disadvantages specific to females, which they experience on the basis of their gender. Women's movements are composed of at least one organization that is independent of control by governmental, political party, or other organizational entities, which in turn are controlled by men. We found that they date no further back in time than the mid-nineteenth century, and can be divided into a first (mid-nineteenth to mid-twentieth centuries) and a second wave (those that have arisen since about 1968). While nations around the world have experienced them (we documented 31 nations for the first wave, 16 for the second), they have varied extensively in size.

The theoretical question we raised was this: What accounts for the emergence and growth of women's movements in particular times and places? We found that women's movements arise when macro-structural change results in "role expansion" for women, that is, in the development of new, nontraditional opportunities for a sizable number of especially middle-class women, who constitute the pool from which the vast majority of activists is drawn. Industrialization, urbanization, and the growth of the middle class constituted the critical structural changes in the first wave. They functioned to expand certain public, but not including employment, roles of married middle-class women (e.g., roles in temperance, socialist, nationalist, and other social movements, and social welfare and philanthropic roles). They also served to increase the access of females to formal education, and to expand the employment opportunities of single women. In the second wave, in highly industrialized societies, vastly increased labor force participation by married women was the critical form of role expansion, and it resulted from extensive economic expansion in the 1950s and 1960s. Further increases in educational access again constituted an important form of female role expansion. The greater the magnitude of the structural changes, the larger the women's movement tended to become.

We postulated that role expansion for women often results in "status/role dilemmas" or strains. We defined this as contradictions between socially defined, ascribed gender norms and those associated with newly emerging social roles. Women may find themselves treated according to traditional norms inappropriate to their achieved status/role, or they may be expected to behave in inappropriate or contradictory ways.

Women who experience expanded roles are likely to come into increasing contact with men whose roles, competencies, and credentials are equal—even inferior—to their own, who nonetheless experience superior opportunities and rewards. Using reference group theory, we argued that this contact prompts at least some of these women to change their comparative reference group from other women— especially those who remain in traditional roles—to men. In turn, change in reference group will prompt feelings of relative deprivation.

Because of their expanded roles, and especially in urban settings, these women are likely to come into increased contact with one another. Their status/role dilemmas and sense of relative deprivation can thereby be shared and refined. As a result, at least some members of this growing pool of women will collectively develop a perception that their problems and disadvantages are not individually caused, but rather are shared on the basis of gender and produced by the social system. They are likely to develop a view that the reward and opportunity systems are unfair and illegitimate. They are, therefore, likely to develop an ideology and set of goals consciously oriented to changing the system that they now perceive as unfairly disadvantaging them. In short, much as Marx argued concerning the development of worker consciousness, we argue for gender consciousness. Moreover, their expanded roles are likely to give women increased access to the tangible and intangible resources that resource mobilization theorists argue are required to mount a social movement, including networks, contacts, organizational and public speaking skills, and money (Gale 1986; Zald and McCarthy 1979; Jenkins 1983). In this they may be aided by men who benefit from ongoing changes in women's roles and/or suffer by dint of the problems faced by women with whom they have familial or other intimate relationships.

Not all—or even a majority—of women who experience expanded roles become activists. However, a larger pool of such women results in a larger-sized movement. The emergence and growth of women's movements, therefore, reflect ongoing changes in the status and roles of women, which in turn result from macro-structural changes.

The Relationship of Unintentional to Intentional Change Efforts: Achieving Goals

Social movements have two basic ways that they can *directly* influence elite members to enact the changes they wish to see. They can make it costly for elites to fail to make change and/or they can make it rewarding for them to do so. The extent to which a movement is able to raise the cost or reward ante for elites depends in part on the size and resources of the movement itself, but also on factors that are idiosyncratic to each case. In what follows I will suggest some means that could or have been employed by women's movements to directly affect the behavior of elites on behalf of their goals.

One way to make the status quo costly is physical violence and property destruction. Black urban riots in the United States during the latter half of the 1960s helped to persuade many public-policy makers and employers to make at least some token changes on behalf of the Black community. However, with the exception of a minority of militant suffragists in Great Britain, women's movements have been overwhelmingly peaceful and nonviolent. Since suffrage, if women are well organized in mass numbers, they have potentially been able to use the ballot to punish political elite members who fail to support their goals. However, women's movements have been unable to command sufficient votes to employ this tactic in other than scattered elections, and then usually on only single-issue grounds (e.g., pay equity for state employees, ERA). Nor have women's movements (as distinct from labor unions chiefly composed of women) used the labor strategies of strike and boycott other than around very specific issues of a relatively minor nature (e.g., the dumping of infant formula in Third World nations by Nestlé) or unsuccessfully (e.g., the boycott of states that failed to ratify ERA). The one cost tactic that women's movement groups, at least in the contemporary United States, have used extensively and fairly successfully has been the legal suit against employers who discriminate. This type of action presupposes the existence of antidiscrimination legislation, which already symbolizes extensive elite action on behalf of women. In general, it appears that women's movements have either largely ignored or been unsuccessful in their attempts at tactics that render too costly elite opposition to major demands. This may be because even mass women's movements have lacked sufficient numbers and resources to employ cost tactics, other than violence, effectively, and violence seems to be especially incongruent with a female gender consciousness.

Nonetheless, since the first signs of the emergence of women's movements in the mid-nineteenth century, they appear to have achieved important intermediate goals. In the first wave, women in numerous societies gained expanded access to educational opportunities, some changes in legal and property rights for married women, the vote, and assorted other changes specific to particular cases. In the case of contemporary women's movements, women in a number of nations have achieved better control over their reproduction through access to contraception and abortion, legislation rendering illegal discrimination in the economy and educational institutions, and assorted other legal changes, policies, and programs that are specific to each society. If, by and large, such changes have not resulted from coercion, how have they been won?

In the last section I argued that women's movements emerge and grow to substantial size largely because of a set of factors associated with industrialization, economic expansion, and urbanization. Recall that earlier I argued that unintentional gender system change results primarily from technological development and economic expansion, which serve to open up new role opportunities to women. When we combine these two theoretical arguments, what we see is that the same basic macrostructural factors that spur unintended change contribute in a fundamental way to the emergence and growth of women's movements; *the emergence and especially the growth of such movements signifies or indicates that change in the gender system is already under way.*

From this vantage point, women's movements do not in fact produce change as much as *they manifest and expedite a process already in motion.* Women's movements that grow beyond an incipient level and attract substantial grass-roots support do so because ongoing changes are producing problems and needed resources for a large pool of women, the pool from which activists are drawn. But that pool is substantially larger than the number who become activists. Moreover, most members of this pool are related to men, many of whom are adversely affected by the problems confronting the women to whom they are attached. In this way, a growing segment of society comes to support at least some of the changes propounded by a women's movement.

The major importance of women's movements is to articulate specific proposed changes and a rhetoric or ideology that legitimates such changes, for the bulk of potential supporters who are not themselves activists, including at least some members of economic, educational, and especially political elites. Women's movements develop a set of social definitions that are counter to the traditional ones that serve to legitimate and perpetuate the status quo. A women's movement ideology falls largely on deaf ears until a sufficiently large pool of women (and the men to whom they are attached) encounter problems that can be made sense of by it. The development and dissemination of such an ideology and programs of specific change targets constitute major mechanisms that allow nonactivists to reformulate into social and political terms their definitions of the origins and solutions to personally experienced problems. In the most recent wave of women's movement activism, this came to be called "consciousness-raising." It is important to note that it occurs not only in self-conscious groups of activists but in varying degrees among significant segments of the mass public. It does so primarily through the dissemination of ideas by activists through the media of mass communication.

Often, especially large movements will be characterized by substantial ideological and programmatic diversity, ranging from calls for moderate, relatively minor rule changes to the radical overhaul of the entire system. Not only will the public rarely if ever subscribe to the full ideology and program developed by activists, it will tend to support the more moderate proposals. Moreover, the public will pick and choose among proposals, supporting those that appear most salient to their own personal problems. In this way, elite response, especially governmental response to public pressure, will also be piecemeal. It too will usually support most readily the least radical policies, programs, and laws (see Giele 1978), namely, those that the majority of the public deem most important for their own lives and those of family members.[1] The women's movement per se does not *directly* reward elites for their support. It expedites public support for change and, therefore, the public rewarding or punishment of elites who support, or fail to support, such change. Activists, even in mass movements, rarely reach sufficient numbers to accomplish this on their own.[2]

In some cases, governments respond to demands made by a women's movement in the absence of such a shift in public opinion. Indeed, they may even respond positively to demands made by a very small women's movement. For instance, four nations enfranchised women before World War I, and in none of these cases had a women's movement grown to mass proportions. Kennedy established a Presidential Commission on the Status of Women and Congress passed the 1963 Equal Pay Act and Title VII of the Civil Rights Act, all before the reemergence of a mass women's movement in this country. These kinds of governmental actions reflect political struggles idiosyncratic to specific times and places. A given political party may have supported (or opposed) female suffrage as part of a calculus of how many additional votes it would net versus its opposition. According to Rupp and Taylor

(1987), Kennedy's commission resulted from pressure by those opposed to ERA, including, especially, organized labor, who felt that such a commission could effectively bury the amendment, thereby maintaining protective legislation for women. Title VII of the Civil Rights Act resulted from a failed attempt by southern senators to defeat that act, which was designed to protect Blacks. This suggests that women's issues may become enmeshed in other political struggles, and whether women gain or not is less a question of their collective actions than of the political fortunes of contending (male) elite factions. It is possible that women's movements could manipulate political struggles in such a way as to gain some of their objectives in the process. However, the historical and cross-national record suggests that when women's movement issues become enmeshed in other political conflicts, women lose more often than they gain in the process (see Chafetz and Dworkin 1986, especially chap. 1).

In summary of this section, I have argued that when women's movements emerge and gather substantial grass-roots support, it is because a change process is already under way that is seriously affecting the roles and status of large numbers of women. Primarily through their development and dissemination of a counterideology and a program of specific targets of change, women's movements affect public opinion. In turn, it is the pressure of changed public opinion that is primarily responsible for new laws, programs, and policies developed by elites. In this way, women's movements expedite rather than directly cause change.

THE LIMITS TO CHANGE

Rarely do social movements achieve all of their specified goals or targets, not to mention their overall goal. In fact, movements on behalf of a disadvantaged group, such as women, Blacks, or workers, typically wax and wane over many decades. Periods of mass activism result in the attainment of some targets. This is followed by a period of substantial quiescence, during which committed activists continue to work, but few grass-roots followers are to be found and public visibility for the activists and the issues is low (e.g., Rupp and Taylor 1987). Indeed, a public reaction, including overt hostility and some reversal of earlier changes, may arise during this time. Subsequently, a new wave of grass-roots activism and public visibility reemerges, focusing attention on the unfinished agenda left over from the previous wave of movement activity.

To this point I have explored the conditions that expedite the emergence and growth of women's movements and the achievement of at least some of their specific goals or targets. In this section I will explore the conditions that limit change and to date have contributed to the failure of women's movements to achieve their overall goal of full gender equality. To do so I will call upon my work with A. Gary Dworkin concerning antifeminist movements (1987a, 1987b, forthcoming).

When we examined organized reactions to women's movements across nations and historically, Dworkin and I found that they comprised two different types of groups. First, there are vested interest groups, namely, those preexisting groups and organizations that represent dominant social institutions and that profit from the status quo. They are usually organized so as to perceive and react quickly to challenges to their interests. As a normal part of their functioning, they have ties with governmental actors whom they lobby in an effort to protect and enhance their interests (Gale 1986). Only if they fail to succeed in blocking the aims of a women's movement through pressure on governmental elites will the second type of antifeminist group emerge: the grass-roots, voluntary organization. Typically, antifeminist vested interest groups are of crucial importance in organizing and providing resources for such voluntary organizations.

We also found that, despite a rhetoric that focuses on value threat and conflict, the fundamental source of threat to antifeminists is to their class and/or status interests. Vested interest groups are threatened by one or both of two things: (1) ongoing change in women's roles and status (e.g., in some nations at the turn of the century, organizations of male clerical workers became ardent antifeminists in response to female incursion into their jobs); (2) specific demands made by a women's movement (e.g., in the first wave, women's movements in a variety of nations were integrally intertwined with temperance movements, and liquor interests became major actors in the development and funding of antisuffrage activism). For voluntary association members, one form of threat is to men's economic or class interests—in the same way as it is to vested interest groups. Men as individuals also confront threat to their patriarchal status. In addition to threats to their husbands', hence their own, economic interests, women antifeminists are typically threatened by newly emerging definitions of women's roles and status. We found that female antifeminists often remained encapsulated in traditional roles in an era of role expansion and change in normative definitions for other women. They experienced a decline in the social status of the traditional roles they continued to play.

We concluded that organized antifeminism arises dialectically as a response to women's movements that become large and/or successful. They arise because social change affects different segments of a society in different ways. Changes that enhance the rewards and opportunities of some women affect other women negatively. Insufficient human capital, insufficient opportunity, familial obligations, and religious or other normative restrictions function to ensure that a sizable number of women will not avail themselves of the new opportunities. At a minimum, their relative status declines. Virtually by definition, social change threatens—or at least appears to threaten—the vested interests of many of those groups that profit from the status quo.

The process of antifeminist movement development—especially that of voluntary associations—is expedited by the very rhetoric of the women's movement against which it battles. Ironically, the ideology of a women's movement, which raises the consciousness of others similarly affected by change and gains at least their partial support, focuses the attention of the potential opposition. By clarifying the issues of contention, a women's movement makes itself a specific target of opposition by others. In the absence of such a rhetoric, potential antifeminist individuals may have no better explanation or understanding of the source of their problems and frustrations than potential supporters of a women's movement.

Antifeminist movements may enjoy more political clout than their numbers and public support warrant. In this way, they may have an advantage over their opposition. One reason for this is the involvement of vested interest groups. Such groups typically have access to extensive resources. They themselves often comprise members of socioeconomic and political elites. Moreover, they have long-term, ongoing relationships of influence with politcal elites. A second reason is that antifeminists have one very clear goal: to resist (and/or reverse) change in the gender system. Consensus around this issue is relatively easily maintained (see Mottl 1980, p. 627). Especially large, change-oriented movements typically comprise a multitude of groups and organizations espousing different change targets, priorities, strategies, and ideologies. What may appear to an outsider as trivial differences in ideology, priorities, or strategies can take on immense importance to insiders, regardless of their consensus on the most general goal (in this case, gender equality). The result is the splintering of groups and the use of scarce resources, energy, and time on internecine battles. This not only diverts movement organizations from pursuing their primary goals, it may alienate many activists and sympathetic nonactivists from the larger cause. In fact, the very sense of a larger cause may be a casualty of this process.[3]

Countermovements arise in response to real or imminent intermediate goal achievement by the movements they oppose. They, therefore, arise later in time than their opposition. Antifeminist movements typically fail to prevent or retract the early round of changes sought by a women's movement—if the conditions discussed earlier are "ripe" for such changes. Nonetheless, they do arise in time to all but ensure that the full agenda of the women's movement will not be met. In this they are aided by the fact that, while much of the public is sympathetic to aspects of the women's movement, most do not subscribe to its full ideology and complete program. Many such members of the public will be placated by the initial changes made in response to their problems, after which they become apathetic to the further goals of the women's movement. It may be especially difficult to generate enthusiasm in a younger generation of women, who are actively taking advantage of the recently won changes (Schneider 1988). To the extent that a women's movement succeeds in eliminating the most blatant and obvious forms of female disadvantage and drives sexism "underground," younger women may fail to perceive the now more subtle forms of discrimination to which they are subject (see Safilios-Rothschild 1979).

In summary of this section, I am suggesting that activism on behalf of gender equality has a wavelike quality. Structural changes, which, in enhancing many women's opportunities, create strains and problems for them, produce increased activism and public support for further change. But social change also negatively affects both certain vested interests and other women who, for whatever reasons, do not avail themselves of the new opportunities. Over time, opposition from these people combines with increasing public apathy, which follows upon limited, albeit usually important legal, policy, and definitional changes that benefit women. Together, they reduce the impetus for, in fact, actively impede, further change, which must await a new wave of structurally induced change and mass activism. This process is summarized graphically in Figure 7.1. Each wave begins at a different point than its predecessor, with many of the earlier gains having been substantially consolidated and made part of "normal" social life.

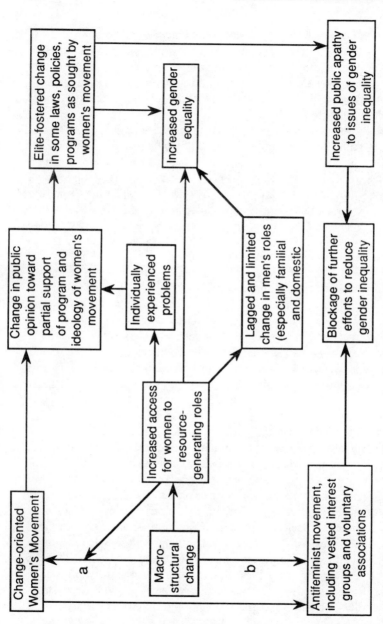

Figure 7.1 Major Components of the Gender Change Process Model

a. For a detailed depiction of this linkage, see charts in Chafetz and Dworkin (1986, 1987b, and forthcoming).
b. For a detailed depiction of this linkage, see charts in Chafetz and Dworkin (1987b and forthcoming)

CONCLUSIONS: TARGET AND PROCESS

I have argued that the chief target of change must be the gender division of labor, especially the demand for substantially greater access of women to elite positions. In the last section, I also argued that, to the extent that change and change efforts threaten vested interests, organized opposition to further change in the gender system is likely to emerge and eventually contribute to the end of a change phase. What can threaten most the powerful vested interest groups, which are overwhelmingly male in composition, more than the large-scale incursion of women into elite positions? That is, the most important target of change is precisely that which can be assumed to mobilize the most powerful actors in a society to resist such change.

Yet vested interest groups have public constituencies that they cannot afford to alienate, be they consumers, voters, workers, congregants, or some other group. It is possible that in successive "steps" women will gain sufficient power resources, primarily through reductions in the gender division of labor, to be in a position finally to use their resources as consumers, workers, voters, and so on to make their continued exclusion from elite positions too costly for male elites to sustain. Or they may use those resources to up the reward ante for male elites who are in a position to allow them entry.

I do not think that this will happen any time soon for women. The impetus of *mass* women's movement activism seems to have about played itself out for now, with a substantially incomplete agenda left. Barring economic calamity, the remainder of this century and the early years of the next should witness increasing societal accommodation to the fact that most women spend almost their entire adult life in the labor force in advanced industrial societies.[4] Issues such as child care, male contribution to household and family work, parental leave, and comparable worth require solutions just to resolve the strains already produced by the wholesale addition of women to the labor force. None of these seriously addresses the issue of the *deployment* of women within the labor force and especially elite roles. Perhaps when it comes, the next major wave will deal primarily with the unresolved issue of deployment. If it does, it may eventuate in full gender equality.

NOTES

1. Nonpolitical elites respond to public opinion just as elected officials may. Economic institutions may alter their hiring practices and advertisements; the media of mass communication may make changes in their programming; universities may institute new courses, programs, and admissions policies; foundations and community agencies may fund new types of projects; religions may change wording and admit women to ritual and organizational roles; police and courts may alter their policies toward rape and family violence victims; and so on.

2. In our research on women's movements, Dworkin and I (1986) found that, in the few cases where nations experienced an unambiguously mass movement, only about 3% of the public belonged to movement groups or organizations.

3. There is a positive aspect to intramovement diversity. To the extent that radicals propose strategies, goals, and/or ideologies that are completely unacceptable to the public, the proposals of moderate activists are likely to appear more reasonable and legitimate than they would in the absence of yet more extreme demands. This enhances the likelihood that some of the movement's goals will be met.

4. A more depressing scenario is also quite possible. As advanced industrial societies continue to lose traditionally male manufacturing jobs to both automation and inexpensive Third World labor, men may move into the female service occupations that currently provide jobs for most employed women. If these jobs fail to continue to expand at a rapid rate, it is possible that men will displace women from them, lowering the demand for women's labor outside the home, and thereby increasing gender inequality.

REFERENCES

Barron, R. D. and G. M. Norris. 1976. "Sexual Divisions and the Dual Labour Market." Pp. 47–69 in *Dependence and Exploitation in Work and Marriage*, edited by Diana Leonard Barker and Sheila Allen. London: Longman.

Bell, Colin and Howard Newby. 1976. "Husbands and Wives: The Dynamics of the Deferential Dialectic." Pp. 152–68 in *Dependence and Exploitation in Work and Marriage*, edited by Diana Leonard Baker and Sheila Allen. London: Longman.

Berch, Bettina. 1982. *The Endless Day: The Political Economy of Women and Work*. New York: Harcourt Brace Jovanovich.

Blumberg, Rae Lesser. 1978. *Stratification: Socioeconomic and Sexual Inequality*. Dubuque, IA: William C Brown.

———. 1984. "A General Theory of Gender Stratification." Pp. 23–101 in *Sociological Theory, 1984*, edited by Randall Collins. San Francisco: Jossey-Bass.

Cahill, Spencer. 1983. "Reexamining the Acquisition of Sex Roles: A Symbolic Interactionist Approach." *Sex Roles* 9(1):1–15.

Chafetz, Janet Saltzman. 1984. *Sex and Advantage: A Comparative, Macro-Structural Theory of Sex Stratification*. Totowa, NJ: Rowman and Allanheld.

———. 1988a. *Feminist Sociology: An Overview of Contemporary Theories*. Itasca, IL: F. E. Peacock.

————. 1988b. "The Gender Division of Labor and the Reproduction of Female Disadvantage: Toward an Integrated Theory." *Journal of Family Issues* 9(March):108–31.

Chafetz, Janet Saltzman and A. Gary Dworkin. 1986. *Female Revolt: Women's Movements in World and Historical Perspective.* Totowa, NJ: Rowman and Allanheld.

————. 1987a. "In the Face of Threat: Organized Antifeminism in Comparative Perspective." *Gender & Society* 1(March):33–60.

————. 1987b. "Action and Reaction: An Integrated, Comparative Perspective on Feminist and Antifeminist Movements." Paper presented at the annual meetings of the American Sociological Association, Chicago.

————. Forthcoming. "Action and Reaction: An Integrated, Comparative Perspective on Feminist and Antifeminist Movements" (revised and expanded from the oral paper). In *Cross-National Research in Sociology,* edited by Mel Kohn. Beverly Hills, CA: Sage.

Chodorow, Nancy. 1978. *The Reproduction of Mothering: Psychoanalysis and the Sociology of Gender.* Berkeley: University of California Press.

Constantinople, Anne. 1979. "Sex-Role Acquisition: In Search of the Elephant." *Sex Roles* 5(2):121–33.

Coser, Rose Laub. 1986. "Cognitive Structure and the Use of Social Space." *Sociological Forum* 1(Winter):1–26.

Cramer, James C. 1980. "Fertility and Female Employment: Problems of Causal Direction." *American Sociological Review* 45(April):167–90.

Curtis, Richard. 1986. "Household and Family in Theory on Inequality." *American Sociological Review* 51(April):168–83.

Ferguson, Kathy. 1980. *Self, Society, and Womankind.* Westport, CT: Greenwood.

Fishman, Pamela. 1982. "Interaction: The Work Women Do." Pp. 170–80 in *Women and Work: Problems and Perspectives,* edited by R. Kahn-Hut, A. K. Daniels, and R. Colvard. New York: Oxford University Press.

Fox, Mary Frank and Sharlene Hesse-Biber. 1984. *Women at Work.* Palo Alto, CA: Mayfield.

Friedl, Ernestine. 1975. *Women and Men: An Anthropologist's View.* New York: Holt, Rinehart & Winston.

Gale, Richard. 1986. "Social Movements and the State: The Environmental Movement, Countermovement, and Government Agencies." *Sociological Perspectives* 29:202–40.

Giele, Janet Zollinger. 1978. *Women and the Future: Changing Sex Roles in Modern America.* New York: Free Press.

Goffman, Erving. 1977. "The Arrangement Between the Sexes." *Theory and Society* 4(3):301–31.

Harris, Louis. 1987. *Inside America.* New York: Vintage.

Hartmann, Heidi. 1984. "The Unhappy Marriage of Marxism and Feminism: Towards a More Progressive Union." Pp. 172–89 in *Feminist Frameworks: Alternative Theoretical Accounts of the Relations Between Women and Men,* edited by Alison Jaggar and Paula Rothenberg. New York: McGraw-Hill.

Hertz, Rosanna. 1986. *More Equal than Others: Women and Men in Dual Career Marriages.* Berkeley: University of California Press.

Huber, Joan and Glenna Spitze. 1983. *Sex Stratification: Children, Housework, and Jobs.* New York: Academic Press.

Jenkins, Craig J. 1983. "Resource Mobilization Theory and the Study of Social Movements." *Annual Review of Sociology* 9:527–53.

Kanter, Rosabeth Moss. 1977. *Men and Women of the Corporation*. New York: Basic Books.

Kessler, Suzanne and Wendy McKenna. 1978. *Gender: An Ethnomethodological Approach*. New York: John Wiley.

Lever, Janet. 1976. "Sex Differences in the Games Children Play." *Social Problems* 23–24(April):478–87.

Lipman-Blumen, Jean. 1976. "Toward a Homosocial Theory of Sex Roles: An Explanation of Sex Segregation of Social Institutions." *Signs* 1(Spring):15–31.

Martin, M. Kay and Barbara Voorhies. 1975. *Female of the Species*. New York: Columbia University Press.

Mottl, Tahi L. 1980. "The Analysis of Countermovements." *Social Problems* 27:620–35.

Nielsen, Joyce. 1978. *Sex in Society: Perspectives on Stratification*. Belmont, CA: Wadsworth.

O'Kelley, Charlotte G. 1980. *Women and Men in Society*. New York: Van Nostrand.

Oppenheimer, Valerie K. 1970. *The Female Labor Force in the United States*. Berkeley: University of California Press.

Ortner, Sherry B. 1974. "Is Female to Male as Nature Is to Culture?" In *Woman, Culture and Society*, edited by Michelle Z. Rosaldo and Louise Lamphere. Stanford, CA: Stanford University Press.

Parker, Seymour and Hilda Parker. 1979. "The Myth of Male Superiority: Rise and Demise." *American Anthropologist* 81(2):289–309.

Rupp, Leila J. and Verta Taylor. 1987. *Survival in the Doldrums: The American Women's Rights Movement, 1945 to the 1960s*. New York: Oxford University Press.

Sacks, Karen. 1974. "Engels Revisited: Women, the Organization of Production and Private Property." Pp. 207–22 in *Woman, Culture, and Society*, edited by Michelle Zimbalist Rosaldo and Louise Lamphere. Stanford, CA: Stanford University Press.

Safilios-Rothschild, Constantina. 1979. "Women as Change Agents: Toward a Conflict Theoretical Model of Sex Role Change." Pp. 287–301 in *Sex Roles and Social Policy*, edited by Jean Lipman-Blumen and Jessie Bernard. Beverly Hills, CA: Sage.

Sanday, Peggy. 1974. "Female Status in the Public Domain." Pp. 189–206 in *Women, Culture, and Society*, edited by Michelle Zimbalist Rosaldo and Louise Lamphere. Stanford, CA: Stanford University Press.

———. 1981. *Female Power and Male Dominance: On the Origins of Sexual Inequality*. Cambridge: Cambridge University Press.

Schneider, Beth. 1988. "Political Generations and the Contemporary Women's Movement." *Sociological Inquiry* 58(1):4–21.

Schur, Edwin. 1984. *Labeling Women Deviant: Gender, Stigma, and Social Control*. New York: Random House.

Stewart, Abigail J., M. Brinton Lykes, and Marianne LaFrance. 1982. "Educated Women's Career Patterns: Separating Social and Developmental Changes." *Journal of Social Issues* 38:97–117.

Trey, J. E. 1972. "Women in the War Economy—World War II." *Review of Radical Political Economics* 4(July):1–17.

Vogel, Lise. 1983. *Marxism and the Oppression of Women: Toward a Unitary Theory*. New Brunswick, NJ: Rutgers University Press.

West, Candace and Don Zimmerman. 1987. "Doing Gender." *Gender & Society* 1:125–51.

Zald, Mayer and John McCarthy. 1979. *The Dynamics of Social Movements*. Cambridge, MA: Winthrop.

Chapter 8

TOWARD A FEMINIST THEORY OF DEVELOPMENT

RAE LESSER BLUMBERG
University of California, San Diego

DEVELOPMENT MAY BE SEEN as a Janus-faced concept. One face involves the contemporary world capitalist system and the political-economic processes that affect both the positioning of a state within it and the well-being of different classes of its citizens. Its other face is a historic vision of development, from our foraging forebears to the creation and continuing change of today's world economy. Extant nonfeminist theories concerning both faces of development range from the neoclassical to the radical. But they share a common trait: near "gender blindness" that pays only peripheral attention to half the human race.

In this chapter, I focus on the contemporary face of development. Broadly speaking, explanations of development are provided by two dominant competing paradigms—a neoclassical "modernization" approach and a more radical alternative (embracing Marxist-dependency-world system variants). In two aspects, however, there is little competition: (1) attention to women is rare in either approach, and (2) both tend to view the household as a "black box" and a basic unit of analysis. According to this conceptualization of the household, it doesn't really matter who brings in the information, who does the work, and who gets the rewards. Somehow, whether by perfect dictatorship or perfect democracy, information, labor, and returns are redistributed internally. Indeed, the neoclassical approach describes the household by a single production function (Becker 1981).

AUTHOR'S NOTE: I gratefully acknowledge the helpful comments of Bennett M. Berger, Debbie Bernstein, Mary Freifeld, and Joseph R. Gusfield. Gershon Shafir's cogent critique of the kibbutz material proved especially valuable. I also wish to thank Huma Ahmed Ghosh for her valuable bibliographic and research assistance.

161

Here, I suggest that development paradigms that give short shrift to gender and ignore what I term the *internal economy of the household* have less power to explain, and, at the policy level, less leverage to ameliorate, major problems of underdevelopment. Actually, this chapter is only a way station toward a feminist theory of development—its hypotheses are still evolving and do not yet constitute a comprehensive, alternate vision of "development with a feminist face."[1]

This chapter first presents hypotheses from my general theory of gender stratification. Second, it posits an "internal economy of the household" that ranges, in different ethnic groups, classes, and countries, from the single production function model of the mainstream paradigms to households marked by "separate purses"—essentially, "his, hers and (sometimes) theirs." Third, it presents a series of hypotheses from my evolving "feminist theory of development." Supporting empirical evidence is provided for the main propositions. The chapter then applies the resulting theoretical model to two wildly disparate phenomena: the African food crisis, considered by many to be caused, in part, by a failure of deliberate development planning, and the Israeli kibbutz, generally considered a much more successful attempt at planned-from-scratch development.

In both instances, I suggest, despite their extreme dissimilarity, *many of the same explanatory propositions apply.* As both show, the programs and structures created by deliberate development planning can affect gender stratification, even when gender is not explicitly taken into account in such planning. In addition, I propose, changes in the level of gender stratification produce second- and third-order consequences that affect the direction and even success of the planned development itself. Furthermore, there is considerable evidence that indicates that the relationship between gender stratification and the success of planned development is inverse (see, e.g., Blumberg 1988a, forthcoming-a; Carloni 1987). With respect to this chapter's case studies, consequences range from exacerbation of the African food crisis to, in the kibbutz, a gender division of labor so stereotyped and inflexible that, over and above its negative impact on many women denied occupational choice, it apparently lowered efficient adjustment to male mobilization in the 1973 war and seems a major reason why most kibbutzim use many short-term international volunteers and/or hire ideologically disapproved outside wage labor.

HYPOTHESES FROM A GENERAL
THEORY OF GENDER STRATIFICATION

In my general theory of gender stratification (Blumberg 1984, forthcoming-c), the most important of the many factors posited as influencing women's overall equality is economic: Specifically, it is proposed that the key variable is relative male/female *control* of economic resources—at a variety of "nested" micro and macro levels from the household to the state. Here is a summary of the relevant aspects of the theory:

(1) Relative male/female economic power is the most important of the major independent "power variables"[2] affecting overall gender stratification:

(a) Women's relative economic power is conceptualized in terms of degree of *control* of key economic resources—income, property, and other means of production. In other words, mere work in economic activities or even ownership of economic resources does not translate into economic power if the person derives no control of economic resources thereby.

(b) Further, the degree of control over *surplus* allocation is held to be more important for relative male/female economic power than the degree of control over resources needed for bare subsistence; that is, in most societies, withholding food from hungry children is rarely an option at the micro level. For both genders, the more surplus controlled, the greater the leverage.

(2) Relative male/female economic power varies—and not always in the same direction—at various "nested" levels ranging from micro to macro, that is, from the couple to the household, the community, the class, the ethnic group, and the state.

(3) The macro levels influence the micro levels more than vice versa, once they emerge historically. For example, Khomeini's decrees drastically restricting the occupational options, dress, and legal situation of Iranian women have apparently diminished their position within the household as well as the larger society. Conversely, in other countries (with a few exceptions, such as Pakistan's 1988 adoption of Islamic law) the twentieth-century trend has been to pass new laws granting women more rights and more control over their personal lives.

(4) Further, the more macro levels of the "pyramid of political economy" in stratified societies are highly male dominated, although the

degree varies—compare, for example, macro-level male dominance in Iran versus Iceland. (Still, no situation in any society today compares with Iroquois women's macro-level economic predominance—see note 2—nor is there a society where women control even half the economy.)

(5) Therefore, the extent to which the more macro levels are male-dominated *and* repressive of females affects how much actual leverage a woman can wield for any given amount of economic resources she controls at the micro level:

(a) In other words, the macro levels act somewhat analogously to a "discount rate" on the exercise of women's relative economic power at the micro levels.

(b) Such "discount rates"—or constraints—are most often *negative;* that is, greater relative male control of the macro levels means that economic, political, legal, religious, and ideological factors—including their internalization in gender socialization patterns—act to *nibble away at* the amount of economic power a woman actually can realize from any given amount of micro-level economic resources.[3]

(c) As a result, we can conceive of a woman's "net economic power" as that which actually can be wielded after the various "discount factors"—at both macro and micro levels, and both negative and positive—have been taken into account. (For example, a woman who feels ideologically bound to hand over her earnings to her husband may have much less "net economic power" than a beautiful, nonearning young wife.)

(6) Women's relative economic power rises and falls in different trajectories with different consequences. But it generally falls more rapidly that it rises:

(a) On the up side, when a woman's relative economic leverage increases (net of the various macro- and micro-level "discount factors" mentioned above), her self-confidence/sense of self also increase (Roldan 1982, 1988; Kusterer et al. 1981; Crandon and Shepard 1985; Blumberg 1985, forthcoming-b). Her say in household decision making (domestic, economic, and fertility issues) also tends to grow, albeit slowly, and not always smoothly or uniformly. During such transitions, violence may result if men use their greater physical force to keep women from consolidating a rising economic position (see, e.g., Roldan 1982, 1988).

(b) On the downside, however, a decline in her base of independently controlled economic resources often portends a quite rapid decrease in her relative power position and say-so in household decisions, including expenditures (Blumberg 1985, 1988a, forthcoming-a forthcoming-b, forthcoming-c).

(7) The greater women's relative economic power, the greater their control over their own lives in a variety of dimensions with broader economic implications:

(a) The greater a woman's relative economic power, the greater the likelihood that her *fertility* pattern will reflect her own perceived utilities and preferences—rather than those of her mate, family, state, and so on.

(b) The greater her relative economic power, the greater her control over a variety of other "life options" as well—including marriage, divorce, sexuality, household authority, and various types of household decisions.[4]

In sum, there is a whole chain of consequences that emerges from a change in the micro-level gender balance of economic power between male and female. It is clear that some of these consequences extend far beyond the micro level and could have a profound impact on economic development. To take just one example, there is empirical support for Hypothesis 7a, above, that with more economic power/(i.e., economic resources under their own control) women will have more say in realizing their own fertility preferences. Generally, but not invariably, women use their greater economic leverage to achieve *lower* fertility.[5] But micro-level fertility aggregates, of course, to a country's fertility rate. And recent empirical evidence based on large samples of Third World countries (e.g., Hess's forthcoming study involving 49 nations over two time periods) strongly supports the hypothesis that reducing fertility contributes to economic growth in Third World nations. In other words, the economic empowerment of women at the micro level—that is, their increased share of the "internal economy of the household"—can generally be expected to help their country's economic growth inderectly by reducing its fertility levels.

Given space constraints, only two examples are presented:

(1) *Mexico City:* Roldan (1982, 1988) studied 140 poor Mexican women who did garment/other industry piecework in their own homes. In 33 of the 53 households selected for intensive study, women and men pooled into a common pot for basic household subsistence expenses. Despite some "borrowing" from the pot by those husbands who drank heavily, women in the "pooling households" managed the spending of the basic subsistence fund. Moreover, the data showed an unmistakable link between the percentage of the total household pool

contributed by the wife and her leverage in fertility decisions. Specifically, in the 11 "pooling" households where women contributed over 40% of the pot, the decisions to use contraceptives or to have more children were the wife's alone in fully 50%. In another 40%, the decision was joint, and in only 10% was it made by the husband alone. In contrast, in the 19 "pooling" households where women contributed less than 40% of the total, wives had less say. Use of contraceptives was the wife's decision in only 40%, a joint decision in 53%, and the husband's in the remainder. With respect to having more children, it was the wife's decision in only 20% of the cases; in another 68% the decision was joint, and the husband's in the rest.

(2) *Guatemala:* Here the evidence is even more dramatic: It shows that fertility has dropped drastically among women who earn—and control—enough money to support their families (Blumberg 1985, forthcoming-b). In 1985, I followed up a 1980 study by Kusterer et al. (1981) of the impact of an agribusiness enterprise on the lives of three villages of poor, largely Indian, contract growers and the mainly Ladina women who worked in its processing plant. The villagers grew broccoli, cauliflower, and snow peas for the wholly owned subsidiary of a U.S.-based multinational corporation, and the women processing plant workers froze and packed the vegetables for export to the United States. The company paid these women the minimum wage, and during the eight- to nine-month "high season," shifts of 12–16 hours a day, six days a week, were not uncommon. The result was a wage level as high as that of an urban, male blue-collar worker—enough to transform their lives. The women kept control of their earnings, and by 1985, the fertility impact was unmistakable. Among 15 "1980 veterans" in the 1985 sample (median age = 32.5 years), only 13 babies had been born between 1980 and 1985. They averaged *only 2.2 children each* and have taken control of their fertility: 7 say they won't have any more children (at median age = 37, mean = 2.3 children). In contrast, in 1985, 20 women from the only contract grower village with a substantial Ladina population (Patzicia) averaged *5.2 children* at median age 33.5. Even though about half of these women helped their husbands in the fields, the company's check was made out solely to the husband. And when asked about further fertility, the Patzicia wife's frequent response: "Well, I don't want any more but my husband does so I'll have to continue."

These examples do more than support the link between women's relative economic power and their say in fertility decisions. They also illustrate that even in households where the husband's power is such that he dominates household decisions, husbands and wives may have differing and even opposed interests and utilities. All these are glossed over in the household-as-basic-unit-of-analysis model that continues to dominate both neoclassical and radical paradigms of development. So the next task of this chapter is to offer a disaggregated view of the household.

THE INTERNAL ECONOMY OF THE HOUSEHOLD AND IMPLICATIONS FOR THIRD WORLD DEVELOPMENT

It is not just among the Third World poor that we can find an "internal economy of the household." However, this chapter limits its focus to the households of poor Third World women. The main point of this section is the contention that, despite considerable regional/cultural variation, most Third World households are not monolithic entities in which all members subordinate their individual advantage and pool their resources to assure a "household survival strategy" masterminded by the household head. Rather, Third World households tend to have their own "internal economy," revolving principally around gender and age.

In this "internal economy of the household," the extent to which *anything* is shared varies considerably. Here are a few of the dimensions that vary:

—With respect to *labor,* time-budget studies invariably find that women work longer total hours (due to the "double day" of productive and reproductive tasks) although the amount varies greatly (see, e.g., Carr and Sandhu 1988).

—With respect to *agricultural information,* several studies have shown that one cannot assume that agricultural extension and technical advice given to the husband are accurately communicated to the wife when she is actually responsible for the farming tasks involved. Studies finding ineffective communication include Fortmann (1982) in Tanzania, Koons (1988) in Cameroon, and Blanc-Szanton, Viveros-Long, and Suphanchainat in Thailand (in Carloni 1987). In the latter case, men were trained by a development project to carry out crop trials; but the men were not the full-time farmers—their wives were. Because the wives received no training:

Crops were planted incorrectly and did not grow, the power tillers provided by the project could not be used, and a nitrogen-fixing crop intended to fertilize rice did not get planted. *Even when the husband was present, advice on crop production was incorrectly transmitted from husband to wife* (Carloni 1987, p.16, emphasis added).

—Even *calories* have been found to be unequally distributed by gender and age within households (i.e., not in proportion to individual size and energy requirements). Senauer (1988) analyzed 1983–84 longitudinal household survey data for a random sample of about 800 poor rural households in three Philippine provinces. Not only were calories distributed unequally by age and sex, but how well women and children fared depended more on mother's estimated wage rate than on father's income (the relation of male/female income control and child nutrition is treated below).

—Furthermore, there are regional/cultural, as well as class, differences in how much control families have over the decisions and income of even *unmarried daughters*—normally thought of as the most firmly subordinated age-gender group within households. Wolfe (1988), on the one hand, has shown how unmarried daughters in Muslim Java ultimately make their own decisions about whether they will get factory jobs—and their own decisions about how much (if any) of their earnings they will turn over to their families. On the other hand, studies in Hong Kong and Taiwan (e.g., Salaff 1981; Arrigo 1980; Kung 1983; Greenhalgh 1985) show much greater patriarchal family control of "factory daughters."

—Most striking, the "internal economy of the household" is manifested in the varying—but surprisingly high—extent to which women have obligations as *providers of food and/or income*. In the Third World, the expectations that women have provider responsibilities are highest in most of sub-Saharan Africa and lowest in rain-fed agrarian societies where women are relatively unimportant in cultivation, and the local interpretation of a patriarchal religion (e.g., Hinduism in Northern India, Islam in Saudi Arabia) stresses men's roles as primary breadwinners.

—Most important for the theories presented in this chapter, however, there are few places in the world where women have *no* access to *income generation*.[6] And there seem to be even fewer places where wives who generate income turn it *all* over to the household head for allocation. Even in the archetypal model of the unitary household, the U.S. midwest farm family, wives earned and controlled their own "butter and egg money." Moreover, while the degree of pooling varies worldwide, all the evidence indicates that "separate purses" for husbands and wives are most predominant in Africa (reasons for this are discussed below; see also Blumberg 1988a, forthcoming-a; Fapohunda 1978; Guyer 1980, 1988; Staudt 1987).

In sum, there are ample data on the "internal economy of the household," whose importance further emerges in the next section, where hypotheses for a still-incomplete "feminist theory of development" are presented and illustrated.

HYPOTHESES FOR A "FEMINIST THEORY OF DEVELOPMENT" AND SOME SUPPORTING DATA

Chafetz (1988) argues that "the acid test of whether a theory is 'feminist' rests with whether it *can be used* (regardless of by whom) to challenge, counteract, or change a status quo which disadvantages or devalues women." Her three other conditions for "feminist theory" also are found in the introduction to this volume:

First, gender comprises a central focus or subject matter of the theory. Feminist theory seeks ultimately to understand the gendered nature of virtually all social relations, institutions, processes. Second, gender relations are viewed as a problem. By this I mean that feminist theory seeks to understand how gender is related to social inequities, strains, and contradictions. Finally, gender relations are *not* viewed as either natural or immutable. Rather, the gender-related status quo is viewed as the product of sociocultural and historical forces which have been created, and are constantly re-created by humans, and therefore can potentially be changed by human agency. (Chafetz 1988, p. 5)

The following hypotheses meet Chafetz's criteria and *are* aimed at changing a status quo that disadvantages women. Ever since Boserup wrote her path-breaking book *Woman's Role in Economic Development* (1970), with the then-novel thesis that development does not necessarily improve women's lot, feminist scholars, activists, and practitioners of development have been attempting to document the disadvantages and influence policy so as to increase its gender sensitivity. At first the studies tended to be aimed at empirically supporting Boserup's contention that, quite frequently, development increased women's workload while undercutting their economic resource base, and that this effect was most frequent in precisely those areas where women had traditionally been most economically active *and* economically independent (e.g., sub-Saharan Africa, Southeast Asia, the Caribbean). But little substantive change occurred, despite the fact that all the major development "donor agencies" soon adopted policies proclaiming their commitment to what soon became known (least controversially) as "women in development" and the U.S. Agency for International Development in 1973 actually even was put under congressional mandate to do so.[7]

The field of women in development (WID) emerged in the 1970s, at a time when there was international concern with *equity issues*, and it was felt that true development could not occur unless it benefited the "poorest of the poor" and the "most vulnerable." Women were viewed as victims, a special interest group, despite the attempts of WID researchers to document their strong roles in economic production in most of the Third World. When the development policy pendulum swung from equity to economic "efficiency" in the early 1980s, the case for paying attention to women and for disaggregating all development data by gender had to be made anew on *economic* grounds: "Look, our data show that women are playing key roles in Third World development and if they are bypassed or undercut, not only the women but also development itself will suffer." The hypotheses and supporting data to follow are feminist in Chafetz's sense, and are part of my continuing efforts to show that gender stratification and the "internal economy of the household" (especially the male/female resource balance and changes therein) have consequences that do affect development far beyond the micro level—in the case of Africa, all the way to the extent of food availability in the region.

It has already been noted that, in much of the Third World, women have substantial responsibilities as family provisioners, although regional and cultural variations are strong. Let us begin the hypotheses with two propositions that better specify the *class location* of women with provider responsibilities:

H_1: *The farther down* within the class structure and particular economic sectors (especially the most poorly measured ones, low resource farming and the informal sector),[8] *the higher the proportion of women who are economically active.*

H_2: *The farther down* within the class structure and particular economic sectors, *the higher the proportion of their family's subsistence women's economic activities provide* (see, e.g., Deere 1977 on Peru;

Matlon 1979, Norman et al. 1982, Blumberg 1988d on Nigeria; Mencher 1988 on India; and Roldan 1988 on Mexico).

This proposition is, of course, patently true in the case of *female-headed households*, a large and growing category throughout the Third World, which tends to be concentrated at precisely the economic levels and sectors specified in H_1 (see, e.g., Buvinic, Youssef, and Von Elm 1978; Sivard 1985, p. 11, who estimates that "women are the sole breadwinners in one-fourth to one-third of the families in the world").

The next two hypotheses propose that men, and *women who have provider responsibilities*—even as "provisioners of last resort"—spend income under their control in different manners:

H_3: *Women tend to contribute a higher proportion of their income to family subsistence, holding back less for personal consumption.* Here is some evidence (much documentation for these assertions is found in Blumberg 1988a, forthcoming-a):

(1) *South India:* Mencher studied samples of desperately poor agricultural laborers in 10 villages in Tamil Nadu and 10 more in Kerala. In each state, samples were random in 6 o´ the 10 villages, and about 48 households were sampled in each village. In India, there is such a loss of status for a woman to do field work for pay that only the poorest do it. But they are crucial for their family's survival. Mencher's data reveal the following aggregate picture: *Earnings*—wives earned a median of 55% as much as their mates (mean = 58%). *Proportion of earnings contributed to family subsistence*—wives contributed a median of 94% of their earnings (mean = 93%), versus a median of only 72% of earnings contributed by their husbands (mean = 71%). Thus because wives held back so little for themselves, their contributions to family subsistence amounted to a median of fully 84% (mean = 92%) as much as their husbands, even though they earned little more than half as much (calculated from Mencher 1988, Table 2).

(2) *Mexico City:* In Roldan's intensive study (1982, 1988) of 53 households of women who did garment/other industry piecework in their own homes, she found men and women pooling income for household subsistence expenses in 33 households. Wives claimed to put in 100% of earnings, while husbands put in 75% or less (given that nearly half the men withheld income information from their wives, in what wives resentfully viewed as a control technique to keep them dependent, men may have held back an even higher percentage). Therefore, even though these women earned woefully little, in 11 of these 33 households, their contributions amounted to 40% or more of the total

common fund. Roldan found, that by earning their own money, the women in all 53 households studied in depth were freer to spend for their *own* priorities. And these were clear: "Of course [working for pay] is important because if you earn your own money you yourself distribute it and you do not have to beg for it. You buy food, or a dress for your daughter, the socks for your son"(1982, p. 30).

(3) *Cameroon:* Guyer (1988) studied two Beti farming villages where women grew most of their family's staple crops; they earned some income primarily from petty trade. Meanwhile, their husbands grew cocoa as a cash crop. As in much of Africa, men and women not only had separate income streams but also had separate expenditure responsibilities (this is discussed further below). Although women farmers earned only about one-third as much cash as their spouses, "of total cash expenses for food and routine household supplies, women contribute two-thirds and men one-third" (Guyer 1988, p. 51; this, it should be stressed, was in addition to women *growing* their family's main food crops).

The last study emphasizes women's greater devotion of both subsistence production and cash income to providing food for their families. This leads to H_4:

H_4: *It is the* mother's, *rather than the father's, income or food production, that is more closely related to children's nutrition.* True, this is not *always* the case, even for women with provider obligations, but once again, evidence presented for Asia, Latin America, and Africa indicates that this effect is widespread.

(1) *South India:* In another study in Kerala, Kumar (1978) found that mothers' gardens or income means better-nourished children. From an initial stratified random sample of 120 households in three rural villages, she selected a sub-sample of 48 desperately poor families with children aged 3–36 months; these she studied for an entire crop cycle. Her regressions are complex but show that the single largest contributor to the child's nutrition was the presence of a home garden—tended and distributed from by the mother. The data also show that there was no positive increase in child nutrition as *paternal* income rose. But increasing *maternal* income *did* benefit the children's nutrition. To reiterate, the regressions show that it was resources under the *mother's* control—her home garden and, if she worked for wages, her earnings—that proved most important in accounting for the level of child nutrition.

(2) *Belize:* Stavrakis and Marshall (1978) studied how the introduction of commercial sugarcane affected women's economic roles and

family nutrition in a Belize village. Sugarcane generated quite a bit of income, but it was men who controlled it and benefited from it ("money flowed out of the system as fast as it came in, spent on drink, trucks, travel and purchased female companionship. By and large it did not benefit the women at home tending the children and animals"— Stavrakis and Marshall 1978, p. 158). Meanwhile, production of corn and other foods declined. Women had depended on corn for food, exchange with kin (a women's exchange network redistributed corn for past favors and provided food to women whose husbands had had a bad crop year), and, most important, food for their pigs. Pigs constituted the women's main independent source of income and they had fed them the 40% of the corn that was spoiled or blighted. So, with less corn meaning less pig production, women's income fell while men's income rose. But, according to the authors' nutrition survey (involving a purposive sample of 59 people in eight households who were surveyed in both 1973 and 1974), men's higher income did *not* increase the generally poor extant level of child nutrition. Ironically, while consumption of healthy foods such as fruits, meats, and fish declined, "consumption of soft drinks and frozen koolaid [*sic*] increased by 255%" (p. 161).

(3) *Northern Ghana:* Tripp (1981) studied the factors associated with good nutrition among a nonrandom sample of 187 children in a Nankane-speaking farm village. Due to uncertain rainfall and declining soil fertility, cultivation is precarious and the area is marked by both a preharvest "hungry season" and periodic food shortages. Tripp found that, given the poor crop conditions, although everyone farms, farming variables were not associated with better nutrition. Rather, it was *trading* income that proved to be linked to children's nutritional well-being. Specifically:

> Of all the variables tested, the trading activity of the *mother* is the one most significantly associated ($p < 0.001$) with the nutritional status of the child. In no case does a woman's trading generate profits that are equivalent to those of the male long-distance traders, but the *relatively small amount of money that a female trader earns is translated more directly to the nutrition of her children. The woman has complete control over her earnings,* and although her trading does not provide her with a lot of money, it does furnish a small steady income which she can use to buy food to augment that provided by the farming activities of herself and her husband. (Tripp 1981, pp. 19–20, emphasis added)

To reiterate, the foregoing section has attempted to show that wherever women have (1) any provider responsibilities whatsoever, and (2) any income under their control, then family well-being—especially chil-dren's nutrition—may be more closely linked to an increase or decrease in *mother's* (versus father's) income.[9] Combining hypotheses from the gender stratification theory and H_1-H_4 above, in fact, we can assert that a decrease in a woman's income will tend to rapidly reduce her household power and input in decisions about everything from major economic decisions to what foods to buy in the store, and from how many children to have to which children should be sent to school for how long. Thus her having less money means that, even if the husband's income rises, the composition of household spending is likely to tilt away from her prefer-ences for children's nutrition and well-being. Accordingly, where women have provider responsibilities, we can hypothesize as follows:

H_5: *Women will tend to allocate their labor (1) toward activities that put income and/or food under their direct control; and (2) to the extent culturally feasible, away from activities that don't*— even if the latter are more profitable.

We shall illustrate the hypothesis with examples from Africa, in order to lay the groundwork for the discussion, below, of the African food crisis. All involve planned development projects that introduced an inter-vention that increased women's work load while giving the returns to their husbands. In terms of the prevailing development view of the household as a monolithic pooling unit, this should have created no problems whatsoever. The facts show otherwise.

How Development Suffers When Women's Returns to Labor Are Ignored

Here, the focus will be on the consequences *beyond the household.*
(A) *The Cameroon SEMRY I Irrigated Rice Project.* Jones's sophisti-cated econometric analysis (1983) provides the best-documented case of a development project suffering because women were not given sufficient compensation for their labor. Specifically, she demonstrated that women's own return to labor affects how much rice they grow. Her data stem from a random sample of 102 Massa women from three villages and demostrate three key findings:

(1) *The project's long-term prospects are in doubt* because it has not *been able to get farmers to grow enough rice* to provide revenues for both operating costs and amortization. Although SEMRY I encompasses about 5,400 hectares of pump-irrigated rice fields, and both yields and

prices have been good, "every year many fields go uncultivated for lack of farmer interest . . . . In the 1981 rainy season . . . only 3,228 hectares were cultivated, despite [a 45%] increase in the producer price in 1980" (Jones 1983, p. 30). To understand why SEMRY can't find takers for its idle fields, we must see who works versus who benefits.

(2) *Women with more incentive raise more rice.* Cultivating rice on irrigated SEMRY fields is a *joint conjugal* activity but the *husband gets all the income.* He then compensates his wife as he sees fit.

> In return for [her] sweat: a woman receives about 7,700 CFA [French African francs] and about 9,200 CFA worth of paddy from her husband after the harvest, or about 16,900 CFA in total. This is less than a quarter of the net returns from rice production—about 70,000 CFA. Valued at the market wage rates . . . a woman's labor contribution is worth about 31,200 CFA, so her husband makes a profit of about 14,300 CFA from her labor. (Jones 1983, p. 51)

Husbands are very aware that their wives' continued participation depends on their own generosity (i.e., their "wages"). This is because, although wives must raise *some* rice or risk a beating, wives' rice labor—especially during transplanting—competes directly with women's sorghum production and other income-generating activities. In fact, one of Jones's regressions shows that women must make literally a one-to-one trade-off between the number of days they work on rice versus sorghum planting and weeding during the peak season for rice transplanting (days rice = $28.57 - 1.04$ days sorghum; $R_2 = .77$; F = 230.93). And women have reason to prefer to work on sorghum, which is cultivated on an *individual* basis by both women and men in 100% of project households: Although a married woman uses her sorghum primarily for feeding her family, it is her *own* sorghum. Consequently, another of Jones's regressions establishes a very strong "relationship between the amount of compensation women receive from their husbands and the number of days they worked on their husbands' rice fields" (Jones 1981, p. 52; $R_2 = .70$). Yet rice gives the better return.

So, it is not surprising that the few independent women (mostly widows) who grew rice on their *own* account spent 24.7 days transplanting it. In contrast, married women spent only 16.4 days transplanting their husbands' rice, a significant difference. As a result, independent women's households transplanted .47 hectare per adult worker versus only .31 hectare transplanted by married women.

(3) Empirically, *women with more incentives cultivate twice as much*

rice land. There was no difference in *yields* between independent and married women: Both obtained about 4,300 kilos per hectare. The difference was in *quantity of land* cultivated. Specifically, the independent women and one subgroup of married women—those who received a significantly *higher rate of compensation* from their husbands—cultivated about *double* the land. Jones compared independent women with two groups of married women—those whose households grew more than .75 "piquet" (1 piquet = .5 hectare) per household worker versus those growing less. The independent women averaged .94 piquet per household worker. Households cultivating .75+ piquet per household worker averaged an almost identical .95 piquet. Households cultivating less than .75 piquet averaged only *half as much*—.47. The secret? Married "women who cultivated .75 piquet or more per household worker were compensated at the mean rate of 363 CFA/day, while the married women who cultivated less than .75 piquet per household worker received only 302 CFA/day from their husbands" (Jones 1981, p. 133; the difference is significant).

In sum, although wives were compensated above opportunity costs, few had *enough* incentive to "take on the cultivation of an additional rice field" (p. 83). And many of SEMRY's irrigated fields still go unused as a result.

(B) *Other African examples.* Space constraints prevent a full discussion but in all of the following three examples from Kenya and one from the Gambia, women were expected to labor but received no direct return. And in all cases, the project suffered. *Kenya:* (1) Apthorpe (1971) documents this for a pyrethrum project (the dried flowers are used for insecticide); (2) Hanger and Moris's study of the Mwea resettlement project (1973) also found that negative consequences ranged from lowered family nutrition and wives' decreased decision-making power to increased male drunkenness as women brewed beer for income, because only their husbands were getting a return from women's labor on the project's irrigated rice; and (3) the findings from Broch-Due's study of the Turkana (1983) echo those of Hanger and Moris on increased male drunkenness and decreased child nutrition, as well as those of Jones in that women with their own irrigated plots spent less time cultivating off-project rain-fed sorghum. *The Gambia:* Dey (1981, 1982) found that rice production *decreased* as women, denied benefits for a crop they traditionally cultivated and controlled, held back their labor on a project for irrigated rice.

In short, incentives for "the household" didn't elicit as much of a response from women farmers as incentives under their own control, and the consequences of women's resulting behavior negatively affected development and family well-being outcomes. Let us posit a *positive* case in the next hypothesis:

H_6: Especially among poor women with provider responsibilities, they may be more *responsive than their male counterparts to either (1) easing of constraints on their production or (2) emergence of new incentives for production.*

Only one case (from Africa) is presented in support, but it is a powerful one. *Cameroon:* Henn (1988), an economist, studied random samples in two Beti villages in the cocoa-growing region of southern Cameroon. In preview, she found that even though they were *already* working over 60 hours a week, women proved more responsive to improved marketing conditions and rising prices for food crops than men, who worked only half as many hours.[10]

A major new road opened in 1982, which enormously improved marketing access for the village of Bilik Bindik; farm-gate prices also rose. Meanwhile, the village of Mgbaba remained quite isolated. Henn found that both men and women in Bilik Bindik increased output of marketed food, but women's response was much greater:

Women in Bilik Bindik reported increasing their food production and processing labor after the road opened . . . [spending] 4.6 *more* hours a week producing food than women in market-isolated Mgbaba. Women's total work week was nearly *sixty-eight hours* in Bilik Bindik versus *sixty-one hours* in Mgbaba . . . [a difference] significant at the ten percent confidence level. Women in Mgbaba worked less than *five hours* a week producing food for the market while women in Bilik Bindik spent *10.75 hours.* The effects of the additional labor on women's incomes, enhanced by the lower marketing costs in Bilik Bindik, were dramatic: women from Bilik Bindik made an average net income of *$570* from sales of processed and unprocessed food, while women from Mgbaba made only *$225* (Henn 1988, p. 323, emphasis added)

The contrast with men is sharp. Men's main source of income is cocoa; overall, only 24% of men sold food crops, versus fully 94% of women. But this small group of men received an exceptionally high rate of return for their production of the only two food crops grown by males: Plantains and bananas brought them an average return of $3.80 per hour. In contrast, cocoa brought them an average of $1.70 for the 1984 crop. Women received only $0.71 for food crops grown on their own account (including peanuts, corn, melons, leafy vegetables, onions, tomatoes, cassava, plantain, banana, and cocoyam). Still, the Bilik Bindik men devoted not quite *one hour* per week to increased plantain and, especially, banana production, versus the Mgbaba men's average of only *twenty minutes'* labor per week on these perishable food crops (from Mgbaba, it's difficult to get them to market without spoilage). At the same time, however, the men in Bilik Bindik "*cut back* on the amount of time they spent helping their wives produce food for the family. Women in Bilik Bindik, therefore, were obliged to make up for disappearing male labor in the subsistence sector" (Henn 1988, p. 324, emphasis added).

Given the small male sample size, these data must be seen as merely preliminary. But it seems that men, despite an average workweek of under 32 hours, proved less responsive than women working *double* that load to attractive new income opportunities for marketing food crops. (The women described themselves as overworked, devoting 26 hours per week to agriculture and 31 to "domestic" activities, versus their husbands' 12 hours per week to agriculture and 4 to "domestic" tasks; for both genders, the remaining work time is devoted to other income-producing activities.) Clearly, the women's additional labor time is approaching physiological limits. Moreover, they run the risk that their husbands will shift more of the burden of family maintenance costs onto women as female income rises—a pattern Henn inferred was occurring from cross-sectional data. Still the women's response speaks for itself: Despite an apparently crushing labor burden, they increased their workweek still futher—to obtain needed income.

The final hypothesis (thus far) for this evolving feminist theory of development builds on the above by positing the conditions under which women give primacy to income-generating activities over their reproductive activities.

Everywhere, women are more responsible than men for the full range of reproductive activities—not only fertility, but also the tasks that nurture and maintain the labor force from day to day and from generation to generation. Indeed, one variant of theorizing on women in development takes off from the notion that women's lives are adjusted more to their reproductive activities (including child care and domestic tasks) than their productive activities (see, e.g., Beneria 1982). While I don't ignore reproductive activities, I have argued the opposite tack (Blumberg 1984). Here I propose the following summary:

H_7: *Women will give primacy to income-generating activities, and accommodate their reproductive activities to fit, under the following conditions:* (1) The returns from the activity are controlled by the woman, (2) she has a need for income for expenditure obligations for her children, herself, and/or her extended kin, (3) she is physically able to accommodate the extra work by extra effort and/or shunting some of the labor burden to others (mainly, her children), (4) it involves a (further) commercialization of what she already is doing, and (5) her extra income will not be matched by a 1:1 withdrawal of resources or assistance from her husband.

In the next portion of the chapter, the macro implications of Hypotheses 5–7 are woven into a discussion of the African food crisis; lack of attention to women producers—*and their returns to labor*—is proposed to be an important, although neglected, cause of the region's persistent food shortfalls.

NEGLECT OF WOMEN FARMERS' MICRO-LEVEL INCENTIVES AND THE AFRICAN FOOD CRISIS

Africa's disastrous deficit in food production: We have seen the end result of the African food crisis on our television screens—periodic famine. The famines usually are traced to such immediate precipitating causes as severe drought and/or war. But the overall trends of the African food crisis are fairly grim even in years that we don't see media coverage of starving mothers holding emaciated babies with swollen bellies and matchstick limbs. Here are some statistics:

According to FAO, food supply grew by about 1.6% per annum during the period 1970–1979, while population grew by between 2 and 3.5%. More recent FAO figures indicate that the situation has since worsened. (Raikes 1986, p. 162)

Food production per capita has fallen over the last decade by up to 15% in some countries and by 6% over the whole of the [sub-Saharan Africa] region. Cereal imports have risen by 117% and food aid by 172%. (World Bank 1985, Annex Table 6, quoted in Lawrence 1986, p. 1)

According to a recent African survey (ECA 1983, pp. 8–9). . . . Food self-sufficiency ratios dropped from 98% in the 1960s to approximately 86% in 1980. This means that, on average, each African had about 12% less home-grown food in 1980 than 20 years earlier. (Hyden 1986, p. 11)

The minimal attention by nonfeminists to the fact that it is females who are the foremost food farmers: It would seem reasonable to suppose that learned discussions of the African food crisis would at least acknowledge the crucial—and, within the "women in development" literature, well documented—role of *women as producers of up to 80% of the locally consumed/marketed food* (e.g., Sivard 1985, pp. 5, 17). But a look at two of the most recent such analyses, Mellor, Delgado, and Blackie (1987; in the "mainstream " paradigm), and *World Recession and the Food Crisis in Africa* edited by Lawrence (1986; in the more radical paradigm) shows that this is not the case. One finds much rhetoric about "peasants" and "producers" but little awareness of the gender of those growing most of the food *and* doing most of the agricultural labor (the Economic Commission for Africa, aggregating from micro-level studies, estimates that females account for 60%-80% of *all* labor hours in agriculture—United Nations 1978, p. 5).

These recent volumes are not alone in largely overlooking women farmers in Africa. In fact, the practices of colonialism overlaid by several decades of postindependence development assistance have created an almost wholly male-oriented approach to farming in most African countries that belies the importance of female producers. Schools of agriculture have overwhelmingly male enrollments and the few females are concentrated in traditional home economics (Gamble et al. 1988). Overall, an estimated 97% of all extension agents in Africa are male (Swanson and Rassi 1981). And, in most countries (although this is *starting* to change in a few places, such as Kenya, Malawi, and Nigeria), the targets of their assistance are also almost always male. Why?

A case of Western agrarian bias? Elsewhere (Blumberg forthcoming-a, forthcoming-c), I have noted that one reason for this virtually all-male orientation is that the colonialists, and the current development experts, came from or were trained in Western countries with heavily male *agrarian* farming systems. The ethnographic data base amply documents that agrarian farming systems are predominantly *male*-based (see, e.g., Murdock 1967). But much (albeit not all) of Africa is *horticultural*.[11] And here the ethnographic data base documents that male-based farming systems are a distinct minority: Of 376 horticultural societies included in Murdock's (1967) 1,170-society *Ethnographic Atlas,* men are the primary cultivators in only about one-fifth. Also, as noted, male development experts almost invariably view both the agrarian farm family and the "modern nuclear family" as solidary entities headed by men and functioning as a single enterprise—a "black box" view of the household, which is least appropriate when extended to horticultural Africa.

Why (at least partly) "separate purses" are so prevalent in Africa: There is ample documentation as to the empirical reality that, in most of sub-Saharan Africa, husbands and wives keep wholly or partly "separate purses"—that is, have at least partly independent income streams and separate expenditure obligations (see, e.g., Fapohunda 1978; Jones 1983; Henn 1988; Guyer 1988; Staudt 1987; Blumberg 1988a, forthcoming-a). "Separate purses" seem linked to several of Africa's distinct structural characteristics: (1) polygyny, (2) patrilocal, patrilineal kinship systems, and (3) horticultural cultivation in which women are important farmers. These three factors are interlinked.

Polygyny is still fairly prevalent: for example, it ranges from 30% to 47% in most of the nine sub-Saharan countries included in the World Fertility Study sample (see United Nations 1987, p. 324). Also, patrilocal, patrilineal kinship systems still predominate, although land title is increasingly passing from kin group elders to individual males. Under such a system, additional wives mean additional resources for a man. This is because, even if a woman does much of her farming on her own account, she has a marital obligation to labor on her husband's fields and/or crops. (In many groups, men and women farm their own crops and plots but women are allowed to intercrop own-account crops on the husband's plots on which they are required to work). But for the woman, a patrilineal, patrilocal system means that her access to land is tenuous. Women typically receive only *use rights* to a plot of land from their husband or his kin group. What they raise is theirs only as long as the land remains in production.

The whole patrilineal, horticultural, often polygynous system puts a premium on maintenance of at least partially "separate purses." How much goes into "his, hers, and theirs" varies. Polygyny almost always means separate purses for co-wives. Co-wives may share *domestic* labor, but typically maintain entirely separate *economic* endeavors and accounts. In a number of ethnic groups, men and women may pool expenditures for certain items, such as their children's school fees. But, in many groups, a woman is seen as having the obligation to provide food, or income to purchase food, for her own children. Especially in groups with high marital instability, it is very important for her to maintain ties with her natal kin. This entails her fulfilling certain financial and ceremonial obligations to them.

In short, under the prevailing system, filling her provider role and keeping up her natal kin ties mean that women not only *must* have separate incomes but also separate obligations for spending it. And, as we have shown above, both positively (Henn) and negatively (Jones, and the subsequent four African examples), women are not passive members of a unitary household. They actively attempt to allocate their labor, to the extent culturally possible, *toward* activities that put cash and/or food under their control, and *away* from those with more indirect returns, even if these provide a higher rate of return.

If development practice would work *with* these realities, women's very needs for incomes—and lower oportunity costs stemming from their lower incomes—would seem to make them more responsive to a reduction of constraints and an increase in prices (as occurred in Henn's study of the two Cameroonian villages that did and did not get a road).[12] But if the development experts' agrarian-influenced view dims the visibility of women farmers to their eyes, the opacity of their "black box" model of the unitary household completely blinds them to the "internal economy of the household"—whereby not only production but also returns and incentives must be looked at in gender-disaggregated terms.

Hardship for naught? "Structural adjustment" and incentives for food producers: One of the major aims of current development practices vis-à-vis Africa—especially the World Bank's "structural adjustment" programs—is "getting the prices right" (World Bank 1981). This involves changing a country's macro-economic policies to reduce government interference in markets and "correct" urban-biased factor prices. The rationale for these policies—which are acknowledged to bring immediate hardship to the urban poor, for whom prices of basic necessities typically skyrocket—is that in addition to thereby increasing "tradables," especially for export, the resulting higher agricultural prices will provide incentives for small-scale food producers. (In many African countries, some 98% of local food output is generated by small-scale producers.) But the above discussion indicates that even the "rightest" of prices won't matter if women producers of the bulk of the food crops don't get enough of the resulting income to provide incentive.

The bottom line: Thus, for much of rural Africa, development aid targeted at males—and ignoring the "internal economy of the household," with women's special constraints and needs—of necessity entails, at a minimum, an inefficient use of scarce resources. At maximum, it appears that insufficient attention to women producers and their *incentives* may be a crucial but little recognized factor in the African food crisis. And yet, ironically, if given appropriate technical/credit aid and incentives, African women farmers may be the single most *cost-effective available resource to alleviate the food crisis* (Grosz 1988).

THE ISRAELI KIBBUTZ, GENDER STRATIFICATION, AND THE INTERNAL ECONOMY OF THE HOUSEHOLD

Let us consider the case of the kibbutz in terms of my evolving theories of gender stratification and development. First, it shows that the theories' scope extends beyond the Third World (with its mix of spontaneous and planned development)—here, to a planned utopia. Second, it examines how some of the kibbutz's deliberately adopted structural features and macro-level policies that were not aimed at gender issues unintentionally bolstered women's equality at the micro level (versus their spouses) while unintentionally limiting their power and occupational choice at the kibbutz macro level (its political economy). One lesson we shall learn is that, unless gender is explicitly considered in the planning stages, outcomes will rarely enhance gender equality, even among those professing such an ideology.

In most respects *other* than gender, the Israeli kibbutz rests secure on its laurels as one of the most successful and enduring experiments in socialist utopias. Older kibbutzim contain three or even four generations and enjoy an upper-middle-class standard of living. At the same time, in none of the three major kibbutz federations has there been compromise on adherence to full socialist equality in several important aspects, including the following: (1) Every adult is a member of the kibbutz in his or her own right—thus a woman's kibbutz membership is independent of her marital status;[13] and (2) all members continue to receive equal shares of the collective product; all the basics and many of the amenities—food, clothing, lodging, health care, vacations, and so on—are equally available to males and females (Rosner, Gluck, and Avnat 1980; Palgi 1978).

These two long-entrenched policies, I suggest, have created a structure where, at the *micro* level of husband and wife, kibbutz women face their mates with something no other women anywhere in the world can match—essentially, full, guaranteed economic equality. Given this micro situation, it is the hypotheses of the gender stratification theory, rather than the evolving feminist theory of development, which are stressed. Kibbutz men and women have equal individual shares of kibbutz resources, and children's needs are fulfilled by the collectivity. But there is a major contradiction. Despite an ideology of gender equality, women are less than equal in two key *macro* areas: First, they are underrepresented in the powerful economic committees and central kibbutz offices (economic manager, treasurer, secretary). Second, an extreme, sex-segregated division of labor has remained remarkably constant for some 40 years: Perhaps 90% of women remain in a narrow range of "services"—child care/childhood education, laundry, kitchen work, and so on. Actually, the two are *interlinked.* Economic committee members are mainly employed in the "productive" branches, so women's jobs limit their access to the positions controlling the kibbutz's macro structure. And it is at the top that policies affecting the kibbutz economic structure and its division of labor are formulated; "town meeting" members' meetings respond to an already created agenda.

A large literature has sprung up on why so many kibbutz women work in traditional "services" and so few hold macro-level positions of power.[14] Explanations range from the sociobiological to the psychological to the structural (see Palgi et al. 1983 for an excellent compilation of the recent positions in this debate). My own explanation (Blumberg 1983a, forthcoming-d) is structural and takes off from my gender stratification theory.

But what I wish to stress in this chapter is the contradiction: The structural conditions responsible for less than full female equality at the *macro* level also—like those responsible for women's extraordinary economic equality at the *micro* level—stem largely from deliberate kibbutz "development policy and practice."

Blasi (1981) states the case succinctly: Kibbutz founders made a concerted efforted to promote *economic* equality; in contrast, they made only a "half-baked attempt" at *sexual* equality, "whose conclusion was also half-baked."

With respect to *economic* equality, there was deliberate manipulation of structural or organizational arrangements, he notes, and constant fine-tuning so that this central goal of the kibbutz would not be compromised. As I have noted above, women benefited—primarily at the micro level—from their economic equality, but benefits to women were secondary or even unwitting consequences of deliberate efforts to create and sustain a structure of economic equality. In parallel fashion, many of the macro-level structural arrangements fashioned by the kibbutz leadership over time worked to women's disadvantage. But this too was an unintended consequence. In other words, I suggest, the story here is similar to that in so many Third World development projects: Women are helped or hurt unintentionally, depending on how deliberate development policies' impact on the prevailing structural and organizational arrangements happens to affect them.

In stark contrast, there was *no* such deliberate manipulation of kibbutz structure to ensure *gender* equality, Blasi asserts.[15] Rather, he notes, even the ideological tenet of sexual equality emerged slowly and to varying degrees in the early kibbutz movement. Moreover, as seen below, practice lagged behind ideology.[16]

Before presenting a brief summary of my explanation of why kibbutz structure inhibited full macro-level female equality, let me restate my hypothesis (5a above) that a less favorable gender equality situation at the macro level acts as a negative "discount rate" on the extent to which a woman can derive full leverage from her micro-level economic power. Hence, although I stress that kibbutz women enjoy more equality at the micro than the macro level, they fall somewhat short of complete equality even here. Still, kibbutz *men* spend more hours in child care and household tasks than men in any other advanced economy—capitalist or socialist—ever included in time-budget research (Rosner 1982). Moreover, kibbutz men participated in nine of thirteen categories of domestic tasks surveyed (Tiger and Shepher 1975; Rosner and Palgi 1980). (Even so, men spent much less time in child care/domestic pursuits and avoided the nastiest chore, cleaning the bathrooms.)

Clearly, more than economic factors are at work: There is strong gender-role stereotyping in the kibbutz, which affects both childhood socialization/expectations (Safir and Dotan 1977; Safir 1982) and adult perceptions (Rosner 1967). Moreover, these stereotypes affect gender equality despite attempts to raise "unisex" children to age 5–6 and an unsuccessful campaign to *assert* that women's child/domestic "service" activities are as important and prestigious as (men's) "productive" tasks.

Focusing now on the macro level, my argument is that, for women, structural disadvantage was built into the kibbutz from the beginning and was intensified and institutionalized by initial and subsequent policies and practices. The initial disadvantage occurred with the base deliberately chosen and constructed by the largely male founders[17] of the early kibbutzim (1909 to the 1920s)—*agrarian* socialist.

Agrarian cultivation, as noted above, is *the* "male farming system" par excellence. Empirically, men predominate in agrarian cultivation and women are subordinated in almost all agrarian societies (see, e.g., Michaelson and Goldschmidt 1971). Why an agrarian base? It was technically possible (soils were deep enough). And, of course, the vision of cultivation brought by the pioneer kibbutzniks from their Eastern European villages—where Jews had been prohibited from being farmers—was of an agrarian mixed farming system, in which males predominated in field work.

Resistance by many of the males (and a few of the females) restricted women's participation in agrarian field work even in the pioneering days of the kibbutz (Reinharz 1987; Safir 1983). It appears that, even in the hardship-filled 1920s and 1930s when agrarian production was being established, no more than 50%-60% of the women managed (or were allowed) to work in production (Tiger and Shepher 1975). In those days, women were largely childless.

An aerial photo of a kibbutz shows how women's problems were compounded when children began to be born. The children's houses are located in the inner core of the kibbutz (for military defense as well as social reasons). Agrarian field crops are located at the farthest perimeter—beyond any horticultural crops (e.g.,vegetables), poultry, or most dairying activities. Fresh milk was not pasteurized and bottled in Israel until 1966 (Safir 1983, p. 127), so nursing mothers generally came in to breast-feed their children during the workday. Additionally, mothers of weaned children were pressured by Freudian-tinged beliefs to visit their offspring during the day (the kibbutz did not exist in an intellectual vacuum; it kept up with European cultural/intellectual fads and paradigms). So although the kibbutz created unique children's houses for communal child rearing (staffed 100% by women), it promoted mother-child contact during the workday. The long journey, for much of the year under a blazing sun, took its toll: Male branch managers disliked having such women—with their diminished production—on their teams (Leshem 1972).

Attrition of mothers from the field crop branches was steady. More women remained in the horticultural, poultry, and dairying branches—activities that tend to be female worldwide, according to the ethnographic data bases (e.g., Murdock 1967). But here they came up against another obstacle: Kibbutz *socialism* as manifest in its accounting standard, "income per labor day." Following the most orthodox socialist definition of the "labor theory of value," the kibbutz counted only labor as a cost of production. They didn't even put shadow prices on land and capital (the common practice in the Eastern European socialist countries; see Barkai 1971, 1973). And by this yardstick, horticultural

branches—which the women preferred (see Viteles 1967)—look greatly
inferior to agrarian ones. Agrarian field crops use less labor per unit of
ground area, and hence look better in the kibbutz books. Because the
kibbutz is economically rational within the parameters of its self-defined
socialist ideology, these labor-intensive horticultural branches were
gradually phased out (or operated on a minimal, less commercial, low-
input basis). Women might have been upset, but they sadly accepted it
as being "for the good of the kibbutz" (Spiro 1975). After all, given the
kibbutz accounting system, everyone could "see" that horticultural
crops were less profitable.

As women with children left agrarian production, their places were
taken by newly immigrated members, who were still mainly single,
young, and male. Increasingly (especially as the horticultural branches
were phased out), women were concentrated in traditional female reproductive activities. But these were now organized as separate occupations: cooking or cleaning or child care or laundry and so on for eight
hours a day. From the mid-1930s through the 1970s, many women
expressed distress with their occupational lot[18]—in vain; their occupational concentration reduced their access to macro-level power. Once
women's small foothold in the "productive" branches was largely
eroded, their access to the economic committees all but dried up, as
noted above. So for decades, kibbutz investment decisions slighted the
disgruntled women's "service" branches. Until the coming of the industrial revolution (i.e., the establishment of manufacturing and other modern enterprises) in the 1960s, investment disparity was such that men
drove tractors while some women scrubbed clothes on a washboard.
(As factories needed more labor, some services such as laundry and
food services finally got capital investment to free female labor. But the
factories stressed hierarchy—see, e.g., Rosner 1981a; Leviatan 1983—
so although they employ a higher proportion of women than agricultural production branches, most of these women have ended up in
bottom-rung jobs.)

The very labor-intensive services absorbed more and more of the
kibbutz women as their niches in farming production shrank. By the
early 1950s, an invidiously ranked, sex-segregated division of labor was
firmly entrenched. It was perpetuated in subsequent generations of kibbutz women not only by socialization but also by kibbutz labor allocation practices among adolescents (Hertz and Baker 1983). High school
girls were *required* to work in the children's houses; boys were given

experience in a wide choice of agricultural assignments.[19] Thereafter, human capital considerations further reified the extant gender division of labor.

Both genders—but especially women who did not work in "productive" branches or occupy key kibbutz positions (Talmon 1972, p. 119; Rosner 1981b)—turned increasingly to the micro world within the walls of their flats. Especially in the most leftist of the three kibbutz federations (Kibbutz Artzi), this "private familism" has been seen as a threat to the public, communal character of the kibbutz (Rosner and Palgi 1980; Rosner 1981b, 1982).

Over time, many female voices of dissatisfaction with the narrowness of their occupational options were muted: many women left, others resigned themselves. After decades of such a division of labor, there has been an almost Darwinian selection in favor of women least opposed—or most resigned—to working in children's houses or traditional domestic chores (Blumberg forthcoming-d).

But the kibbutz has paid a price: There is less flexibility to respond to technological change, shifts in the returns to various economic activities, or the military mobilization of males. Even in an emergency, for example, in Israel's 1973 Yom Kippur War, kibbutz women did *not* step into the breach to cover the absent men's agricultural activities (Palgi 1982; Agazzi 1982). Moreover, the allocation of so many jobs by gender rather than ability creates labor surplus in certain categories and labor shortage in others, in additional to reducing occupational choice. In recent years, some committed women activists and an increased level of concern by national kibbutz leadership have succeeded in pushing through some small reforms (e.g., the reduction in gender-differentiated education and work assignments for teens, the Kibbutz Artzi goal that 20% of children's house workers be male by some unspecified future date—see Palgi et al. 1983, p. 303).

At this point, however, it appears that only fundamental restructuring of the kibbutz economic mix could dramatically broaden women's occupational options (Shefi 1982). And even this wouldn't work unless ways were found to reverse the trend toward ever more labor-intensive child care (from ratios of 1:5 to as little as 1:3 children per child-care worker[20]) and/or to bring in large numbers of men.

Further reducing the probability of thoroughgoing "structural adjustment" of the kibbutz is the inertia created by a keen desire to protect the middle-class standard of living achieved in all but the newest kibbutzim (Shefi 1982). That standard of living was created by the extant structure and "development policies and practices." The probabilities are that they will not be easy to change. In sum, the edifice created over time by kibbutz planning makes most likely a continuation of the extant discrepancy between micro- and macro-level gender equality in the kibbutz.

SUMMARY AND CONCLUSIONS

In this chapter, an emerging model for examining the impact of planned development on gender stratification—and vice versa—has been presented. It combines seven hyphotheses condensed from my general theory of gender stratification with a new focus on what I term *the internal economy of the household*. This concept applies when resources, labor, information, and so on are differentially distributed within the household along gender (and age) lines. Then, seven new hyphotheses from an evolving feminist theory of development were presented, drawing out the implications of the "internal economy of the household" for Third World women with provider responsibilities.

The chapter argues that women's independent control of economic resources, in comparison with counterpart males, has consequences that go beyond influencing gender stratification. Conversely, it also argues that planned development can influence gender stratification, even if unwittingly, with consequences that can then reverberate back to affect macro-level development.

With this theoretical underpinning, two very disparate cases were analyzed: the African food crisis and the Israeli kibbutz. In the former, the "internal economy of the household" was stressed: In Africa, women are the primary food farmers, and several of the region's characteristic structural factors (e.g., a patrilocal-patrilineal, often polygynous, horticultural system) militated both toward "separate purses" for men and women and for women's intense need for an income of their own. (This is due to women's obligations as providers to their children and toward their own natal kin.) A development model that fails to appreciate women's importance as producers and is totally blind to the "internal economy of the household" and women's needs for returns and incentives of their own often resulted in women's position being undercut. Because these women tend to reallocate their labor toward activities that bring income an/or food under their control, the lack of incentives (and technical assistance) to the region's primary food farmers is proposed as an important but unheralded cause of the region's food short-falls. Ironically, women's very needs for income and their lower opportunity costs (due to their lower earnings) make them potentially *more* responsive than men to easing of their constraints and the small price incentives for food crops under their control. Here the price of ignoring the micro-level gender division of labor, resources, and incentives has consequences that affect a continent's food security.

The case of the kibbutz is almost exactly the opposite. Planned development unwittingly had a positive impact on the gender stratification system at the micro level, and a negative impact at the macro level. At the micro level, men and women enjoy full, guaranteed economic equality and it is the roles of men that have been most transformed—their participation in child care and housework far exceeds that recorded for men in other developed societies. Meanwhile, the women are seemingly trapped in a rigid gender division of labor that confines them to child care and domestic-labor-type jobs, and precludes their gaining their proportionate share of positions at the top of the kibbutz's "pyramid of political economy." My explanation combines propositions from my gender stratification theory with the evolving development theory's emphasis on gender-blind planning. But even though there is more resignation among today's kibbutz women to their less than satisfactory macro-level position, the kibbutz has paid a price for its macro-level sex stratification and occupational segregation: It is a less flexible institution whose options for change and adaptation to emergency are sharply limited. Indeed, one reason the kibbutz uses so many short-term international volunteers and employs ideologically disapproved outside wage labor is because its own labor allocation is rendered less efficient by its rigid gender division (Shafir 1989). Despite its laurels, it has yet to become "all that it can be."

Nevertheless, the message gleaned from the theories in this chapter is that neither the African nor the kibbutz situations are immutable. The current situation is caused by particular configurations of structural and policy factors. And these can be changed. Thus, incomplete as it is, the emerging model combining theories of gender stratification, the "internal economy of the household," and the external consequences of the first two may also provide insight into *unplanned development*—the historic sweep from hunters and gatherers to multinationals. Instead of the ahistoric view of "woman as eternal victim," which emerges from explanations of "women's fate" based on biology or even a concept of universal patriarchy, this model provides a basis for examining the "conditions under which" gender stratification can be expected to *vary* from maximal to minimal or even nonexistence. And it may show a direct link between the fortunes and freedom of women and the fortunes and freedom of their societies.

NOTES

1. Others also have begun such a project (see, e.g., DAWN 1985).

2. Per Lenski (1966, p. 197), other main "power variables" include political, force, and, to a lesser extent, ideology. *Economic* power has been the most achievable for women empirically, however, as well as being most important theoretically. We know of prestate societies where women controlled *well over half* of the economy (e.g., the horticulturalist Iroquois of colonial North America; see Brown 1975). In contrast, women are more likely to be victims than wielders of *force*. Moreover, while a few societies' *ideology* considers women equal (none holds them superior), we know of none where women have as much as a 50–50 share of *political* power.

3. Macro-level "discount rates" can, rarely, be positive (e.g., when women are given the vote by fiat from above). Further, there are *micro* level "discount factors" that are more likely to be *either* positive *or* negative for women (e.g., each partner's commitment to the relationship, relative attractiveness and gender role ideology). These, also, affect the "net" male/female balance of power (Blumberg and Coleman 1989).

4. Blumberg (1978, 1984) provides many empirical examples of the link between women's relative economic power and the extent of control over various "life options." In addition, in a pilot study testing my gender stratification theory with a sample of 61 preindustrial societies, regressions explained 56% of the variance in an index of "life options" (i.e., $R^2 = 0.56$). An index of women's relative economic power accounted for over 80% of that. Finally, since Blood and Wolfe (1960), a large U.S. literature on "familial (or marital) power" has emerged (Blumberg and Coleman 1989 give references), almost invariably supporting the relation between wives' employment and/or income and their input into familial decision making.

5. In some parts of the Third World (especially in Africa), however, rural women want and *need* more children than family planners would like them to have—to help fetch water and increasingly scarce firewood and fodder, to provide child care and help with other domestic and farm work activities, to provide for old age, and so on.

6. Studies of rural Hindu farming populations in Northern India and Nepal (e.g., Acharya and Bennett 1981, 1982, 1983) and, especially, research on the Yemen Arab Republic (Howe 1985) draw a picture of women who are apparently wholly unpaid family workers. But even in much of the Arab world, micro-level studies show much higher rates of income generation by women than recorded in national accounts. For example, Nassif (1976, cited in Van Dusen 1977, p. 23) found some 40% of women in a Tunisian village with economic roles from which they derived some income—but officially, only 13.2% of rural Tunisian women were classed as economically active.

7. The "Percy Amendment" (by former Senator Percy [R-IL], Section 113 of the 1973 Foreign Assistance Act) requires that U.S. bilateral development aid "be adminis-

tered so as to give particular attention to those programs, projects and activities which tend to integrate women into the national economies of foreign countries, thus improving their status and assisting the total development effort." Reviews of the extent to which this had occured after a decade or more found little impact (Blumberg 1983b on Latin America and the Caribbean; Blumberg 1982–1983 on Asia; and Carloni 1987 reviewing over 100 Third World development projects).

8. Unfortunately, poor Third World women's activities are drastically undercounted in national accounts (see, e.g., Anker 1983; Beneria 1982; Dixon 1982; Dixon-Mueller 1985; Fong 1980; Wainerman and Recchini de Lattes 1981). The undercount is the worst for nonformal, noncash activities—where many women are found in much of the Third World.

9. It also can be shown that women's spending patterns cannot be accounted for strictly by "Engel's (1857) Law"—that the lower the income, the higher the proportion spent on life's basic necessities (Houthakker 1957). Women in almost all the studies reviewed above earned far less cash income than their husbands, so one might explain females' "altruistic" spending by "Engel's Law" and expect these effects to vanish where women and men's incomes are equal. This is not the case. In one of Mencher's 10 Kerala villages (Allepey-1), women *did* earn equal income, but *still* contributed more to household survival (92% of income, versus 76% for men).

10. Her samples consisted of 40 households: She surveyed each married adult in 21 households in Bilik Bindik (representing 23% of its total households) and 19 households in Mgbaba (representing 17% of its total households). Henn's final sample consisted of 34 men and 47 women (there are more women due to polygyny).

11. *Agrarian* refers to a plow-based farming system that may be rain-fed or irrigated but typically involves "mixed farming" (i.e., crops and animals) on soils deep enough to take the plow. Traditionally, agrarian cultivation involved animal-drawn traction and animal dung for fertilizer; now it increasingly relies on mechanized cultivation and commercial fertilizers. In contrast, hoe *horticulture* generally uses slash-and-burn techniques. In much of Africa, poor tropical soils—thin, acidic, easily leached—predominate, precluding mechanized agrarian cultivation.

12. Even so, there are limits to just how much women can be expected to respond to lowered constraints and increased prices if they are laboring from dawn to dusk. More effort is sorely needed to transform women's necessary but most invisible tasks: (1) fetching water, fodder, and increasingly scarce (given deforestation) firewood, and (2) processing staple crops for storage, sale, or eating.

13. My thanks to Debbie Bernstein for insisting that I emphasize this aspect of my argument. This is the structural underpinning of women's micro-level leverage.

14. Women make up only about 20% of kibbutz economic committees; rarely hold kibbutz central offices except in the 10%-15% of kibbutzim electing *two* secretaries, one male, one female (Tiger and Shepher 1975); and are only 6%-7% of the elite economic managers training program (*merkaz meshek*; Blumberg 1983a; Karnovitch 1982).

15. Blasi (1981, reprinted in Palgi et al. 1983, p. 94) notes that "women were never given affirmative action education in engineering or economic planning to make sure they could serve on those committees or in those work branches. True, they never asked for it. And the men never asked for training in child development, cooking or sewing." The kibbutz never considered "specific organizational solutions" to promote gender equality as they did to ensure economic equality, he continues: "What would have been the effect of

legislating that men and women should make up equal numbers of production and service branches? Or legislating that men should receive training in dealing with young children and make up half of the early schooling systems staff? True, the fact that this seemed weird to people who eliminated wage systems, created total social security, and developed an impressive direct democracy, only indicates that their hearts were not carefully defined on the matter (let us not forget their East European sexist legacy)."

16. Blasi also undercuts the sociobiological explanation of women's concentration in child care/domestic services and their underrepresentation in kibbutz office. This agrument (e.g., Tiger and Shepher 1975; see also Spiro 1979), Blasi notes, rests on the assumption that the kibbutz founders *did* attempt a thoroughgoing sexual revolution that initially included the absence of a gender division of labor—and then *failed* to maintain that initial equality. But there was no initial equality.

17. Only 20%-35% of the kibbutz pioneers were women, according to Talmon (1972, p. 19; see also Tiger and Shepher 1975, pp.79–84), and very few were kibbutz leaders. The few women had to be pioneers on *men's* terms (Izraeli 1981, 1982).

18. For example, Viteles (1967) describes women's protests against being edged out of production dating back to 1936; Rosner's (1967) survey data show lower prestige and morale in women's service jobs; Agazzi (1979, 1980) gives a newer negative view.

19. Hertz and Baker (1983, p. 102) further undermine Tiger and Shepher's sociobiological explanation for the extant gender division of labor in the kibbutz: "Since high school girls do not yet have children, it seems unlikely that they are '. . . seeking an association with their own offspring, which reflects a species-wide attraction between mothers and their young.' " (Tiger and Shepher 1975, p. 272).

20. In my 1981–82 fieldwork updating my earlier study, many women questioned if such low 1:3 ratios were even *healthy*. Palgi (1982) stresses that the low ratios arose from shorter, larger shifts that were adopted to better working conditions. Regardless of reason, the net result has been to increase the pressure on virtually all young women to do a stint as child care workers (almost all are young women; in midlife, women are usually phased out of the children's houses into kitchen, laundry, and so on).

REFERENCES

Archarya, Meena and Lynn Bennett. 1981. *The Rural Women of Nepal: An Aggregate Analysis and Summary of Eight Village Studies.* Vol. 2, part 9. Kathmandu, Nepal: Tribhuvan University, Centre for Economic Development and Administration.
———. 1982. "Women's Status in Nepal: A Summary of Findings and Implications," mimeo. Washington, DC: Agency for International Development, Office of Women in Development.
———. 1983. *Women and the Subsistence Sector: Economic Participation in Household Decision-Making in Nepal.* Working Paper no. 526. Washington, DC: World Bank.
Agazzi, Judith. 1979. "Kibbutz and Sex Roles." *Crossroads* (4, Autumn).
———. 1980. "The Status of Women in Kibbutz Society." In *Integrative Cooperatives in Industrial Societies,* edited by K. Bartolke et al. Assen, the Netherlands: Van Gorcum.
———. 1983. [Personal interviews].
Anker, Richard. 1971. "Female Labour Force Participation in Developing Countries: A

Critique of Current Definitions and Data Collection Methods." *International Labour Review* 122(6, Nov.-Dec.).

Apthorpe, Raymond. 1971. "Some Evaluation Problems for Cooperative Studies, with Special Reference to Primary Cooperatives in Highland Kenya." In *Two Blades of Grass: Rural Cooperatives in Agricultural Modernization*, edited by Peter Worsely. Manchester: Manchester University Press

Arrigo, Linda Gail. 1980. "The Industrial Working Force of Young Women in Taiwan." *Bulletin of Concerned Asian Scholars* 12(2):25–38.

Barkai, Haim. 1971. *The Kibbutz: An Experiment in Microsocialism*. Research Report no. 34. Jerusalem: Hebrew University of Jerusalem.

———. 1973. [Interview and personal communications, January-September].

Becker, Gary. 1981. *A Treatise on the Family*. Cambridge, MA: Harvard University Press.

Beneria, Lourdes. 1982. "Accounting for Women's Work." In *Women and Development: The Sexual Division of Labour in Rural Societies*, edited by Lourdes Beneria. New York: Praeger.

Beneria, Lourdes and Gita Sen. 1981. "Accumulation, Reproduction and Women's Roles in Economic Development: Boserup Revisited." *Signs*. 7(2): 279–298.

Blasi, Joseph. 1981. "A Critique of Gender and Culture: Kibbutz Women Revisited." *Journal of Marriage and the Family* (May):451–56.

Blood, Robert O., Jr., and Donald M. Wolfe. 1960. *Husbands and Wives: The Dynamics of Married Living*. New York: Free Press.

Blumberg, Rae Lesser. 1978. *Stratification: Socioeconomic and Sexual Inequality*. Dubuque, IA: William C. Brown.

———. 1982–83. "At the End of the Line: Women and United States Foreign Aid in Asia, 1978–1980." In *Women in Developing Countries: A Policy Focus*, edited by Kathleen Staudt and Jane Jacquette. New York: Haworth.

———. 1983a. "Kibbutz Women: From the Fields of Revolution to the Laundries of Discontent." In *Sexual Equality: The Kibbutz Tests the Theories*, edited by Michal Palgi et al. Norwood, PA: Norwood.

———. 1983b. "To What Extent Have Women Been Taken into Account in U.S. Foreign Aid in Latin America and the Caribbean? Clues from the 'Paper Trail' of Agency for International Development Projects." Washington, DC: Agency for International Development, Bureau for Latin America and the Caribbean.

———. 1984. "A General Theory of Gender Stratification." In *Sociological Theory, 1984*, edited by Randall Collins. San Francisco: Jossey-Bass.

———. 1985. "A Walk on the 'WID' Side: Summary of Field Research on 'Women in Development' " in the Dominican Republic and Guatemala. Washington, DC: Agency for International Development, Bureau for Latin America and the Caribbean.

———. 1988a. "Income Under Female Versus Male Control: Hypotheses from a Theory of Gender Stratification and Data from the Third World." *Journal of Family Issues* 9(1):51–84.

———. [with the assistance of Lorna Lueker]. 1988b. *The Half-Hidden Roles of Rural Nigerian Women and National Development*, draft. Washington, DC: World Bank, Women in Development Division.

———. 1988c. "Gender Stratification, Economic Development, and the African Food Crisis: Paradigm and Praxis in Nigeria." In *Social Structures and Human Lives*, edited by Matilda White Riley. Newbury Park, CA: Sage.

———. Forthcoming-a. *Making the Case for the Gender Variable: Women and the Wealth and Well-Being of Nations.* Technical Monograph in Gender and Development no. 2–89. Washington, DC: Agency for International Development, Office of Women in Development.

———. Forthcoming-b. "Work, Wealth, and a Women in Development 'Natural Experiment' in Guatemala: The ALCOSA Agribusiness Project in 1980 and 1985." In *Women in Development: A.I.D.'s Experience, 1973–1985.* Vol. 2, *Ten Field Studies.* Washington, DC: Agency for International Development.

———. Forthcoming-c. *Women and the Wealth of Nations: Theory and Research on Gender and Global Development.* New York: Praeger.

———. Forthcoming-d. "As You Sow, So Shall You Reap: Updating a Structural Explanation of Gender Stratification in the Kibbutz." *Gender and Society.*

Blumberg, Rae Lesser and Marion Tolbert Coleman. 1989. "A Theoretical Look at the Gender Balance of Power in the American Couple." *Journal of Family Issues* 10(2).

Boserup, Ester. 1970. *Woman's Role in Economic Development.* New York: St. Martin's.

Broch-Due, Vigdis. 1983. *Women at the Backstage of Development: The Negative Impact on Project Realization by Neglecting the Crucial Roles of Turkana Women as Producers and Providers.* Rome: Food and Agricultural Organization.

Brown, Judith. 1975. "Iroquois Women: An Ethnohistoric Note." In *Toward an Anthropology of Women,* edited by Rayna Reiter. New York: Monthly Review Press.

Buvinic, Myra, Nadia Youssef, and Barbara Von Elm. 1978. *Women Headed Households: The Ignored Factor in Development Planning.* Washington, DC: International Center for Research on Women.

Carloni, Alice Stewart. 1987. *Women in Development: A.I.D.'s Experience, 1973–1985.* Vol. 1, *Synthesis Paper.* Washington, DC: Agency for International Development.

Carr, Marilyn and Ruby Sandhu. 1988. *Women, Development and Rural Productivity: An Analysis of the Impact of Time and Energy Saving Technologies on Women.* Occasional Paper. New York: UNIFEM.

Chafetz, Janet Saltzman. 1988. *Feminist Sociology: An Overview of Contemporary Theories.* Itasca, IL: F. E. Peacock.

Crandon, Libbet and Bonnie Shepard. 1985. *Women, Enterprise and Development.* Chestnut Hill, MA: Pathfinder Fund.

DAWN (Development Alternatives with Women for a New Era). 1985. *Development Crises and Alternative Visions: Third World Women's Perspectives.* Norway: Author.

Deere, Carmen Diana. 1977. "Changing Social Relations of Production and Peruvian Peasant Women's Work." *Latin American Perspectives* 54(1,2).

Dey, Jennie. 1981. "Gambian Women: Unequal Partners in Rice Development Projects?" In *African Women in the Development Process,* edited by Nici Nelson. London: Frank Cass.

———. 1982. "Development Planning in the Gambia: The Gap Between Planners' and Farmers' Perceptions, Expectations and Objectives." *World Development* 10(5):377–96.

Dixon, Ruth. 1982. "Women in Agriculture: Counting the Labor Force in Developing Countries." *Population and Development Review* 8(3):539–66.

Dixon-Mueller, Ruth. 1985. *Women's Work in Third World Agriculture.* Geneva: International Labour Organization.

Dwyer, Daisy and Judith Bruce, ed. 1988. *A Home Divided: Women and Income in the Third World.* Palo Alto, CA: Stanford University Press.

Economic Commission for Africa (ECA). 1983. *ECA and Africa's Development 1983–2001: A Preliminary Perspective Study.* Addis Ababa: Economic Commission for Africa.

Fapohunda, Eleanor. 1978. "Characteristics of Women Workers in Lagos: Data for Reconsideration by Labour Market Theorists." *Labour and Society* 3:158–71.

Fong, Monica. 1980. "Victims of Old-Fashioned Statistics." *Ceres: F.A.O. Review of Agriculture and Development* 13(3):29–32 Rome: Food and Agricultural Organization.

Fortmann, Louise. 1978. "Women and Tanzanian Agricultural Development." Economic Research Bureau Paper no. 77.4. Dar Es Salaam: University of Dar Es Salaam, Economic Research Bureau.

———. 1982. "Women's Work in a Communal Setting: The Tanzanian Policy of Ujaama." In *Women and Work in Africa,* edited by Edna G. Bay. Boulder, CO: Westview.

Gamble, William K., Rae Lesser Blumberg, Vernon C. Johnson, and Ned S. Raun. 1988. *Three Nigerian Universities and Their Role in Agricultural Development.* Project Impact Evaluation Report no. 66. Washington, DC: U.S. Agency for International Development.

Greenhalgh, Susan. 1985. "Sexual Stratification: The Other Side of 'Growth with Equity' in East Asia." *Population and Development Review* 11(2):265–314.

Grosz, Ron. 1988. [Personal communication].

Guyer, Jane. 1980. "Household Budgets and Women's Incomes." Working Paper no. 28. Boston: Boston University, African Studies Center.

———. 1988. "Dynamic Approaches to Domestic Budgeting: Cases and Methods from Africa." In *A Home Divided: Women and Income in the Third World,* edited by Daisy Dwyer and Judith Bruce. Palo Alto, CA: Stanford University Press.

Hanger, Jane and Jon Moris. 1973. "Women and the Household Economy." In *Mwea: An Irrigated Rice Settlement in Kenya,* edited by Robert Chambers and Jon Moris. München: Weltforum Verlag.

Henn, Jeanne Koopman. 1988. "Intra-Household Dynamics and State Policies as Constraints on Food Production: Results of a 1985 Agroeconomic Survey in Cameroon." In *Gender Issues in Farming Systems Research and Extension,* edited by Susan V. Poats, Marianne Schmink, and Anita Spring. Boulder, CO: Westview.

Hertz, Rosanna and Wayne Baker. 1983. "Women and Men's Work in an Israeli Kibbutz: Gender and Allocation of Labor." In *Sexual Equality: The Israeli Kibbutz Tests the Theories,* edited by Michal Palgi et al. Norwood, PA: Norwood.

Hess, Peter. Forthcoming. *Population Growth and Socioeconomic Progress in Less Developed Countries: Determinants of Fertility Transition.* New York: Praeger.

Houthakker, H. S. 1957. "An International Comparison of Household Expenditure Patterns, Commemorating the Centenary of Engel's Law." *Econometrica* 25:532–51.

Howe, Gary Nigel. 1985. *The Present and Potential Contribution of Women to Economic Development: Elements of Methodology and Analysis of the Yemen Arab Republic.* Washington, DC: Agency for International Development, Office of Women in Development.

Hyden, Goran. 1986. "The Invisible Economy of Small Holder Agriculture in Africa." In *Understanding Africa's Rural Households and Farming Systems,* edited by Joyce Lewinger Moock. Boulder, CO: Westview.

Izraeli, Dafna N. 1981. "An Empirical Test of the Effects of Sex Proportions: A Study of

Union Officers in Israel." Paper presented at the International Interdisciplinary Conference on Women, Haifa.
———. 1982. [Personal inteviews].
Jones, Christine. 1983. "The Impact of the SEMRY I Irrigated Rice Production Project on the Organization of Production and Consumption at the Intrahousehold Level." Washington, DC: Agency for International Development, Bureau for Program and Policy Coordination.
Karnovitch, Ora. 1982. [Interview, January].
Koons, Adam Surla. 1988. "Reaching Rural Women in the Northwest Province: A Presentation of More Ways in Which Women Are Not Men." Paper prepared for the Conference on Development and Cameroon, "The Role of Food and Agriculture," University of Florida, Gainesville, April.
Kumar, Shubh K. 1978. "Role of the Household Economy in Child Nutrition at Low Incomes: A Case Study in Kerala." Occasional Paper no. 95. Ithaca, NY: Cornell University, Department of Agricultural Economics.
Kung, Lydia. 1983. *Factory Women in Taiwan.* Ann Arbor: University of Michigan Press.
Kusterer, Ken et al. 1981. *The Social Impact of Agribusiness: A Case Study of ALCOSA in Guatemala.* A.I.D. Evaluation Special Study no. 4. Washington DC: Agency for International Development.
Lawrence, Peter, ed. 1986. *World Recession and the Food Crisis in Africa.* Boulder, CO: Westview.
Lenski, Gerhard E. 1966. *Power and Privilege: A Theory of Social Stratification.* New York: McGraw-Hill.
Leshem, E. 1972. [Interview, Jerusalem, June].
Leviatan, Uri. 1983. "Why Is Work Less Central for Women? Initial Explorations with Kibbutz Samples and Future Research Directions." In *Sexual Equality: The Israeli Kibbutz Tests the Theories,* edited by Michal Palgi et al. Norwood, PA: Norwood.
Matlon, Peter J. 1979. *Income Distribution Among Farmers in Northern Nigeria: Empirical Results and Policy Implications.* Washington, DC: A.I.D.; Michigan State University.
Mellor, John W., Christopher L. Delgado, and Malcolm J. Blackie, eds. 1987. *Accelerating Food Productivity in Sub-Saharan Africa.* Baltimore: Published for the International Food Policy Research Institute by Johns Hopkins University Press.
Mencher, Joan. 1988. "Women's Work and Poverty: Women's Contribution to Household Maintenance in Two Regions of South India." In *A Home Divided: Women and Income in the Third World,* edited by Daisy Dwyer and Judith Bruce. Palo Alto, CA: Stanford University Press.
Michaelson, Evalyn Jacobson and Walter Goldschmidt. 1971. "Female Roles and Male Dominance Among Peasants." *Southwestern Journal of Anthropology* 27:330–52.
Murdock, George P. 1967. "Ethnographic Atlas: A Summary." *Ethnology* 6:109–236.
Nassif, Hind. 1976. "Women's Economic Roles in Developing Tunisia." Paper presented at the meetings of the Association of Arab-American University Grads, Middle-East Studies Association.
Norman, David W., Emmy B. Simmons, and Henry M. Hays, eds. 1982. *Farming Systems in the Nigerian Savanna: Research Strategies for Development.* Boulder, CO: Westview.
Palgi, Michal. 1978. *Women Members in the Kibbutz and Participation.* Haifa: University of Haifa, Kibbutz University Center.

————. 1982. [Personal communication, May].

Palgi, Michal, Joseph Blasi, Menachem Rosner, and Marilyn Safir. 1983. *Sexual Equality: The Israeli Kibbutz Tests the Theories*. Norwood, PA: Norwood.

Raikes, Philip. 1986. "Flowing with Milk and Money: Agriculture and Food Production in Africa and the EEC." In *World Recession and the Food Crisis in Africa*, edited by Peter Lawrence. Boulder, CO: Westview.

Reinharz, Shulamit. 1987. "Why Is the Kibburtz Not a Utopian Society for Women?" Paper presented at the symposium, "The State of Kibbutz Utopian Aspirations," Harvard University, March.

Roldan, Martha. 1982. "Intrahousehold Patterns of Money Allocation and Women's Subordination: A Case Study of Domestic Outworkers in Mexico City." Unpublished paper circulated to participants in Women, Income, and Policy Seminar, Population Council, New York, March.

————. 1988. "Renegotiating the Marital Contract: Intrahousehold Patterns of Money Allocation and Women's Subordination Among Domestic Outworkers in Mexico City." In *A Home Divided: Women and Income in the Third World*, edited by Daisy Dwyer and Judith Bruce. Palo Alto, CA: Stanford University Press.

Rosner, Menachem. 1967. "Women in the Kibbutz: Changing Status and Concepts." *Asian and African Studies* 3:35–68.

————. 1981a. *Participatory Political and Organizational Democracy and the Experience of the Israeli Kibbutz*. Haifa: University of Haifa, Kibbutz University Center.

————. 1981b "Women's Self-Defeating Struggle for Institutional Change in the Kibbutz." Paper presented at the International Interdisciplinary Congress on Women, Haifa.

————. 1982. [Interviews].

Rosner, Menachem, Y. Gluck, and A. Avant. 1980. *Satisfaction with Consumption in the Kibbutz*. Haifa: University of Haifa, Institute for Study and Research of the Kibbutz and the Cooperative Idea.

Rosner, Menachim and Michal Palgi. 1980. *Family, Familism & the Equality Between the Sexes*. Haifa: University of Haifa, Kibbutz University Center.

Safir, Marilyn. 1982. [Interviews].

————. 1983. "The Kibbutz: An Experiment in Social and Sexual Equality: An Historical Perspective." In *Sexual Equality: The Israeli Kibbutz Tests the Theories*, edited by Michal Palgi et al. Norwood, PA: Norwood.

Safir, Marilyn and Irit Dotan. 1977. "Vocational Aspiration Expectancies: City-Kibbutz Comparison with Pre-School Children." Paper presented at the meeting of the Israeli Psychological Association Congress.

Salaff, Janet W. 1981. *Working Daughters of Hong Kong*. New York: Cambridge University Press.

S.E.M.R.Y. 1981. *S.E.M.R.Y. I dans l'ensemble S.E.M.R.Y. Rapport de Synthese*. Document 81–52. Yagoua: Author.

Senauer, Benjamin. 1988. "The Impact of the Value of Women's Time on Food and Nutrition." Minneapolis: University of Minnesota, Department of Agricultural and Applied Economics.

Shafir, Gershon. 1989. [Personal communications, March-April].

Shefi, Eliza. 1982. [Interview, January].

Sivard, Ruth. 1985. *Women—A World Survey*. Washington, DC: World Priorities.

Spiro, Melford E. 1975. [Interview, San Diego, April].

————. 1979. *Gender and Culture: Kibbutz Women Revisited*. New York: Schocken.

Staudt, Kathleen. 1987. "Uncaptured or Unmotivated? Women and the Food Crisis in Africa." *Rural Sociology* 52(1):37–55.

Stavrakis, Olga and Marion Louise Marshall. 1978. "Women, Agriculture and Development in the Maya Lowlands: Profit or Progress?" Paper presented at the International Conference on Women and Food, Tucson, AZ.

Swanson, Burton and Jaffer Rassi. 1981. *International Directory of National Extension Systems*. Champaign: University of Illinois, Bureau of Educational Research.

Talmon, Yonina. 1972. *Family and Community in the Kibbutz*. Cambridge, MA: Harvard University Press.

Tiger, Lionel and Joseph Shepher. 1975. *Women in the Kibbutz*. New York: Harcourt Brace Jovanovich.

Tripp, Robert B. 1981. "Farmers and Traders: Some Economic Determinants of Nutritional Status in Northern Ghana." *Journal of Tropical Pediatrics* 27:15–22.

United Nations, Report of the Secretary General. 1978. "Effective Mobilisation of Women in Development." New York: Author (UN/A/33/238).

United Nations. 1987. *Fertility Behaviours in the Context of Development. Department of International Economic and Social Affairs*. New York: Author (ST/ESA/SER.A/100).

Van Dusen, Roxann A. 1977. "Integrating Women into National Economies: Programming Considerations with Special Reference to the Near East." Paper submitted to the Agency for International Development, Office of Technical Support, Near-East Bureau.

Viteles, Harry. 1967. *A History of the Cooperative Movement in Israel: A Source Book in Seven Volumes*. Vol. 2, *The Evolution of the Kibbutz Movement*. London: Vallentine-Mitchell.

Wainerman, Catalina H. and Zulma Recchini de Lattes. 1981. *El Trabajo Feminino en el Banquillo de los Acusados: La Medicion Censal en America Latina*. Mexico: Population Council.

Wolfe, Diane L. 1988. "Female Autonomy, the Family, and Industrialization in Java." *Journal of Family Issues* 9(1):85–107.

World Bank. 1981. *Accelerated Development in Sub-Saharan Africa: An Agenda for Action*. Washington, DC: Author.

————. 1985. *World Development Report 1985*. Washington, DC: Author.

Chapter 9

REFLECTIONS ON FEMINIST THEORY

ROSE LAUB COSER

Boston College and
Henry A. Murray Center, Radcliffe College

AN ADJECTIVE CAN GIVE TROUBLE. How am I to understand the qualifier *feminist*? Is it a theory of feminism? Or is it the use of theory by feminists? Or is it a different kind of theory altogether? It is quite possible, nay probable, that there exists no one sociological theory that will give us the tools to explain gender differences or gender discrimination. Yet, sociological theories can be used in part, or they may have to be refined, and other sociological theories may have to be developed, in order to deal with the problems that feminists have articulated.

In order to understand the Protestant ethic, and especially what follows from it, we need the theories of Durkheim, Weber, and Merton, among others. In order to understand specific phenomena pertaining to the division of labor, to which I shall come back later, we need explanatory schemes that come from Durkheim, Marx, and others. Beyond this, theorists make certain assumptions from which they derive their hypotheses. Marx assumed that all societies are characterized by antagonisms between social classes, and this provided the basis for his theorizing. Weber assumed, and provided evidence for the fact, that value systems, if held collectively, can help determine the course of history. Durkheim assumed that societies must be based on a binding force— cohesion—that derives both from material conditions and from the ideational world. And Freud—to name one more—assumed, and spent a lifetime theorizing about it, that human behavior is to be explained by sexual drives and their repression.

It doesn't help to call these theories middle-class, or male, or nineteenth-century ideas. They may well be one or the other or all of these, but I believe that this is epistomologically irrelevant. What we can agree upon is that various sociological theories offer partial explanations for some problems, and that none of them is sufficient for understanding all. And some propositions in extant theories may well prove to be useless, such as Marx's proposition of the inevitability of socialism, and some of Parsons's (or Freud's, or Durkheim's) notions of the social roles of women. Yet, Miriam Johnson in this volume shows how Parsons, who has been attacked by feminists more than any other social theorist, can help us understand that, for women to achieve equality with men, the family has to undergo radical structural change.

In their theorizing, feminists make certain assumptions, namely, that, as Janet Chafetz (in this volume) has said, sex is the most salient variable in every society, that all societies have as part of their basic structure the division between genders, that the most important aspect of any society is its gender structure, and that all societies have kept women in subordinate positions. Different societies have done it in different ways, but common to all is the fact of gender differences and women's subordination as a main structural component.

These are empirical generalizations, of course. I don't think that this has to continue. And this is where theorists who are feminists have a task to perform: On the basis of these assumptions, which they will prove are based on facts, they will have to select the problems they deal with, ask questions that derive from these assumptions, and search for explanations that show, implicitly or explicity, that it "ain't necessarily so," that other arrangements are possible. They may even go further and try to articulate, as Janet Chafetz does in this volume, what it would take to accomplish such a change, and how it would come about.

A theory based on such assumptions will use sociological theories that can help answer our questions even if only partially. In the course of our theorizing, we may be led to refute, or to refine, or simply to abandon, some existing theories. So much the better. It will be our opportunity to contribute to sociological theory generally.

Theories that help us in our endeavor do not necessarily have to be based on our assumptions, as Miriam Johnson shows in her chapter on Talcott Parsons. We would dismiss such theories—under the pretext that they are part of "male science"—only at our peril. There is no male science, or female science. True, the experience of women differs from that of men. I would rather state this differently: Some women's experiences (in plural) differ from some of men's. Does this mean that their scientific methods have to differ? Scientific activity, especially in the social sciences, is based on the same principle as social interaction generally: the human ability to put oneself in the position of the other person. If this were not the case, we would have a Black theory, a White theory, a lower-class theory, an upper-class theory—you name it. There would be no way of testing our theory or some of its propositions, and hence there would be no way of convincing those who do not share our specific experiences. We would not understand one anothers' theories, and everything would fall apart. This would indeed be deconstructionist, to mention a modern fad.

In this connection I am reminded of my teacher some decades ago, the psychologist Gardner Murphy. In discussing interviewing techniques, he spoke about the notion that the interviewer should have the same characteristics as the interviewee. He asked: What characteristics? If a Black person interviews another Black person, the objection may be raised that the interviewer is middle class and the interviewee lower class, or the other way around. When the hurdle is overcome, it will be said that the interviewer is short, the interviewee tall, or vice versa. Does one have to be sick to interview a sick person, even if one does not have the same experience? Murphy concluded that one should stop paying more than minimum attention to matching interviewer and interviewee, and that the most important thing is that the interviewer be both as sensitive and as reasonable as possible. Granted, no interviewer will ever be perfect on both counts, but must try to approximate the ideal.

The same is true with theorizing. I am not arguing that we should ignore or suppress all our experiences—of gender, race, national origin, social milieu, or even personal ones. There is no need to. Our experiences, different as they are for each individual, or for women collectively, add to our intuition and our thinking. We should indeed try to add our sensitivity to our reasoning. If by relying too much or too little on our experiences we fall short of sensitivity or objectivity to get closer to the truth, someone will come and criticize. And this is as it should be.

To be useful, social theory must be critical, implicitly or explicitly. To theorize means to detach oneself from the given. In sociology this means that we cannot take existing social conditions, or their explanations, for granted. Meisenhelder's chapter gives me the opportunity to state my annoyance with the use of the term *critical theory*, as if to be critical were something special, something that other theories are not. Just as those who call themselves critical theorists don't want to separate body and mind, emotion and reason, I don't want to separate critical from other theorizing. A theory is either fruitful or not fruitful in our understanding of social phenomena, and any theory implies, as I suggested earlier, that it ain't necessarily so. Even theories based on assumptions of the positive aspects of the status quo implicitly consider other alternatives, as Miriam Johnson has shown, and at the very least are critical of those who question the status quo or the benefits of social change.

The notion that there is unity of body and mind, of emotion and reason, should be treated, I believe, in pragmatic fashion. Where we find out more or understand better by making some separations and distinctions, by all means let's do so. Where our purpose is better served by abolishing distinctions, let's do that. Whether we do or not depends on the problem and on our data.

I don't think it is useful, as Meisenhelder does in this volume, to speak of the existence of a "feminist conception of the totality of human reason." Are we feminists making claims of understanding more than anybody else? Are we saying that feminists, or women, at the exclusion of nonfeminists or men, can conceive of some "totality," whatever that is? Can we ever understand the totality of anything? I would like to be a bit more humble.

Does our experience of women as women entitle us to a claim to better understanding? Are our experiences reliable informants of the truth? Specifically, what experiences? How are we going to select experiences that help us understand, and those that prevent us from understanding? Who is there to help me make such selection, given that no one else shares my individual experience? As to common experiences, there is a tendency in feminist theorizing to extoll one experience that women have in common: the experience of the female body and female sexuality. I believe that this is a variant of sociobiology, namely, the notion that women must be different because their body is different. Such an assumption, while based on truth, is neither original nor helpful. This is only one in an "array of elitist doctrines which have maintained that certain groups have, on biological or social grounds, monopolistic or privileged access to new knowledge" (Merton 1973). Using women's bodily experience as a basis for theory building reduces the gender gap to biological differences. It does not yield an explanation as to why women are being underpaid, why they are being kept subordinate to men, why they are considered to be inferior generally. In other words, it does not help overcome gender inequality.

Just as Marx's aim was to find ways to bring about equality between all men, to abolish the exploitation of man by man (if not of woman by man), and to eliminate class differences, so our feminist assumptions are to serve knowledge about how to bring equality between men and women. I shall use any theories that will enrich my understanding of the factors that hinder, and those that help, approach this goal. I will use as much reason and objectivity as I can muster, all the while using my feelings and those of my sisters, and my own and their experiences, if these turn out to be helpful in formulating some theoretical propositions that will in some small way serve these goals.

Janet Chafetz's chapter in this volume is a fine example of theorizing by a feminist, one who wants to explore the possibilities and processes of social change in the direction of gender equality. She asks what specific social structures and processes are fundamental in maintaining social stability; and she asks how change can occur, what the effects of change will be on various subpopulations of the society. These questions are similar to those raised by Karl Marx, and her preliminary answer is similar as well: The social system is being maintained through the division of labor. Gender systems, she says, are being maintained by a gender division of labor in society at large. This is the basis upon which Chafetz will build her theory of social change.

There are some formulations that I would encourage her to modify:

(1) She says that the gender division of labor "reinforces" superior male power. I would say that it is the basis for male power. It creates male power and maintains it. However, as I shall argue, it may not even be necessary to insist on what is the basis of what, as long as we agree that male power and the division of labor sustain each other to keep females in subordinate positions.

(2) Talking about the part that the women's movement and social movements in general play in bringing about social change, she states that social movements "expedite rather than directly cause" social change. This seems indeed to be the case, but I think the term *expedite* seems to me to minimize the effectiveness of the women's movement. I would suggest that in our theorizing we don't get ourselves into a corner by trying to find causes, or original causes, or first causes, or main causes. It reminds me of the question Tolstoy raises in *War and Peace*. He asks what makes the apple fall from the tree? Is it the weight of the apple? Is it the ripeness of the apple? Is it the wind? Or is it the law of gravity? He concludes that all these causes are at work. I suggest that while it is true that the women's movement came about after the gender division of labor in our society had already produced some change on the macro level, it further contributed to bringing about more change.

Similarly, as I have noted, when Chafetz says that the gender division of labor *reinforces* male power, she implies that male power is the *real* cause of gender inequality. Though true, I think it is irrelevant because without the gender division of labor men would have a hard time maintaining their power. I don't care what the real cause is, because I am concerned about solutions. Let me put it in medical terms: The diagnosis of an illness in terms of its origin does not necessarily point to its therapy. I may have gotten an infection by swimming in a polluted river, but that doesn't mean that I have to get back into an unpolluted one or, god help me, wait till it be unpolluted, to get rid of the infection. This doesn't mean that we shouldn't also clean up the river. It seems to me that it is more difficult for every wife individually to persuade her husband to spend a few more minutes a day on household chores than to help to bring about a change in employment legislation, even though this change may not be as fundamental as we would wish. And this is where the women's movement comes in to help.

Nancy Chodorow's theory of mothering (1978), much as I agree with and admire her theory as a whole, offers a solution that I am not quite happy with. She argues that because the little girl remains tied to mother and thus grows up to be dependent, especially on men, and the little boy is made to move away from mother and hence becomes independent, the solution for bringing about gender equality is to change the division of labor in the household. I am thinking along Chafetz's lines when I say that although in the history of the individual the household division of labor (coupled with the authority structure) comes first, in the history of society at large and of the culture, which dictates and sustains this systems, what comes first is the division of labor in the economy. In other words, a radical change in the division of labor in society would do much to undermine the division of labor in the household. True, in line with my earlier argument one might object that the household division of labor has its own consequences, but given that it remains in the private sphere, it is likely to be less efficient. This does not preclude, of course, also working on the micro level.

It may well be, as Miriam Johnson argues in this volume, that "the status of wife . . . as defined by the marriage contract and our informal expectations concerning husband superiority, lies behind women's secondary status in the wider society." This does not mean that we have to wait till the family structure changes to bring about a different and egalitarian division of labor on the macro level. And even if the family structure were to change, I am not sure it would have far-reaching consequences for the division of labor in society. I agree with Janet Chafetz that social change is not likely to proceed the other way around, just as sex-role attitudes changed after, and not before women's massive entry into the labor force (Giele 1988, p. 309, quoting Oppenheimer 1982, p. 30).

To clean up the country from the pollution of sex inequality, it may be helpful to look at some small results. Whenever women are gainfully employed, they gain power in the family (Coser, 1987), and men lose power. As Sorenson and McLanahan have shown (1987), if women work at home they are completely dependent on husbands. They decrease their dependency in the measure in which they are gainfully employed. "In 1940, white married women, on average, relied on their husbands to provide 86 per cent of their economic support. By 1980, their dependency had been reduced to 58 per cent" (Sorenson and McLanahan 1987, p. 670). The problem in our society, however, is that women are usually employed in lower-paying jobs than men, and although they may have more power in the household than those who are not gainfully employed, this helps maintain men in superior power positions.

That the sex division of labor in society is the basis of gender inequality is brought home dramatically by Rae Lesser Blumberg, in this volume. She shows that, in some African societies, the more women contribute to production, the more control they have over the allocation of the product. Her analysis of kibbutz society is especially relevant: Although the ideology of the kibbutz has been outspoken in its insistence on gender equality, women are underrepresented on powerful committees and have remained in traditional women's work—children, kitchen, and laundry. In agriculture, they were employed from day one in more labor-intensive, hence less profitable, jobs, and ever since industrialization began, they were employed in bottom-rung jobs. Sex segregation of labor was being perpetuated not only by socialization but also by labor allocations in adolescence. High school girls were required to work in children's houses while boys were given experience in a wide choice of assignments. As a result, women fall short of equality on the micro level as well, and there is strong gender stereotyping.

In the kibbutz example there was complete equality between men and women on the micro level. Yet, this had no impact on achieving equality in the economic and occupational spheres.

This is because household problems are likely to remain private troubles. Equality in the occupational sphere, which is public, would do much to elevate the status of women, thereby doing much to destroy the stereotype of women's inferiority and elevating their bargaining power on the private level.

The kind of work that Chafetz, Blumberg, and other authors in this volume have been doing are good examples of fine feminist scholarship and fruitful social theory.

REFERENCES

Chodorow, Nancy. 1978. *The Reproduction of Mothering: Psychoanalysis and the Sociology of Gender.* Berkeley: University of California Press.

Coser, Rose L. 1987. "Power Lost and Status Gained: A Step in the Direction of Sex Equality." *Koelner Zeitschrift fuer Soziologie und Sozialpsychologie* (March).

Giele, J. 1988. "Gender and Sex Roles." In *Handbook of Sociology,* edited by N. J. Smelser. Newbury Park, CA: Sage.

Merton, Robert K. 1973. "The Perspectives of Insiders and Outsiders." Pp. 99–136 in *The Sociology of Science: Theoretical and Empirical Investigations,* edited by N. Storer. Chicago: University of Chicago Press.

Oppenheimer, V. K. 1982. *Work and Family: A Study in Social Demography.* New York: Aldine.

Sørenson, Annemette and Sara McLanahan. 1987. "Married Women's Economic Dependency, 1940–1980." *American Journal of Sociology* 93(November): 659–77.

ABOUT THE CONTRIBUTORS

JOAN ACKER is Professor of Sociology at the University of Oregon and, since 1987, Guest Research Professor at Sweden's Center for Working Life, where she is the adviser to the research group on women and work. She has published on organizational theory, women and work, gender and class, life experiences of middle-aged women, and qualitative research methods. Her most recent article, "Class, Gender, and the Relations of Distribution," appeared in *Signs* (Spring 1988). A book, *Doing Comparable Worth: Gender, Class and Pay Equity*, will be published by Temple University Press.

JESSIE BERNARD is Research Scholar, Pennsylvania State University. Her research interests are women, marriage, family, feminism, and the history of sociology in the United States. She is the recipient of nine honorary doctorates and numerous awards, and is a founding member of Sociologists for Women in Society. Her recent publications include *The Female World, The Female World in Global Perspective,* and *The Feminist Enlightenment* (in process).

RAE LESSER BLUMBERG is Associate Professor in the Department of Sociology at the University of California, San Diego. Her publications include *Stratification: Socioeconomic and Sexual Inequality,* the forthcoming *Women and the Wealth of Nations: Theory and Research on Gender and Global Development,* and "A General Theory of Gender Stratification" (in *Sociological Theory,* 1984). She has done field research on development and/or gender issues in about a dozen countries around the world, most recently in Guatemala, the Dominican Republic, and Nigeria.

JANET SALTZMAN CHAFETZ is Professor of Sociology at the University of Houston, where she has taught since 1971. Her major research interests are gender theory and gender stratification. She is especially interested in the development of integrated, middle-range theory in the area of gender. Recent publications include *Sex and Advantage* (1984),

Female Revolt (with A. G. Dworkin, 1986), *Feminist Sociology: An Overview of Contemporary Theories* (1988), and "The Gender Division of Labor and the Reproduction of Female Disadvantage" (*Journal of Family Issues,* March 1988). That paper, along with the chapter in this volume, form the basis of a book in progress, titled *Stability and Change in Gender Systems: An Integrated Theory.*

ROSE LAUB COSER is Adjunct Professor of Sociology at Boston College and Professor Emerita at the State University of New York at Stony Brook. For 1988–89 she is a Visiting Scholar at the Henry A. Murray Center at Radcliffe College. In the past she was on the faculties of Wellesley College, Harvard Medical School, and Northeastern University. She is the author of several books, including *Training in Ambiguity: Learning Through Doing in a Mental Hospital* (Free Press, 1979). Her *In Defense of Modernity: Complexity of Social Roles and Individual Autonomy* is forthcoming (Stanford University Press). Her latest theoretical papers from a feminist perspective are "Cognitive Structure and the Use of Social Space" (*Sociological Forum,* 1, 1986), and "Power Lost and Status Gained: A Step in the Direction of Sex Equality" (*Kolner Zeitschrift für Soziologie und Sozialpsychologie,* 39, 1987).

MIRIAM M. JOHNSON is Professor in the Department of Sociology at the University of Oregon and is an affiliate of the Center for the Study of Women in Society. She does research and writes articles in the area of gender development and family structure. She is the author of *Strong Mothers, Weak Wives: The Search for Gender Equality* (University of California Press, 1988), and is coauthor, with Jean Stockard, of *Sex Roles: Sex Inequality and Sex Role Development* (Prentice-Hall, 1980). She currently holds a Rockefeller Foundation grant for a project titled "Gender, Structural Differentiation and the Family."

EDITH KURZWEIL is Professor and Chair, Department of Sociology at Rutgers, Newark. Her book, *The Freudians' Freud: A Comparative Perspective,* is forthcoming from Yale University Press. Among her publications are *The Age of Structuralism: Levi-Strauss to Foucault* (Columbia, 1980), *Italian Entrepreneurs: Success Out of Chaos* (Praeger, 1983), *Literature and Psychoanalysis* (coeditor, Columbia, 1983), and *Cultural Analysis* (coeditor, Routledge, 1984). She is executive editor and a frequent contributor to *Partisan Review,* as well as other cultural and professional journals.

THOMAS MEISENHELDER is Professor of Sociology at California State University, San Bernardino. His publications include articles in *Human Studies, Sociological Inquiry,* and *Qualitative Sociology.* He is currently involved in a project investigating state and class relations in Southern Africa. Among his interests in sociology are Marxist theory and the sociology of the Third World. He recently completed a monograph-length manuscript on feminism and critical theory, which includes the piece published here.

DOROTHY E. SMITH is currently Professor in the Department of Sociology in Education at the Ontario Institute for Studies in Education, Toronto, Canada. She has published extensively in feminist studies and in the social organization of knowledge. She has recently published a book, *The Everyday World as Problematic: A Feminist Sociology* (Boston: Northeastern University Press, 1987), exploring the implications of women's standpoint for sociology.

RUTH A. WALLACE is Professor of Sociology at George Washington University, where she has taught for nearly two decades. Her recent publications include *Contemporary Sociological Theory* (with Allison Wolf, Prentice-Hall, 1986), *Gender in America* (with Patricia Lengermann, Prentice-Hall, 1985), and "Catholic Women and the Creation of a New Social Reality" (*Gender and Society,* March 1988). She is past Chair of the Theory Section of the American Sociological Association.

NOTES

NOTES

NOTES

NOTES